CONISTON

MICHAEL BRADLEY

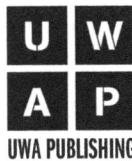

U W
A P
UWA PUBLISHING

Michael Bradley is a lawyer and writer. He is the managing partner of Marque Lawyers, a commercial law firm in Sydney which he and his colleagues founded in 2008. He practises in media, administrative and regulatory law. Michael is also a widely published writer, with a regular op-ed column in *Crikey* and previously with *The Drum* and *The Australian Financial Review* as well as articles in *The Saturday Paper*, *The Sydney Morning Herald* and other publications. He writes on law, politics and social justice.

To Charmaine, my reason

First published in 2019 by
UWA Publishing
Crawley, Western Australia 6009
www.uwap.uwa.edu.au

UWAP is an imprint of UWA Publishing,
a division of The University of Western Australia.

THE UNIVERSITY OF
WESTERN
AUSTRALIA

Copyright © Michael Bradley 2019
The moral right of the author has been asserted.
ISBN: 978-1-76080-103-8

NATIONAL
LIBRARY
OF AUSTRALIA

A catalogue record for this
book is available from the
National Library of Australia

Cover design by Peter Long
Typeset by J&M Typesetting
Printed by Lightning Source

uwapublishing

CONTENTS

FOREWORD

Makarrata is the culmination of our agenda: the coming together after a struggle. It captures our aspirations for a fair and truthful relationship with the people of Australia and a better future for our children based on justice and self-determination.

We seek a Makarrata Commission to supervise a process of agreement-making between governments and First Nations and truth-telling about our history.

Coniston is, for me, one of the first post–Uluru Statement from the Heart histories. The Uluru Statement from the Heart and its call for structural reform, Voice, Treaty, Truth was motivated by the need to propose a staged and sequenced approach to a formal settlement in this country where First Nations have never ceded the land. *Coniston* is about truth. The Coniston story is one of the more well known, at least among Aboriginal people, because it is cited frequently as the bookend of the killing times. Coniston is less known among Australians. Yet, as Michael Bradley makes plain in this book, there is plenty of information about Coniston. In fact, the forensic research herein, piecing together the truth of Coniston, presents an important counter-factual to the common refrain *Why Weren't We Told?* Before and post-federation, the colony/nation conducted many public inquiries into the very lengthy period of dispossession through killing over many, many decades. The nation has voluminous state records, parliamentary committee reviews and other inquiries into the frontier wars and massacres. *We Were Told.*

I was the only Aboriginal constitutional lawyer on the Referendum Council that set up the constitutional dialogues, designed and conducted to ascertain from a sample of First Nations what form of constitutional reform would be acceptable to them. This was an exercise in the Australian government retrofitting consultation with First Nations people six years after the modern-day recognition project was set in train by Prime Minister Gillard. What we, Noel Pearson, Pat Anderson, Dalassa Yorkston, I and others, experienced as Aboriginal and Torres Strait Islander Referendum Council members in the dialogues was something extraordinary. We designed the dialogues to build in an early discussion on what recognition may mean in the local region; that is to say, how would reforms to the Australian Constitution (that Turnbull and Shorten agreed we could present to the dialogues) make a difference to their lives on the ground. However, from Hobart to Broome to Thursday Island, before we could even contemplate moving to assess constitutional proposals, each dialogue raised as a first order priority the question of truth and Australian history. We know as Aboriginal people that Australia's history begins with the invasion, first contact, the short-lived conciliation phase, the frontier wars or killing times, the protection era, the assimilation period and, eventually, the self-determination era ushered in by Whitlam. Many referred to this as the true history of Australia. Participants in the dialogues earnestly wanted to know whether Australians wanted to know about what happened to them. 'Do they want to know?' they asked.

Bradley's *Coniston* answers that question.

The Northern Territory was the location for two dialogues that led to the national constitutional convention at Mutitjulu. The first was run by the Northern Land Council in Darwin. The second was run by the Central Land Council in Ross River. Both referred to the massacres and killings that opened up the country to pastoral development and, eventually, mining. The following is an extract from the record of meeting from the Ross River dialogue we used in the Uluru Statement's Aboriginal history of Australia, titled 'Our Story'.

> Participants expressed disgust about a statue of John McDouall Stuart being erected in Alice Springs following the 150th anniversary of his successful attempt to reach the top end. This expedition led to the opening up of the 'South Australian frontier' which led to massacres as the telegraph line was established and white settlers moved into the region. People feel sad whenever they see the statue; its presence and the fact that Stuart is holding a gun is disrespectful to the Aboriginal community who are descendants of the families slaughtered during the massacres throughout central Australia.

Bradley talks about McDouall Stuart in his book, and captures powerfully in the book the consequences and, as absurd as life is, the future good fortune of those who were intimately involved in or sanctioned the killings. The sentiments of the people at Ross River about truth-telling and the humiliation of overt displays of Australian idolatry towards 'explorers' who also led massacres and reprisals were shared across the nation. The story of Australia that we tell ourselves is asymmetrical and impedes progress towards justice. After all, as Brennan J put it bluntly in *Mabo v Queensland*

(No 2), 'Their dispossession underwrote the development of the nation'. This is why the Australian reconciliation process was so severely criticised in all the dialogues. Reconciliation processes around the world involve truth and justice. Australia, it seemed to many dialogue participants, seeks to elide both of these. And this is why reconciliation is a failing framework in which to unite the nation. As the dialogues repeatedly stated, the concept is flawed because to 'reconcile' means to restore friendly relations. It implies a prior relationship that, to many First Nations, did not exist.

Michael Bradley's crisp retelling of Coniston is a jarring but necessary read for all Australians. May it inspire more Australian writers and lawyers and historians to consider the ways they can contribute to the truth-telling of the nation. The Uluru Statement from the Heart concludes with an invitation to all Australians:

> In 1967 we were counted, in 2017 we seek to be heard. We leave base camp and start our trek across this vast country. We invite you to walk with us in a movement of the Australian people for a better future.

I am sure I speak for many First Nations people when I say that we are very pleased that civic-minded lawyers like Michael Bradley have accepted this invitation to walk with us in a movement of the Australian people for a better future. *Coniston* is his contribution to truth-telling, the journey of educating a nation to know itself. It is only from the truth that justice will emerge.

Professor Megan Davis
UNSW

The Northern Territory, 1928

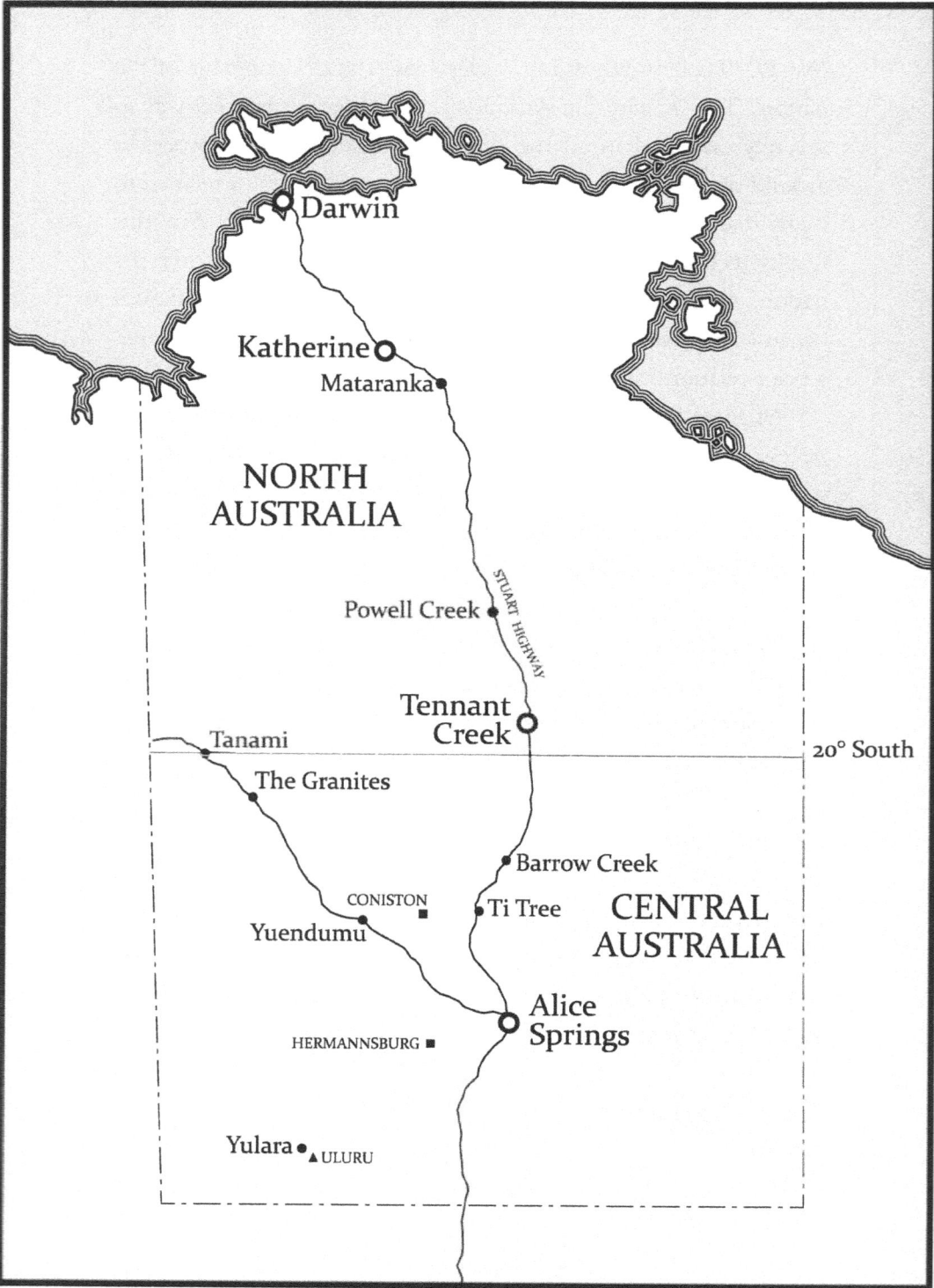

Darwin

Katherine

Mataranka

NORTH
AUSTRALIA

Powell Creek

STUART HIGHWAY

Tennant
Creek

Tanami

20° South

The Granites

Barrow Creek

CONISTON

Ti Tree

CENTRAL
AUSTRALIA

Yuendumu

HERMANNSBURG

Alice
Springs

Yulara

ULURU

Area around Coniston

Lander River

Curlew Waterhole ✗

● Lake Surprise

✗ Dingo Waterhole

✗ Tomahawk Waterhole

Boomerang Waterhole

✗ Rabbit Bore

Hanson River

✗ Circle Well
✗ Baxter's Well

✗

● Broadmeadows
✗

✗ Mt Theo

✗

✗ Tipinpa

● Barrow Creek

✗ Tennant Creek ○

White Stone ✗

● Mt Barkly

Boundary Soak ✗

Anningie ●

Harper Springs

Yurrkuru

Cockatoo
Spring ✗
✗

✗
● Mt Denison

Coniston ●

Pine Hill ●

● Ti Tree

● Woolla Downs

✗

Mission Creek

● Yuendumu

Napperby

Ryan's Well ●

STUART HIGHWAY

TANAMI ROAD

Alice Springs ○

✗ = locations where killings of
Aboriginal people reported to
have taken place, Aug–Oct 1928

AUTHOR'S NOTE

In this book I have quoted directly from many contemporary sources, including diaries, letters, newspapers, books and government records. The way that many Australians during the relevant period spoke about Aboriginal people, the language they used to describe them and their attitudes to them, are frequently shocking in their brutality, contempt and naked racism.

I have not sanitised or censored any of it because I believe it is important, as part of rediscovering and comprehending this episode in our history, that we understand what was considered acceptable, indeed uncontroversial, in Australian society at the time. It often made me catch my breath; it should do yours, too.

Whenever men can form no idea of distant and unknown things, they judge them by what is familiar and at hand.

Giambattista Vico

What we are not facing is the results of what we've done. What one begs the American people to do, for all our sakes, is to simply accept our history.

James Baldwin, 1965, 'The American Dream'

PROLOGUE

Entry for Saturday 11 August 1928, Alice Springs Police Station Day Journal: 'Reported over phone from Tee Tree by Mr Stafford that Mr Fred Brookes prospector had been killed by natives out west from Staffords Station.'[1]

Fred Brooks was indeed dead; he had been bludgeoned to death by Aboriginal men on 7 August at his remote camp, 14 miles west of his mate Randal Stafford's Coniston Station, itself a couple of hundred miles north from Alice Springs. The harmless old dingo trapper lay where he had been stuffed in a rabbit hole by his killers, feet sticking out, rapidly decomposing in the drought-stricken desert.

For the few scattered pastoralists struggling for survival in the insanely harsh conditions of Central Australia, an undeclared war had broken out. The desperate urgency of the situation was compounded a few weeks later when another local man, William 'Nugget' Morton, was the victim of a second unprovoked attack by Aboriginal men, set upon at his camp by up to fifteen of them. Fortunately, Morton, a former boxer, was able to fight them off, shooting one of his assailants dead, but narrowly surviving grave injuries himself.

Within a few months there would be two more murderous assaults on white pastoralists: Harry Tilmouth also survived by shooting his attacker, but Harry Henty was not so lucky, dying face down in the dirt after being shot in the head by an Aboriginal man called Willaberta Jack.

This was, in the minds of the few hundred white residents of the Centre, the black uprising which they had long dreaded. Memories of earlier fatal attacks on unsuspecting workers, miners and explorers dating back fifty years and more were vividly revived. White people were physically outnumbered in this part of the country by twenty or more to one, with the total police force for the 250,000 square miles of Central Australia numbering a paltry seven officers.

The sudden explosion of violence was, everyone agreed, the work of a black tide, as the legendarily untameable tribe called the Warramulla came out of the desert to the west of the Granites, way out in the barren country towards the Western Australian border, surging east on a pre-proclaimed mission to wipe the whites out of Central Australia altogether. It was, as a contemporary historian put it, the Aboriginal people's 'last battle stand against the white man on this continent...perhaps also the last stand of the Stone Age against Western civilisation'.[2]

The white residents now reflected that the Warramulla had given plenty of warning for those who cared to hear it. Two years earlier, one of their number had told a cattle drover working near Mount Peake to go away, saying, 'This no more longa white feller, longa black feller. White man can't sit down longa black feller. White man shift.'[3] Cattle killing by Aboriginal people had become an endemic and increasing problem, exacerbated by the drought which had been ravaging the Centre since 1925. Tensions had simmered for a long time.[4]

In late December 1927, Pastor Albrecht of the Hermannsburg Mission station south-west of Coniston was the recipient of a visit by the recently appointed Government Resident for Central Australia, J. C. Cawood. Albrecht recounted their conversation:

> [Cawood] seemed preoccupied with the worsening drought and the complaints by European settlers that Aborigines coming in from the bush were becoming aggressive in their demands for food. They had to be taught a lesson, he told Albrecht, before they drove the whites off the land in Central Australia.[5]

Cawood well knew what being 'taught a lesson' promised for the Aboriginal people on the pastoral frontiers of Australia. Eight months later, he would have the perfect opportunity to ensure that the lesson was delivered.

The boiling point came in August 1928, with the launch of the Warramulla invasion. Their first target was Coniston, the westernmost cattle station, and its leaseholder, Randal Stafford. They had sent word ahead that they were coming. Fred Brooks unluckily found himself in their path and became their first victim.

The Warramulla uprising immediately degenerated into a sporadic insurgency, with isolated attacks their only tactic. In truth, they were on the defensive as soon as the war began, as the white response was instant and deadly.

By the end of October, the war was over. A series of expeditions, led by Mounted Constable George Murray from the Barrow Creek police post under instructions from Cawood, and including various volunteer posse members as well as Aboriginal trackers, had traversed thousands of square miles around the Lander and Hanson river valleys to the north of Coniston, and out among the Granites hills to the west almost as far as the border, tracking

Brooks' and Morton's attackers. In the course of the hunt, they had shot dead an acknowledged thirty-one Aboriginal people, including several women.

The true death toll was more likely over 100 – perhaps 200 or even more. Murray, a war veteran and experienced policeman, had led what turned out to be the last great punitive expedition against Aboriginal people in Australian history, and the carnage had been extreme. However, unlike earlier such mass-reprisal killings, the changing times meant that the news from the desert could not be suppressed. There was an outcry from southern newspapers and church and Aboriginal welfare groups, and the Federal Government of Prime Minister Stanley Melbourne Bruce, which had responsibility for Central Australia, was forced reluctantly to respond.

The Coniston story culminated eventually in an official Board of Enquiry, stacked by the government with police appointees, and including the Government Resident in Alice Springs (who was also the Commissioner of Police and intricately implicated in the killings himself). After a perfunctory three-week inquiry, the board delivered a whitewash report for the ages, exonerating everyone and declaring that all thirty-one Aboriginal victims had been killed in self-defence – including two who were shot in the back while running away from Murray. There was nothing more to be said, and Coniston faded quickly from history.

These are the bare bones of Coniston. The war of the Warramulla, as I have related it, was a figment of a fevered white imagination; August 1928 did see a sudden upsurge in Aboriginal violence, but it was neither planned nor coordinated, and the Warramulla of the western desert didn't even exist. However, the fear which the violence triggered was real, and its result utterly devastating to the Warlpiri and Kaytetye people of

Central Australia. They were decimated, and their land was desecrated and rendered alien to them.

This story is about unpicking the truth of Coniston: why it happened; how many died; and how that truth came to be buried so deeply that, whenever we talk about Australia's graphic history of war and large-scale death, Coniston is no part of the conversation.

Chapter 1

CENTRAL AUSTRALIA, 1928

We then gave three hearty cheers for the flag, the emblem of civil and religious liberty, and may it be a sign to the natives that the dawn of liberty, civilization, and Christianity is about to break upon them.[1]

In 1932, an expedition commissioned by Frank Packer and Keith Murdoch set out for the Granites, an area of wilderness 380 miles north-west of Alice Springs. A mini–gold rush was brewing in this desolate patch of desert, and the newspaper barons were keen to know whether they should be promoting it or calling it a bust. The expedition concluded that there was 'no payable gold in quantity at the Granites', quickly terminating one of Australia's last gold fevers before it had properly begun.[2]

The gold, or lack of it, in the Granites was par for the course in Central Australia. It is as unforgiving an environment as can be found on Earth. In the early decades of the twentieth century, it was barely populated – at least, not by white people.

Among the expedition members was F. E. (Eric) Baume, who wrote a detailed account of its travels. He met a number of the central characters of the Coniston story and left a compelling picture of the harsh existence endured by the few white inhabitants of the Centre in 1928.

Coniston Station lies almost exactly halfway along the 380-mile trek from Alice Springs north-west to the Granites. Baume, writing in 1932, noted that in the 200 miles between Alice Springs and Coniston 'live three white men and no blacks and the permanent water is, virtually, at the stations owned by these men'.[3]

The country here was, according to Baume, inhospitable to the extreme:

> the hospitality of the far-out station owner must not be overtaxed. The fact that he would share with you his last piece of damper, ounce of sugar or piece of beef should not be remembered lightly. Food is as difficult to obtain on his part, miles out in the lonely bush, as it is for a native.[4]

Baume's expedition set out from Alice Springs with enough fresh water to make it to the next available source, Thompson's Rockhole, 140 miles past Coniston, and enough petrol to keep their trucks going for 800 miles. The water at Coniston, Baume found, was impregnated with mineral and undrinkable.[5] Coniston was no oasis; the only relief it brought the traveller was the reassuring presence of its owner, the redoubtable Randal Stafford, 'the soul of hospitality', according to Baume. But the whole journey from the Alice to the Granites was, he recorded, 'a tragedy of desolation – 380 miles of heat and flies, dust and spinifex'.[6] This country had claimed many men's lives for thirst and starvation: 'no man can live in this desert without a drink for more than twenty-four hours', Baume wrote.[7]

Out from Coniston, Baume and party visited Brooks' Soak (Yurrkuru), the place where Fred Brooks had been murdered four years earlier. As Baume explained, a soak was the commonest source of water in the desert, a tiny human-made well not easy to find if you didn't know what to look for.

> It is in the bank of a dry creek, the bottom of which is filled with rippling sand, with never a trace of moisture. It looks like a miniature geyser hole, its mouth built up by the earth scooped out for many years.
>
> The Brooks' Soak water had a pungent taste, which mixed with the dull water-bag mud, was unappetising. But it was water...[8]

As impossibly harsh as the environment appeared to its white explorers, beginning with John McDouall Stuart from 1860, Central Australia had been home to a large population of Aboriginal people for tens of thousands of years. Around Coniston and the Lander region, the dominant local groups were the Warlpiri to the west and north, and the Kaytetye to the east. Bordering them to the south were the Anmatyerre.

The Northern Territory has, ever since its 'discovery', been a land of misplaced white dreams. In 1863, the colony of South Australia annexed the whole thing, pinning its hopes for economic sustainability on the promise of endless fine grazing pastures which early reports had misleadingly offered. Ambitions for a high place at the Imperial table focused on the slightly lunatic plan to build a telegraph line all the way from Adelaide to Darwin, an epic feat which was surprisingly achieved by the 1870s.

In the course of this construction a precursor to the Coniston massacres took place, at the same Barrow Creek telegraph station from which Mounted Constable Murray would ride half a century later. In 1874, a war party of Kaytetye men staged a full-scale assault on Barrow Creek and the seven white men living there, spearing several of them – two fatally. As old-timer Alec Ross related many years later, the response was swift:

> They sent out messages on the wires everywhere, and the police and parties of men came up from The Tennant and The Alice and from lots of other places. And I can tell you, they did some pretty serious shooting too – taught the blacks a lesson they've never forgotten…and for quite a few more months blacks would get shot in twos and threes in the whole of this district. The blacks had needed a good lesson and they got it right in the neck: they never attacked another white man along The Line after that.[9]

The carnage was wholesale; perhaps as many as several hundred Aboriginal people died in the long-lasting reprisals. Barrow Creek was not the only incident of major bloodshed in the Centre before Coniston; there were numerous attacks on isolated white men, and no shortage of payback.[10] The police were prime movers in the unofficial policy of retributive, and frequently indiscriminate, violence, being directly involved or implicated in all of the major reported incidents of mass killing.[11] For a notorious period in the late nineteenth century, the Northern Territory even briefly emulated the experience of Queensland by establishing a Native Police corps which, as in Queensland, engaged essentially in the wanton slaughter of Aboriginal people in response to every report from white settlers of interference with their peaceful occupation.[12]

It had been, by all accounts, fifty years of hate-filled and frequently violent enmity between the isolated white pastoralists and the incumbent Aboriginal population. The cause was obvious: land. As was by the late nineteenth century a familiar pattern in Australia, the irreconcilable conflict between traditional landowner and the ever-expanding colonial frontier could only end one way; sharing of the finite resource was not an option.

A typically plainspoken Centralian, Mrs Isobel Price of Woolla Downs Station, gave as clear a perspective on this history as one could want, by reference to her own bitter experiences. Her daughter and son-in-law had taken up the adjoining Harper Springs Station and selected a soak as the location of their home-stead, but the local Aboriginal men were anxious that it not be built there as it was a sacred site. Mrs Price explained her reaction:

> Those niggers made no end of a fuss about those few stones and trees and that dirty old soak of theirs. Even old Bob Purvis, who had been the first white man to open up this district for settlement, begged us not to establish Harper Springs Station at that soak, but to sink a well a few miles away. But I put my foot down. I told Ted not to be a dish-rag; you can't afford to take any notice of these thieving dirty wretches; and if Bob Purvis was frightened of the niggers, I was not. We had got our lease from the Government, and it was up to Government to see to it that the law-abiding settlers who opened up this new country were protected from all thieving niggers. Besides, we did have guns ourselves, didn't we? So we got the trees around the soak chopped down, and tossed those white stones away, and then Ted got the soak timbered and cleaned out. He had a job to get any of his stockboys to help him with the work, but I kept on telling him – 'We can't give in to any niggers; we've got our legal rights; and if we let them scare us

now, they'll have us where they want.' Everywhere we went, those thieving rogues seemed to stand in our road with their silly stones and trees, and I wasn't going to put up with any of their stupid nonsense.[13]

Mrs Price's audience for this diatribe was T. G. H. Strehlow, an extraordinary man who diarised his comprehensive travels through the Centre in the 1930s and met most of the principal players in the Coniston tragedy. Having heard Mrs Price out, Strehlow recorded his sad reflection on her story:

> the soak which had been desecrated with such deliberate obstinacy by Mrs Price had been no other place than Ratakapa, the ancient and venerated ceremonial centre of ragia clansmen through the Northern Aranda and Unmatjera areas.[14]

In this single incident was encapsulated a great deal of the colonial history of Central Australia. In any event, whether Aboriginal spiritual traditions and sacred places were to be respected or ignored, there was an unavoidable practical conflict with no obvious solution:

> Aborigines did not recognise white land ownership, and Europeans did not recognise Aboriginal land laws, perceiving 'unoccupied' lands as belonging to the Crown. Without bothering with treaties, the would-be settlers took up pastoral leases on what they viewed as vacant, untamed or 'virgin' country, and set about exploiting the land, the material and religious basis of Aboriginal society.[15]

White settlement of Central Australia had largely followed the building of the Overland Telegraph Line, with the first cattle station being established in 1872. Randal Stafford was granted the lease for Coniston in 1917, and it was still the westernmost pastoral holding in 1928.[16] His close neighbour Nugget Morton's station, Broadmeadows, was to the north up the Lander River.[17] They and a handful of other pastoralists formed the whole white population to the west of the telegraph line; the total for the whole of Central Australia in 1928 was fewer than 400.[18] Sharing the region with them was an Aboriginal population numbering perhaps 10,000.[19]

Unsurprisingly, the uncertain promise of Central Australia had attracted a particular type of settler. These were hard men: mostly single, used to living extremely rough, and uninterested in being governed. The conditions suited the self-sufficient.

The Northern Territory had been under South Australia's control until 1911. However, it had proved to be nothing more than a constant drain on the state's finances, so in that year South Australia finally ceded the Territory to the Commonwealth Government. Neglect was the overarching feature of federal control in the ensuing decades, the main consequence being that the residents were left to fend for themselves.[20] The South Australian Government had finally passed the first legislation specifically dealing with the Territory's Aboriginal people just before handing the land over to the Commonwealth, which largely replicated it in its own law.[21] Its spirit and intent was 'protection'. As was the case in other states, its effect was to remove all possibility of self-determination from Aboriginal people and leave them with the legal status of orphaned children. They were at the total mercy of their official Protectors, who were for the most part the police. For example, all Aboriginal children, whether they had parents or not, were automatically made wards of the Chief Protector.

It is beyond the scope of this work to fully describe the social and legal context in which the Aboriginal people of Central Australia found themselves in 1928. It is summarised brilliantly thus: 'From 1911 Commonwealth policy, like that of South Australia, was based on the assumption that Aborigines were a dying race in need of protection while they died off.'[22] This assumption was near universal in 1911, and still close to pre-dominant in 1928. The primary driver was lived experience – the 'full-blooded' Aboriginal population was, by the 1920s, less than a tenth of what it had been at the time of European settlement in 1788. There was no obvious reason to suppose that this rate of decline would lead to a different result throughout the country from what had already occurred in Tasmania (and all but that in Victoria and New South Wales). The expectation of eventual extinction of the Aboriginal race was supported by three overlapping factors: basic racism; the pragmatic desirability, at least from a pastoral perspective, of the 'native' problem resolving itself by natural means; and the popularity of 'Social Darwinism', the pseudoscience which presupposed that Aboriginal people were inherently inferior to whites and that natural selection would inevitably wipe them out.[23]

In 1927, for no obvious reason, the Territory was cut into two separate zones, North Australia and Central Australia, with independent administrations under the control of the Minister for Home and Territories in Canberra (after 1927; before that, the Federal Government sat in Melbourne). For Central Australia, this made no practical difference.

It was the Wild West. Official authority consisted of the Government Resident, J. C. Cawood, representing His Majesty in Alice Springs, along with his secretary. He was also the Commissioner of Police, commanding a force of seven officers: three in Alice Springs and a single officer in each of four outpost stations. The law which he and his deputy, Acting Sergeant Charles Noblet, administered consisted of sparse Ordinances issued sporadically from Canberra.

There was an inevitability to what followed when the growing tension between traditional landowners and white settlers was exacerbated by the extreme drought which hit the Centre, especially to the west of the telegraph line, from 1925. By 1928 the contest for the remaining water sources between the Aboriginal people and the settlers' cattle was dire and at risk of turning deadly.[24]

This was the situation in August 1928: the historical pattern of white settlement on the frontier inexorably pushing the Aboriginal inhabitants off their land and away from their sacred places and water sources was reaching crisis point. The fact that the same thing had been repeated, with the same violence, in every part of Australia over the previous 140 years supported the assumption of white superiority and confirmed the assumed inevitability of the outcome.[25] The drought was only accelerating this 'normal' trend.

At Coniston, Randal Stafford was simply trying to survive and keep his stock alive. His compatriots like Morton at Broadmeadows and Tilmouth at Napperby were doing the same, having shifted their cattle closer to the Lander River and some of the few remaining places where they could be watered. Fred Brooks was out west at his lonely soak, trying to make some money trapping dingoes (the federal government was offering a bounty on dingo scalps at the time).

Other white men were at large in the wild lands west of the Lander. The legendary bushman Joe Brown was out there somewhere prospecting in the Granites with Bruce Chapman and Alex Wilson, who would each have a major role to play in the events to come. Michael Terry, a peripatetic explorer, was nearing the Lander from the west, part-way through an epic journey across the unmapped territory all the way from the Kimberleys in Western Australia. He, too, would have an influence on the story as it unfolded.

There was another factor at play: the almost complete absence of white women from Central Australia. It takes little imagination to guess where this led, and the colourfully labelled practice of 'comboism' (white men cohabiting with Aboriginal women) would be, arguably, central to the Coniston story.[26] Writing forty years earlier, William Sowden had taken indignant note of the widespread 'taking' of Aboriginal women by white men in the Territory in his report back to the South Australian Parliament:

> When men calling themselves by the name of Britons shamelessly abuse the female relatives of the blacks... when through their disgraceful conduct they bring down the vengeance of an infuriated tribe of blacks upon them, and then, because they are the stronger, shoot the poor wretches down like dogs...The evil has decreased of late; so have the blacks.
>
> Experienced men throughout both colonies tell you that they never knew a so-called native trouble arise but that a lubra was at the bottom of it.[27]

The Warlpiri and Kaytetye, their lands respectively situated roughly around the Lander and Hanson rivers, were struggling too. Their access to water was constantly undermined by white insistence that they move on from the bores and wells when these places were needed for the settlers' stock.[28] Cattle killing was on the rise, as native game and even the feral rabbits had disappeared; it was the settlers' persistent complaint.[29] At Barrow Creek Police Station, Mounted Constable Murray and his trackers were principally occupied in hunting down cattle poachers.[30]

The morning of 7 August 1928 dawned clear and bright. The Centre was tense, but quiet. Fred Brooks was about to be beaten to death.

Chapter 2

THE MURDER OF FRED BROOKS

Be kind to the wild native if you want trouble. He mistakes kindness for fear all over Australia.[1]

Fred Brooks and Randal Stafford were old mates. The two archetypes of the Australian outback had met many years earlier while working on stations in the Innamincka country around Lake Eyre in South Australia.[2] Stafford was a native South Australian, coming from a well-off family but having apparently gone bush at a young age. About Brooks' background nothing is known. Both men were in their sixties in 1928.[3]

Stafford had taken up the Coniston lease in 1917, and Brooks arrived there to help out sometime in the late 1920s. It seems that he had spent his whole adult life apart from white civilisation, working on outback stations, doing some prospecting, scraping an existence from the dirt. He had no family, money or ties. Most contemporary accounts call him 'harmless', although he was hardly helpless. He was a big man, 6 foot 2 inches tall,[4] toughened by vast experience of survival in the harsh extremes of Central Australia.

Conditions at Coniston were bad. Stafford was barely keeping things going, and he had no pay to offer his old mate. A few waterholes on the station were the only remaining decent water source in the region as the drought had run into its fourth year. As

Stafford related the story a few years later, Coniston was becoming a dangerous place to be.

> It was a bad drought year; and Harry Tilmouth from Napperby, and Nugget Morton from Anningie, had both taken out large mobs of cattle into the myall country on the Lander River [within Coniston's boundaries]. Alice [Stafford's Aboriginal partner who lived with him at Coniston] and my boys here often used to pass on to me threatening messages sent in by the myall blacks, telling us all to get out of their country and take our cattle away with us. Coniston Station is on the border between two different tribes, and the waterholes northwest from here are a part of the territory of the Lander River myalls. Alice used to be very frightened whenever these messages came in; for the myalls had said they would kill her first.
>
> Well, there was nothing to be done about it. Harry and Nugget stayed out there, and I sometimes killed an extra bullock for the camp blacks here so that they would not have to starve in the drought.[5]

The 'myall' or 'bush blacks' Stafford was worried about were Aboriginal groups who so far had had little or no contact with white settlers and were considered by whites to be uncivilised and thus distinguished from so-called 'camp' or 'semi-civilised' Aboriginal people. Stafford may well have been receiving warnings as he said but, if so, they were coming from the local Warlpiri who were being pushed off the remaining water sources and were probably losing their patience.

When Brooks told Stafford he was going to head out from Coniston to do some dingo trapping, Stafford warned him that it would be too dangerous to venture any further out than a soak about 14 miles west of Coniston on the edge of the Tanami Desert, which Stafford had named Naval Action after a race horse he had once owned.[6]

Brooks was unconcerned about the danger, telling Stafford that he'd lived with blacks all his life and could handle himself. So he set off, with plenty of provisions from Stafford. In Stafford's words, what happened next had a tragic inevitability:

> Now this is what happened – and it shows that one can never trust any of these bush blacks: their minds must work differently from ours. A party of myalls came in one night, and later came and asked him for some food. While Fred was giving it to them, they all jumped on him and attacked him. One of the gins held him by the hands, while some of the men hacked him down with their tomahawks. Then they stuffed his body down a rabbit burrow, and took all the stores from his camp.[7]

So Stafford said. What was undeniably true about his story, which he started telling a few days after it happened and from which he never wavered, was that Fred Brooks had been clubbed to death by a small group of Aboriginal men. He had been camped at Yurrkuru for a few days, and a party of Warlpiri were also camping there, a few hundred yards or so distant. Early on the morning of 7 August, he was savagely attacked and killed, in an assault which was premeditated and without warning. His mutilated body was indeed shoved in a rabbit hole, his legs grotesquely sticking out in the air.

But why? The immediate question every white in Central Australia would want urgently answered was this: did he do something to provoke his murder – was it payback for a specific grudge – or had the much-feared native rising begun? Brooks had been camping on the western edge of civilisation, so it would make sense if he was first to feel the thrust of the myalls' spearhead as they came out of the desert heading east.

The anxiety is understandable. The first human instinct upon learning that something horrible has happened to someone else is to know its reason, so that we can either rest easier because the cause does not apply to us, or react because it might. In the circumstances of August 1928, being a white man in the Centre meant feeling like you were on the edge of a dark abyss. A panicked public response to the news of Brooks' death was close to inevitable.

How the news came out is an interesting story in itself. Yurrkuru was 14 miles from Coniston, which had no telephone and was a long ride from the nearest place that did. There were no white witnesses to Brooks' murder. However, Stafford was able to say exactly what had happened, down to the details of how Brooks had been tricked and the involvement of a treacherous 'lubra' who held his hands while the men hacked him to pieces. He even knew why Brooks had died, as he explained to Strehlow several years later:

And let me tell you this: Fred Brookes was a decent man who had never harmed anyone all his life. He was what you would call a 'white' man in every way. Fred was the kindest man that ever lived, and he always shared his rations with the blacks. He had always looked on them as his friends.

Old Fred Brookes was the best mate any man could have had, and those myall blacks murdered him without any reason at all. Whatever those myalls might have had against the rest of us, old Fred was entirely innocent. And they murdered him at one of my soaks, on my own land. Even Alice agreed that that party had really come to murder her and me. Only Fred was unlucky enough to cross their tracks. So they killed him instead, because it was easier. Since that day Naval Action has been called Brookes' Soak, and I have named the mountain on the other side Mt. Treachery.[8]

The journalist Eric Baume got the same story from Stafford, with an important extra detail:

When the blacks were hungry he gave them food. It was his invariable practice. He did not interfere with their women – though the practice of the desert tribes is to send in their gins as an offering for food. But his kindliness did not prevent the blacks he had befriended from cutting him to pieces one day, near the soak which bears his name, and hiding (or attempting to hide) the poor butchered remains in rabbit holes.[9]

Stafford was certain that his old mate Fred had been the victim of cruel luck, simply because he had chosen to camp in the warpath of the invading 'myalls' who were on a coordinated mission to wipe out the whites, starting with Stafford himself. So far as most of his contemporaries were concerned, he was obviously right. All of their darkest fears stood confirmed, not just by the fact of Brooks' killing, but by its means.

Michael Terry, a gold prospector who had crossed from Western Australia into Central Australia, happened to be close to Coniston in August 1928, and met most of the main characters in this story (but not Brooks). He recounted the full story in his book *War of the Warramullas*,[10] pinning the blame on a desert tribe called the Warramulla who, he wrote, went on a 'marauding expedition' that year with a plan to first go to Coniston and kill Stafford, then hunt down all the other whites in the Lander River area.

Brooks' misfortune, according to Terry, was to be a kind-hearted innocent in the wrong place at the wrong time. The Warramulla, stumbling upon Brooks' camp laden with chunks of meat from an animal they had just wrongfully killed, realised that their plan of extermination may be exposed if Brooks were allowed to live; so they decided to kill him. The infamous 'gin' (like 'lubra', a derogatory term then in common usage for Aboriginal women) grappled with him and called for the men, who cut the helpless Brooks down with tomahawks and heavy clubs called waddies.

Terry went on: after disposing of Brooks, the Warramulla continued to Coniston, intent on murdering Stafford as well. However, Stafford had been forewarned by a brave little black boy who had been with Brooks and managed to sneak away unseen, running the whole way back to Coniston to deliver the dreadful news. Stafford fired at the warriors as they approached, which was enough to scare them away.[11]

The story told by Stafford in 1932, augmented by writers such as Baume and Terry, was no different from the one that emerged within days of Brooks' death in 1928 and almost immediately attained general acceptance and official sanction. In a memorandum written in November 1928, well before there had been a proper inquiry into the circumstances of Brooks' death and in the absence of any credible evidence at all, J. A. Carrodus, a public servant in the Department of Home and Territories, recorded in a memorandum:

> It is reported that a lubra was sent into Brookes' camp to ask for food. Awaiting a favorable opportunity, she grappled with Brookes and called to the aboriginals. The latter rushed upon Brookes and murdered him with boomerangs, nulla nullas and other weapons. It is stated that the number of aboriginals in the party was 50.[12]

What, then, was the source for this tale of a murder, depicted by white men but witnessed only by Aboriginal people? The Board of Enquiry, which later investigated Brooks' killing and the reprisals that followed, did not interview anyone who claimed to have witnessed the events at Yurrkuru.

The starting point is the initial report of the murder, and about this there is considerable uncertainty. The official record begins with the brief notation in the Alice Springs Police Day Journal at 7 am on 11 August of a phone call from Randal Stafford, then at Ti Tree Well (a tiny settlement on the telegraph line north from Alice Springs, due east from Coniston), reporting that Brooks had been killed. The note was written by Acting Sergeant Charles Noblet, officer in charge of the station and second-in-command of the Central Australia Police Force.

Noblet's superior in Alice Springs was J. C. Cawood, who was both the Commissioner of Police and, as Government Resident for Central Australia, the Commonwealth Government's principal representative in the territory. On 30 August, Cawood submitted his first official report of the incident to the Department of Home and Territories in Canberra.[13] Oddly, he claimed that it was he who received the call from Stafford, contradicting the record in the police station day journal. Of more significance, Cawood appended to his report 'statements from Bruce Chapman and Randle Stafford'. The appended typewritten document is headed 'Statements received by Commissioner of Police Central Australia with report of murder by Blacks of Fredrick Brooks, west of Coniston Station'.[14] The typewritten document is a transcription; the original documents from which it was apparently taken have not survived. Apart from Cawood's letter, they are not referred to anywhere in the historical record, so their provenance is uncertain.

The first item is a 'Letter received by Randle Stafford from Bruce Chapman':

> Dear Randle,
> I am at your place now and have some bad news to tell you that the blacks have killed old Fred Brooks, so I am sending Percy in to wire down to the Police. Alex. Wilson also came in yesterday from old Joe Brown, and he said that he is very bad and cannot move, and so we are waiting for some of your buggy horses, and as soon as we get them I am going out with Alex. to bring them in, so I will tell you all about it when you come.

Bruce (sometimes referred to as Mick) Chapman was a prospector who had been out in the Granites region with the legendary Joe Brown. According to the Territory historian Dick Kimber, the twenty-year-old Chapman was camped a day's ride away from Yurrkuru on the Lander River.[15] Based on his note to Stafford, it was long assumed that Chapman was the first to discover Brooks' body.[16]

This story is based on an unsupported assumption about the movements of two little Aboriginal boys. Brooks did have two boys, aged about nine or ten, with him at the camp at Yurrkuru, tasked mainly with looking after his camels. Skipper and Dodger (we only know their 'white' names) were the first of all to learn of Brooks' death, according to the statement from Stafford appended to Cawood's report, supposedly 'taken down by Robert Purvis at Tee Tree Well':

> Fred Brooks left for a waterhole or soakage 14 miles from Staffords after asking me to cut out green hide for pack bags. Two young boys (half castes) named Skipper and Dodge, who Fred sent out to get the camels said that when they came back they saw bush blacks, and then saw blood about the camp, and track where the blacks had killed Fred Brooks. They also saw where he had been partly buried. The bush blacks told the boys who were crying by this time not to tell whitefellow, 'tellem him been fall down self'. They (the boys) then cleared out and came into Coniston, and Mick Chapman had just got there and sent in the note. Fred Brooks would never allow bush blacks around his camp. Brooks had a supply of rations and this is apparently the cause of the trouble. There was no other trouble.

This is a curious document. We know it was created sometime before 30 August (the date of Cawood's report which appended it). Cawood did not say where or how it had been obtained. Purvis gave evidence to the subsequent Board of Enquiry but said nothing about taking Stafford's statement. Stafford never mentioned Purvis in subsequent statements, nor how he had learned the details he supposedly dictated to Purvis. Stafford could write, so it isn't clear why he needed to dictate his statement at all.

On 2 September, Mounted Constable Murray, who Noblet had sent to Coniston to investigate the report of Brooks' murder, wrote his first report at Alice Springs. In it, he recorded that Skipper and Dodger, on coming into Coniston Station, found that there were no white people there; so, 'a native employee proceeded to Bruce Chapman's camp, twenty miles distant and reported the matter. Chapman proceeded to Brooks' camp and located the body of deceased.' Chapman reburied the body and 'reported the matter to the Police'.[17] This last statement is certainly untrue (it was Stafford who made the report), but whether the boys went to Chapman's camp or he came into Coniston by coincidence is impossible to confirm.

If Chapman's note to Stafford is genuine, then Stafford was not at Coniston when Chapman arrived there. If Stafford was at Ti Tree and Chapman sent his note from Coniston, it would have taken several days for the note to get to Stafford. The only other people at Coniston were Aboriginal servants and 'camp blacks', and they could only get from there to Ti Tree on horseback or foot. This means that Stafford might have received Chapman's note by 10 August, or more likely 11 August, when he telephoned the police.[18] There is no reason to think he would have delayed making this report, as there was no possibility of his finding out more details without travelling himself the hundred or so miles back to Coniston, where there was no telephone.

Of course, Chapman's note only recorded that Brooks was dead, killed by blacks. Stafford did return to Coniston; presumably he left Ti Tree on 11 August after telephoning the police and would have arrived at Coniston about 13 or 14 August.

The Adelaide newspapers were first to report Brooks' murder, on 13 August (two days after Stafford's call from Ti Tree).[19] They reported only the bare details consistent with Chapman's note. By 14 August, however, they (and the main Darwin paper, and even *The Sydney Morning Herald*) were running stories with all of the details from Stafford's 'statement' dictated to Purvis.[20] It's safe to assume that the source for the 13 August newspaper reports was either the Alice Springs Police Station or Cawood. From where they got the detail for their 14 August reports is a mystery; none of the newspapers disclosed their source.

There is no possibility that, when Robert Purvis supposedly took down Stafford's statement at Ti Tree Well, sometime between 11 August when Stafford made his initial report and 13 August in time for it to be communicated to the newspapers for their 14 August publication, Stafford could have spoken with Skipper or Dodger, or learned from any source any of the details of Brooks' death other than the scant outline in Chapman's note.

Coniston had no telephone service or any means of reporting news other than by physical delivery back to Alice Springs. It is also impossible that Stafford could have returned to Coniston after 11 August, spoken with the little boys to learn their story, and made it back to Ti Tree by 13 August. Nor could he have gotten himself to Alice Springs in time, not that there's any suggestion that he did. Chapman did go to the Alice, but not until early September.[21] He was already fatally ill with meningitis, dying on 9 September in the Alice Springs hostel. Noblet later testified that he had tried to obtain a statement from Chapman about what had happened at Yurrkuru, but he was already delirious and unintelligible.[22] His story died with him.

The newspaper reports of 14 August were, in the main, consistent with Stafford's purported statement to Purvis, but with some differences in detail. They all reported that Skipper and Dodger had gone straight from the scene of the murder not to Coniston but to Chapman's camp 14 miles away. The Adelaide papers said that Chapman had sent one of them on to Coniston, where Stafford received the news, and that he then rode to Ti Tree to raise the alarm. The *Northern Territory Times* had Chapman himself riding to Ti Tree. There is no obvious explanation for why the details in the 14 August newspaper reports weren't available to them the day before.

Obviously, the newspapers didn't make their stories up; the consistency of their simultaneous reporting means that they had the same factual source. That must have been someone in Alice Springs. The person who gave the story to that someone – the ultimate source – was surely Stafford. He maintained the same version forever afterwards, but never recorded how it came to him. Even if he did somehow speak with Skipper or Dodger, or someone they'd spoken to, before 13 August, they hadn't witnessed the actual murder. He certainly hadn't spoken with any of the Aboriginal people who saw Brooks die. The most logically inviting conclusion is that Stafford made his story up.

This is a critical understanding, mostly missed by previous histories of the Coniston story. Shortly after Fred Brooks' body had gone cold, his old mate Randal Stafford knew he'd been killed. Exactly how he found out, we can't be sure. However, from 14 August – when the newspapers ran with the lurid details of the slaying – and forever more, what Stafford said had befallen

Brooks (and why), none of which he could possibly have known, had become fact.

Of course, there was available all along an alternative source with a quite different explanation for why and how Brooks died that day. The Aboriginal version of events is reliant on oral history, mostly related in the 1970s and 1980s by people who were children at the time.

The first thing to note is that the Aboriginal people camped at Yurrkuru at the same time as Brooks were not 'Warramullas' or 'Wallmullas' at all. They were of a local tribe, the Warlpiri. Coniston was on their land. The mythical Warramulla 'myalls' of the western desert were just that: a myth. (There was a group called the Warumungu or Warramunga, whose lands were to the north of the Warlpiri and whose language was similar; but they played no part whatsoever in the events of this story.)

The only contemporary recording of the Warlpiri story, albeit of uncertain veracity, was told to the subsequent Board of Enquiry by Annie Lock, a missionary who at the time was single-handedly maintaining a mission camp of starving Aboriginal people at Harding Soak some 100 miles south of Coniston:

> Brooks had two young black boys working for him looking after his camels. This is the story told me by the natives. Brooks fed and clothed them. They would have to give some of their clothing and food to the older natives. Brooks told the little boys they must not do that and made them bring the clothing back. The natives were angry with Brooks and went to his camp and killed Brooks. They did not tell me who took the active part in the killing. They did not tell me that a gin held his

hands while the blacks came up. They did not tell me of any gin that was mixed up in the murder in any way.[23]

More detailed versions were told to various researchers many years later. For example, Peter Horsetailer, a Kaytetye man who was a child living at Barrow Creek at the time of the killings and said he knew Brooks' actual killer, told Grace and Harold Koch in 1991 (as translated by them):

> The Kaytetye people knew nothing about [the killing of Brooks]. It was a Warlpiri who killed that bloke. And he didn't kill him for nothing. He killed him because of a woman.
>
> That's what I was told because that man [who killed Brooks] survived. Not too long ago that old fella passed away, the one who killed Brooks. He passed away at Yuendumu. They held his ceremony not too long ago. I saw him, and that's the story he told me.
>
> 'He had been keeping my wife with him and was humping her. That's why I had to get wild and kill him!' That's what happened with them. It wasn't the Aboriginals' fault.[24]

The man described by Horsetailer was Kamalyarrpa Japanangka, a Warlpiri man known as 'Bullfrog' and with a reputation for being hot-headed. The Aboriginal retellings consistently place him as the main instigator of Brooks' killing, and his wife (or one of his wives) at the centre of the dispute which led to it.

Rosie Nungarrayi, a Warlpiri, was Japanangka's granddaughter. She told her story in the 1990s:

At Yurrkuru, my grandfather killed a whitefella. He hit
the whitefella because the whitefella stole his wife. That
old lady was my grandmother, a Napurrula. She was
frightened when that whitefella took her — that's why
the old man hit him.[25]

The two most detailed handed-down versions of the murder
were related by Warlpiri men Tim Japangardi in 1978[26] and D. M.
Jakamarra in 1990.[27] According to Japangardi, Brooks was camped
near the soak at Yurrkuru and using his camels to dig out waterholes and make a dam. The Warlpiri were camped some distance
to the south, and would come to the soak to get water.

The white man used to go into the camp and drag off
women in front of the men whom he threatened with
his rifle.
One day he took off north with Jangari Japangardi's
mother, Napurrula, and slept with her. He kept her for a
long time in his tent as his woman. Back at the camp at
Yurrkuru they looked for her but when night came she
still wasn't to be found. He kept her for two nights and
didn't send her back home. He continued sleeping with
her the next day and although they went north looking
for her, the men didn't find her. The white man kept her
for three days. After that he sent her back home.

The men conferred, coming to the conclusion that they would
have to kill Brooks because 'he might take our women from us'.
The next morning, they sent Napurrula back to Brooks' camp and
three men — Japangardi, Japaljarri and Japanangka, respectively

Napurrula's son, uncle and husband — followed via the creek bed.[28] They lay in wait while Napurrula followed Brooks into his tent, then they attacked.

> Napurrula yelled out. The old men ran straight up to the tent with their boomerangs. Japaljarri was the first one to strike the white man and he struck him a blow on the back of the jaw. The white man staggered and caught hold of the tent posts. Then another man, Japanangka, broke a club over the back of his neck.
>
> The white man was now staggering around and falling down all over the place. Japanangka took his axe and struck the white man on the neck and killed him outright.
>
> Then they dragged the body west towards the creek and shoved it into a rabbit burrow.

Jakamarra's story likewise avers that Brooks had taken Japanangka's wife and kept her for a long time. However, rather than being the victim of a kidnapping, Napurrula was in this version the subject of a trade: domestic services for food and tobacco. Jakamarra says that Napurrula and her niece

> used to give them [the men] their supper in the late afternoon. They gave them their tea and meat and then went away. They said they were going back to wash the dishes, but back at his [Brooks'] camp he did not have any dishes. They used to go back to the other camp for the whole night. He kept them there. He had taken them for himself.

Two other Warlpiri men, Blind Alec Jupurrula and Engineer Jack Japaljarri, said that Japanangka had agreed to loan his wife to Brooks to wash his clothes, in return for food. Brooks kept the woman but gave Japanangka nothing, so Japanangka killed him for failing to honour the bargain – 'One boomerang he puttem right through here [*indicating throat*] and he cut him with stone knife. Finish.'[29]

However it was that Napurrula had come to be with Brooks (and the more credible account seems to be that some kind of trade had been involved, although there's no basis for assuming that this necessarily involved sexual favours), the men believed she had been detained against their wishes and had concluded that the only answer was to kill Brooks. Jakamarra has Brooks and Napurrula sleeping outside his tent in the early morning warmth when Japanangka and Japaljarri snuck up, and says that Japanangka killed him with a single axe blow that went 'right through him into the ground'.

If Brooks was killed over a woman, then his murder followed a long tradition in the Territory. The lack of white women on the frontier had had the obvious consequence. In 1909, Alfred Searcy published his memoirs of fourteen years in the north during the late nineteenth century:

> There can be no doubt that many of the murders [of white settlers] were caused by the white men taking away the black women from their tribes. Nearly all the drovers, cattlemen, and station hands had their 'black boys' (gins). No objection was raised by the black men to interference with their women so long as they were not abducted. It is the taking away of the women that

has been the cause of so many white men having been rubbed out by the niggers.[30]

Every account of the period of colonisation of the Northern Territory refers to the racial mixing that was an open secret and produced increasingly large numbers of 'half-caste' children who were never referred to as anything other than a 'problem'.[31] No doubt there were both consensual and non-consensual elements involved – everything from mutually consenting relationships, to open trading of sex for food and other goods and, at the far end of the spectrum, kidnapping and rape. In this sense, the Territory was genuinely 'wild', one of the reasons why missionary groups targeted it from early on and maintained a relatively prominent presence. For more than one reason, sex was a source of constant racial tension and provided long-ranging context to the circumstances which led to Brooks' death.

Although every white version had an Aboriginal woman as an active participant in Brooks' killing, this detail is completely absent from all Aboriginal tellings of the story. Consistently present is a clear motive. The conflict between the received, official white narrative and the Aboriginal tradition could not be more stark. On the former basis, Brooks' murder was unprovoked, wanton and vicious. On the latter, at least on the basis of Aboriginal custom at the time, it was defensible or even justified.

Of course, although Aboriginal law may have permitted or even mandated that Brooks be killed, English law did not. That law applied in Central Australia, to Aboriginal people as well as the whites. It also said that the facts that Aboriginal people were ignorant of its provisions, had not consented to its application to them, and were in the bizarre position of being subject to the law while also being denied the basic human rights which white people had as a birthright were irrelevant. So, the law said, Brooks' killers were answerable to it for what they had done. In those terms, what they had done was commit a murder.

The contradictions cannot be resolved now. Randal Stafford's certainty as to how Brooks died and why can be safely discarded as a convenient fiction. The surviving Aboriginal stories give a strong clue, but no more than that. Those who knew why were never asked by any investigator. All that can be said for certain is that Fred Brooks was beaten to death by Warlpiri men in the early morning of 7 August 1928. His life had ended in the most brutal way; the anonymity of his existence, lived out on the fringes of the known world, was about to end too. His death would carry a much larger resonance than anything he had ever done.

Chapter 3

THE HUNTERS

This is the story of the application of the white man's law, with all its constitutional and statutory complexities, to a land where magic and superstition are still potent forces. The policemen of the Northern Territory of Australia must satisfy the white man's law, and at the same time educate the aborigines in its virtues, and establish their confidence in it.[1]

Cometh the hour, cometh the man, goes the saying; and in the immediate aftermath of Fred Brooks' brutal slaying the perfectly suited man would have appeared to be Mounted Constable George Murray. Every frontier vengeance epic needs its hero. Murray fitted the bill.

In August 1928, George Murray was a nine-year veteran of the Central Australia Mounted Police, in sole charge at the Barrow Creek Police Station. His reputation was as a tough and effective policeman, perfectly suited to the extreme harshness of the postcolonial frontier.[2] Physically he was imposing: 'a fine character, quiet, methodical, six feet two in height and of powerful physique'.[3]

Coniston was located within the thousands of square miles of wild country for which Murray was responsible, so it was certain that he would play a leading role in the investigation of Brooks' murder. As it turned out, for the next several months he would be doing a lot more than that. His place in Australian history, for fame or infamy, was going to be suitably fitting for a war hero.

Murray was not a native Territorian, but his origins were rural. He was born in the tiny town of Yarck, in Victoria's upper Goulburn Valley, in 1884. When he volunteered for military service less than three weeks after the outbreak of World War I, the unmarried Murray put his occupation as 'Farmer'.

Murray also noted down at enlistment that he had previously served for nearly nine years in the 7th Australian Light Horse Regiment (which appears to have been a mistake since that unit had not existed prior to 1914).[4] In fact, he had already been to war. Murray's name appears in the Nominal Roll with the rank of Saddler (later promoted to Saddler-Sergeant) for the 5th Victorian Mounted Rifles, a unit which fought in the Boer War as part of the Colonial forces supporting the British Empire. Murray was seventeen years old when he shipped to South Africa in March 1901. The 5th saw extensive action over the ensuing year, fighting some significant battles and suffering relatively substantial casualties.[5]

Twelve years later, Australia was sending its young men to defend the Empire once more, and Murray joined up. At thirty years of age, he was a relatively old recruit. His war service was, by any measure, exemplary. Attached to the 4th Australian Light Horse Regiment as a Private and shipped straight to Egypt in October 2014, he participated in the Anzac landings at Gallipoli and fought in that campaign until the Anzac forces finally withdrew from the peninsula in December 1915. In the meantime he was wounded twice: shot in the left shoulder and left arm.

After regrouping in Alexandria and a promotion to Lance Corporal, Murray was sent to join the 2nd Anzac Mounted

Regiment on the battlefields of the Western Front. There he remained until the end of the war, attaining the rank of Sergeant and sustaining two further wounds (as well as picking up a case of gonorrhoea). One of the confronting features of World War I is that not many men lived long enough to be able to say that they were on active frontline service for the whole thing, but Murray was one of those few. What he endured, and the permanent psychological impact it had on him, can only be imagined. There is no record that he ever spoke about it himself.

Murray was finally shipped back to Australia in October 1918, a few weeks before the Armistice, then discharged from the army in March 1919. He was assessed as unfit for further service due to his war wounds, with a 25 per cent reduction in his capacity for work, but this was not sufficient to qualify him for any form of pension or other compensation. In his application for postwar employment, he said he would like to work as a lorry driver.[6]

The labour market was struggling to absorb tens of thousands of returning servicemen, and perhaps the most obvious employment for a man with extensive military service at one of the highest non-commissioned ranks was in the one peacetime civilian occupation that also involved wearing a uniform and a gun. Perhaps the freedom promised by the outback was also a lure for a man hardened by years of wartime service, free of personal ties and now at a loose end.

In April 1919, Murray applied successfully for a job with the Northern Territory Police.[7] He received no training and was sent immediately to various remote police posts.[8] On 22 July 1926 he took up his posting at Barrow Creek.[9]

Barrow Creek in 1928 was a dot on the map some 200 miles north of Alice Springs, consisting of the police post and a telegraph station (its population today is about eleven). It had

been established in the 1870s during the epic construction of the
Overland Telegraph Line between Adelaide and Darwin. Its place
in Territory history was already significant, following the 1874
attack by the local Kaytetye and subsequent reprisal massacres
which had decimated the Aboriginal population in the area. The
Kaytetye were to play a substantial role in the Coniston story as
well, but not as aggressors.

If the day journal of the Barrow Creek Police Station is any
guide, Murray was a punctilious and efficient police officer. Each
day has an entry in Murray's neat handwriting, noting his and
his Aboriginal trackers' movements and the exact distances travelled. His time was occupied pursuing reports from local pastoralists
of their cattle, sheep or goats being killed by Aboriginal
people. This involved him and his trackers covering enormous
distances on horseback, hunting and occasionally apprehending
Aboriginal suspects, who would be brought in neck chains
down to Alice Springs for prosecution. In mid-1928 Murray had
two Aboriginal police trackers, called Sandy and Dan, officially
attached to him.

Before the events of August to October 1928, Murray enjoyed
a solid reputation – at least, among the white population. The
Aboriginal people living around Barrow Creek had a different
perspective, according to Kaytetye man Peter Horsetailer, who
was a child living there at the time:

> Yeah, I saw him here. When he was around in the early
> days. He was a cheeky man. He'd never speak nicely.
> He'd always talk a bit rough and be quick to start a
> fight. He'd only fight with them [Aboriginal people].
> He didn't make polite requests.[10]

If Murray was fair-minded and straight with the white people of his area, but an entirely sinister presence in the lives of the local Aboriginal people, that was hardly an unusual dichotomy.

On 27 July 1928, Murray was on duty at Barrow Creek, recording a report from Tracker Sandy

> that natives had killed sheep in the vicinity of Barrow Creek Telegraph Stn on Saturday July 21st. M. C. Murray made a search, discovered natives tracks & evidence of a sheep having been killed & cooked in the bush. The feet skin & contents of stomach hidden in the rocks.[11]

The next day, Tracker Dan was sent off 'to bring in certain natives whom suspicion fell on owing to their foot tracks being around scene where sheep had been killed & cooked'. Five days later on 2 August, Dan

> returned with a number of natives. M. C. Murray arrested Aboriginals 'Cadney', 'Sam' & 'Rattler' on a charge of unlawful possession of a carcass of sheep. Each native admitted having killed and eaten sheep.[12]

The last entry in the Barrow Creek Day Journal before a long gap which ended on 21 October 1928 was made by Murray on 6 August: 'M. C. Murray with prisoners Cadney Sam & Rattler to Alice Springs. Trackers Sandy & Dan attending horses.'

When he finally returned to his day journal, Murray made this spare entry on Sunday 21 October: 'From August 7th to October 21st M. C. Murray absent from Station on duty in Alice Springs district. Total distance travelled 3002 miles.'[13] That was a vast amount of ground covered, and Murray had been doing a lot more than chasing after cattle poachers.

———

Arriving at Alice Springs on the morning of 6 August with his human cargo of three Aboriginal alleged cattle thieves, Murray found the headquarters of the Central Australia Police Force operating at its ordinary level of indifference. On duty were Acting Sergeant Noblet and Tracker Tommy. Tracker Peter and 'Native Paddy' were out hunting an escaped Aboriginal prisoner.[14]

Charles Noblet was, by his account, an extraordinarily busy man. Apart from his role as second-in-command of the police force at Alice Springs, Noblet was in August 1928 also the Clerk of the Local Court, Health Inspector, Chief Protector of Aborigines, Warden of Mines and Keeper of the Gaol.[15]

Noblet's many official roles give a clue as to the practical extent of governmental authority in the Territory of Central Australia. In fact, to suggest that at this time it had an administration at all is to mislead. Not that, from the Federal Government's perspective, it needed much governing, with only a tiny white population. The police force comprised eight white men (supplemented by Aboriginal trackers): Commissioner Cawood and Acting Sergeant Noblet in Alice Springs, Mounted Constable Murray at Barrow Creek, four other mounted constables at Alice Springs, Alice Well, Arltunga and Lake Nash and one 'relieving' constable. There were in addition two police officers from South Australia on loan and attached to the construction camps on the north–south railway then being laid. West of the main highway and telegraph line between Alice Springs and Darwin were no police at all.[16]

Noblet was forty-eight years old, a police veteran of twenty-five years' experience. Born in rural South Australia, he volunteered in 1901 with the 5th South Australian Imperial Bushmen, which formed part of the Imperial volunteer force fighting for British prestige in the Boer War and saw considerable action.[17] On his return in 1903, he joined the South Australian police force, serving mainly in the Northern Territory, and then transferring to the Central Australia Police Force. He had been appointed to act in the newly created position of Sergeant at Alice Springs in April 1928, and got the job permanently on 1 September.[18]

Noblet occupies a curiously passive place in the Coniston story. Throughout the events that Fred Brooks' murder unleashed, he remained fixed at the Alice Springs station, apparently at no point contemplating taking more positive action himself. This omission raised eyebrows among some Territorian old hands; musing a few years later on the decision to send Constable Murray to investigate Brooks' killing, Nugget Morton told T. G. H. Strehlow:

> By rights Sgt. Noblet from Alice Springs should have come out himself; for he had been in the country long enough to know how to handle these thieving, murdering niggers. But Noblet was a shrewd guy. He wasn't going to get himself into any trouble with the Government just in case the people that run the newspapers should poke their dirty noses into the whole business. And so he sent out Murray, because Murray was a new chum who had only recently come into this country.[19]

Noblet's superior, the grandly titled Police Commissioner, was John Charles Cawood, fifty-five. He also occupied more than one role, having been appointed the inaugural Government Resident for Central Australia, as well as commissioner, when the Northern Territory was formally divided into North Australia and Central Australia with separate administrations in February 1927.

Cawood's appointment hadn't come without controversy. In his application for the Residency position, Cawood had included in his qualifications sixteen years in the New South Wales Civil Service followed by seventeen years of 'commercial life', during which he had also been elected President of Bellingen Shire Council. In addition, he beefed up his credentials by claiming that he had been 'an Honorary Magistrate and a District Coroner for N S Wales in which capacity I have conducted many Magisterial inquiries'. Among his listed referees was Earle Page, then the Deputy Prime Minister.[20]

Cawood got the job, but a Major Ernest Black of Edgecliff in Sydney was quite stirred up. He had also applied for the job, and been rejected. In a long letter of complaint to the Minister for Home and Territories, Major Black stated his objection:

> It is definitely proved that Mr J C Cawood (who left the Forestry Department in 1909 and was for 16 years employed by a timber firm in a small country town) did not possess the two most essential qualifications not having had war service or medical experience and I can find no evidence of his having the necessary legal tropical and administrative experience.[21]

The Major was ignored, but it seems he had a point. The advertised requirements were considerably more extensive than Cawood's resume. And it appears that he was guilty of some padding. In his own application for re-appointment as Government Resident in

September 1929, Cawood confirmed that he had no war service, 'being ineligible at the time', but stated that he had '13 years service in the Military Forces and qualified for Commissioned Rank'.[22] The Australian National Archives have no record of military service by Cawood, and it's difficult to see where he might have fitted in thirteen years of it. The other oddity is the absence of detail on his supposed work as a magistrate and coroner in NSW; this obviously relevant credential was omitted from a comprehensive list of his qualifications and experience which was placed in the government's file 'for Record Purposes'.[23]

As with Noblet, Cawood's importance to the Coniston story is mostly about what he didn't do. As the dramatic events unfolded around him, he would display an almost comical mix of inaction and ineptitude. He was, in almost every possible way, precisely the wrong man for his time and place.

Cawood may have thought Alice Springs was going to be a quiet enough backwater for his final public posting, and before Fred Brooks died it mostly was. The torpor was broken only by a steady flow of Aboriginal prisoners being brought in from the bush charged with cattle killing, and Cawood had been pestering Canberra for more police resources to head off what the pastoralists were warning was becoming a dangerous increase in Aboriginal 'cheekiness'. Still, for all his and Noblet's protestations of overwork, the prevailing state of Cawood's domain was lazy inactivity.

For Murray, used to fairly constant patrolling at his outback postings, Alice Springs may have offered a welcome break. In any event, he only had a few days to enjoy it before, on 10 August, he and Paddy were despatched by Cawood to the stations of two pastoralists, Jim Moar at Woodford and Randal Stafford at Coniston, in response to 'complaints received over natives killing stock'.[24]

The next day, the first report from Stafford of Brooks' murder came in to the station, and Murray was diverted to take up that case. How he was intercepted on the road is unclear. Murray recorded much later that he 'heard F. Brooks had been murdered' and returned to Ryan's Well, along the highway north of Alice Springs, where he 'communicated with Com'r of Police for confirmation of report'.[25] Cawood said he had 'intercepted' Murray at Ryan's Well and instructed him to head straight for Coniston to investigate the murder.[26] Neither of them said who actually caught up with Murray and caused him to go back to Ryan's Well.[27] Still, by 11 August the bush telegraph would have been buzzing with the news, and anyone who bumped into Murray might have been the one to fill him in. Presumably he decided to go back to Ryan's Well, where there was a telephone, so he could call in to Cawood for instructions. Murray then proceeded directly to Coniston with Paddy, arriving there on 12 August. The next communication he would have with his superiors in Alice Springs would be on 1 September.

Awaiting Murray at Coniston was Randal Stafford. Whether he was 'a tall spare figure, with a patriarchal white beard' and 'an admirably upright carriage' as Strehlow described him, or the 'little man, slightly bent with a brick-red face and white beard and moustache' as he was described by Baume, each at Coniston in 1932, Stafford was an institution of the Territorian world.[28]

The Coniston homestead consisted of a small group of buildings roughly constructed of gum trunks with thatched roofs, set on a rise next to Warburton Creek. The creek was usually dry but, in rainy season, might swell to a quarter of a mile wide. Extremely humble as the Coniston homestead was, and difficult to get to, its location on the absolute fringe of the desert wilderness made it 'an oasis for the wanderers', according to Baume, who described Stafford as 'a password wherever decent men assemble and a Northern Territory figure whose individual courage and capacity for work have made him respected by all'.

Stafford may have fulfilled many of the attributes of the archetypal bush paladin – tough, gruff, suspicious of strangers but endlessly hospitable to 'straight men according to his light' – but there were some significant departures from the cliché. He had come from a well-off, educated family. He was notoriously, and it seems uniquely, nonviolent towards Aboriginal people; and he had even developed a genuine affection for them, at least of a sort.

For Stafford had a 'dark sweetheart'. Her name was Alice, and she had been living with Stafford as his common-law wife for some time. Strehlow recorded an illuminating exchange when he visited Coniston:

'Lots of the black gins around here are so very slovenly and dirty, and yet look at Alice: you wouldn't find a cleaner and nicer white girl in Adelaide than her.' A happy smile stole across Stafford's honest, weather-beaten face. 'And now I must show you a picture of my daughters. But wait, I'll call Alice too: she is their mother, and she is always so proud when I show this picture to my visitors.'

Alice came in, and Stafford put his arm around her waist proudly and affectionately while he told me of the fine progress their two little girls were making at school in Adelaide.

'I want them to have a chance to make good in life', he remarked. 'Everything up here would be against them. In Adelaide my sister looks after them, and they have a good home.'

It was good to see Stafford looking so proud of his family. He seemed to have found a marital happiness for which many men in the southern cities would have envied him.[29]

For 1932 Central Australia, this was radical stuff, marking Stafford in relative terms as an enlightened man. He explained his general views on Aborigines to Strehlow:

I don't dislike the blacks myself: I have lived among the blacks all my life...and I realize that they are human beings like myself. It's just that I don't understand them and their ways. I've been good to them on every station I've been on – I've fed them – I've treated them well – I've never interfered with them much on their walk-abouts; and yet I feel sure that they don't like me much any more than they like those other whites who treat them as though they were dogs. But it doesn't matter to me. I know that these myalls here sometimes spear one of my bullocks; but as long as it doesn't happen too often, I say nothing about it. It was their country before I came into it, and I know they often have a pretty tough time in making a living for themselves.[30]

His live-and-let-live attitude to interracial relations was, it seems, unique to Stafford in the region and it earned him considerable scorn from some of his contemporaries. A somewhat different take on the situation was also recorded by Strehlow when he encountered another local legend, Harry Tilmouth of Napperby Station, 32 miles south-east of Coniston.

old Randall's never been known to hurt any of them niggers neither all his life. That's what I think the real trouble was: Randall let them myalls run around all over his place and never said nothing when they speared one of his bullocks on the quiet, and in the end the niggers thought they could do bloody well what they liked. I don't mind old Randall myself, but I think he's a silly bloody fool about them myalls. It's all because he's had a young myall gin himself for years, Alice he calls her; and old Randall is in love with that gin. Imagine any bloke with any bloody sense ever being in love with any gin! Most of us have got to have gins – no white woman will ever come out into these bloody god-forsaken parts; but most of us try to use our common sense a bit. We all know that no gin can be trusted – she'll go to any nigger as soon as your back's turned.

He's sent his two half-caste girls down to his sister in Adelaide to have them brought up like white ladies. I think he's quite mad myself, just a poor bloody lunatic in fact. My flamin' oath, it's men like him that teach the niggers to be cheeky to us whites.[31]

All the same, in the days following the murder of his close mate Brooks, Stafford was as keen as anyone to see a rough form of justice done. As proprietor of Coniston and Brooks' employer, he was quickly and uncomplainingly co-opted by Murray to provide men and horses for an avenging posse.

Already at Coniston was Alex Wilson, pre-emptively diminished in all contemporary accounts because he was a 'half-caste'. Wilson's role in the succeeding events is maddeningly obscure; he did not give evidence before the Board of Enquiry and there is no record of any first-person statement made by him. He lived a long time in the Territory afterwards, and some later writers were able to interview him.[32] But he was never particularly forthcoming about what he actually saw and what he personally did in those weeks in the desert after Brooks' murder. Consequently, he has tended to take on footnote-status in the telling of the Coniston story. He deserves, for better or worse, a far more prominent part.

Dick Kimber met Wilson in the 1970s and says they became good friends. He records Wilson as being born in Hall's Creek around the turn of the century, to a white father, a bushman who drank himself to death, and an Aboriginal mother who was fatally speared.[33] There is no historical evidence to support this, or the colourful background story Kimber tells in the lead-up to Coniston.

According to Kimber, Wilson came to Central Australia sometime in the 1920s with a young Aboriginal wife. He began working for Nugget Morton, who took Wilson's wife by force. When Wilson protested, Morton opened up his back with a stock whip.[34]

At the time that Fred Brooks was at Yurrkuru getting himself murdered, Wilson was camped near Mount Hardy in the Granites (about 60 miles north-west of Coniston) nursing his employer Joe Brown, the legendary bushman of the Centre, who had fallen fatally ill. Wilson was trying to keep Brown alive while getting him to such help as was available at Coniston. As Brown was rapidly failing, Wilson eventually decided to ride on to Coniston alone, arriving there on 6 or 7 August. Chapman's note to Stafford, apart from announcing Brooks' murder, also told Stafford that Wilson had arrived at Coniston the day before and that Chapman and Wilson were going to head back to rescue Brown, who was in a bad way.[35]

By some accounts, Wilson was in fact the first person to find Brooks' body in its rabbit hole, by coincidence as he passed through Yurrkuru on his way to Coniston.[36] He left it undisturbed and rode on. If this were true, it would mean that Wilson only narrowly missed witnessing the murder or even possibly saving Brooks' life. It doesn't matter, but seems unlikely.

Kimber reckons that, before Wilson and Chapman set off to find Joe Brown, Chapman made a flying trip to Yurrkuru to re-bury Brooks in a deeper grave. He and Wilson then set off for Mount Hardy, making it just in time for Brown to die. They buried him there and headed back to Coniston, where Wilson arrived by 12 August.[37] The round trip for Wilson would have been some 120 miles, supposedly achieved in under five days – quite the feat.

Chapman, whether or not he rode out with Wilson, did not in fact return to Coniston; Murray never mentioned him and it appears they never met. Michael Terry recorded that he bumped into Chapman, along with a man called Mathews, near Ryan's Well on 1 September. Mathews had come from Jimmy Wyckham's station at Mount Peake, and had picked Chapman up somewhere along the way. He told Terry that Chapman had 'gone out to get Joe Brown and afterwards saw Brooks after he was murdered'. Chapman was very ill and accepted Terry's offer of a lift to Alice Springs. They got in on 3 September and Chapman went straight to the hostel to die there a few days later. Terry made no mention of Wilson.[38] What Chapman was actually doing between 7 August and 1 September is a mystery.[39]

Regardless of whether anyone had really seen him die, Brown was dead and Wilson was consequently temporarily unemployed. He was the first conscript to Murray's hunting party, and he would prove a handy addition due to his genuine bush skills and ability to shoot straight with a rifle.[40] He also spoke, at least to some extent, the local dialects.

The next recruit was John 'Jack' Saxby, a 'tall dark cattleman-prospector'[41] who had been in the Territory for twelve years[42] and was somewhere on the Coniston property at the time, sinking a well for Stafford.[43] He joined the party at the homestead sometime before 16 August. What little has been written of Saxby has him as a young bushman with a marksman's dead eye and a willingness to shoot to kill when confronted by Aboriginal people.[44]

The final white member of Murray's party was William 'Billy' Briscoe, another experienced bushman[45] who was employed by Stafford on Coniston, and said he was camped about 18 miles from where Brooks was killed on 7 August. Stafford sent a boy to call him in, and he turned up at Coniston about a week later with extra horses for the hunt and, like the rest of the party, armed to the teeth.[46]

So was the investigative expedition comprised: Mounted Constable Murray, Stafford, Saxby, Briscoe, the 'half-caste' Wilson and three Aboriginal trackers, Paddy, Major and Dodger. Paddy had come from Alice Springs with Murray, but Major was a 'station black' at Coniston, and reportedly the uncle of Dodger, one of the two boys who had reported Brooks' murder. Neither Paddy nor Major was an official police tracker (and Dodger was a young boy, about nine or ten years old). None of the other members of the party was properly deputised by Murray and there is no indication that he had been instructed or authorised to enlist non-police assistance. In fact, apart from Murray himself, nobody in the party had any official or semi-official function or legal authority. This was, in law and practicality, a vigilante group.

Chapter 4

AUGUST

When the Warramullas made the last doomed stand of the conquered Aborigines, they had no idea what they were up against.[1]

The first thing Murray did at Coniston when he arrived there on 12 August, according to his later report to Noblet, was to 'make enquiries' and ascertain the details of Brooks' murder.[2] The version he wrote in his report was essentially the same as what the newspapers had said on 14 August. Since he didn't write it until September, it adds no credence to Stafford's original story, which by then had become folklore.

Murray's next investigative step, he reported to Noblet, was this:

> From enquiries I ascertained the names of twenty adult male aboriginals whom it is alleged were implicated in the murder. Furthermore, I was informed that the natives were still camped near the scene of the murder, and had boasted that they would kill any person who came to their camp, and that they were not afraid of Police.[3]

For the officer investigating a week-old murder, this was (you would suppose) highly significant; he had obtained a list of identified suspects and confirmation of their present location only 14 miles away. Murray would of course have kept a careful note of this evidence, including its source. He would place this record front and centre in his report to his superiors and in his testimony to the subsequent Board of Enquiry. Or so you would think.

In fact, he did none of these things. Despite telling Noblet in September that he had acquired the names of twenty suspects, Murray never mentioned this to the Board of Enquiry during his supposedly exhaustive detailing of the relevant events in sworn testimony. The twenty names are lost to history, if they ever existed. Who gave these names to Murray he never stated. In reality there are two possibilities: either Murray made this up entirely or he treated it as a relatively unimportant detail. Untrained as he was in investigative police work, Murray was not an idiot. His report to Noblet, it must be concluded, was a lie. It was not a promising start to his investigation.

On arrival at Coniston, Murray had instructed Paddy and Major to stand guard over the 'native camp' there, allow nobody to leave 'that may spread the news of my arrival', and detain any other Aboriginal people who turned up.[4] The native camp was, as was the norm on stations, a distance from the main homestead. Murray had no legal authority to detain anyone who wasn't under arrest – not that anyone at the time, or later, appeared to have a problem with his taking this measure.

On 15 August, there was a commotion in the native camp.[5] Two Aboriginal men, strangers to Coniston, had walked into the camp. They were big men, well armed with boomerangs and spears. Paddy and Major, following Murray's orders, immediately moved to intercept and detain them, without giving them any warning. Paddy got hold of one of the men by the arms, while Major grabbed his boomerang, and they tried to drag him over to Murray's car, where the neck chains were kept. They managed to get a neck chain around both men's necks with the cuff attached to one of them.

The intruders were not going down without a fight, however. From their perspective, why would they? Neither Paddy nor Major was wearing a police uniform (remember, they were not official police trackers), and there's no indication that the two visitors had any violent intent.

One of the men managed to pull away from Paddy and, using the neck chain as a weapon, struck Paddy in the back. At this point Murray, having heard the sounds of fighting, ran over from the homestead – with his rifle, according to Paddy, but only with a holstered revolver by Murray's own account – to see Paddy struggling with one of the captives. This man went for Murray, trying to hit him with the chain. The second prisoner got free at the same time. Murray, considering the position 'dangerous', as he later said, pulled out his revolver and shot the man who was attacking him at point blank range, in the face. The bullet entered above the left temple, fracturing his skull and knocking him unconscious. The second prisoner was then subdued as well, and both were tied securely to a tree.

The evidence for this encounter comes from later statements made by Murray and Paddy, which were largely consistent but had some major discrepancies, including whether it happened before Murray's party had commenced the manhunt (as Murray claimed) or after they had already been out for several days and had returned to Coniston briefly (according to Paddy). Paddy neglected to mention at all that Murray had shot one of the prisoners, until asked specifically later by the Board of Enquiry.

And Murray and Paddy each claimed that it was he who brought the second prisoner to heel. None of this matters terribly much but, oddly, Paddy included in his sworn statement the immediate follow-up to the fight, when the prisoners were apparently identified, while Murray omitted this part altogether.

According to Paddy, after the prisoners had been re-secured, Murray called Dodger over and asked him if he knew them.

> Dodga [sic] said 'Yes me been see em longa spring'. I asked Dodga in blacks language what were their names. Dodga said Padygar. I have forgotten the name of the other one. The name of the other black as supplied by Constable Murray is Willingar.

Willingar was the man who Murray had shot in the head. According to Paddy, Dodger identified the two men as being from the mob at Yurrkuru. Murray never said whether their names were on the list of twenty suspects which he was supposedly holding. That would have been an obvious necessity; otherwise, on what possible basis could he maintain their forced imprisonment? After all, all they had done was walk into Coniston and then try to defend themselves when Paddy and Major attacked them.

There is one more mystery to unravel in the capture of Padygar and Willingar. While his report to Noblet and statements to the Board of Enquiry and the Coroner (given at the same time as the board's hearings, early in 1929) were broadly consistent, in early September Murray had also made a deposition to the Magistrate of the Police Court in Alice Springs, in support of the charge of Brooks' murder which he was then promoting against Padygar.[6]

In this brief deposition, Murray told an entirely different story from the one he'd reported to Noblet only a few days earlier.

After repeating the assertion that he had acquired twenty suspects' names, he swore:

> I then proceeded to the locality and arrested Prisoner Padygar. He stated that he had killed the old man so as to get possession of his flour and tobacco. I took him to the scene of the murder. He showed me where Brooks had been camped and stated that Brooks had been sitting down repairing pack bags when a number of natives including himself, crept up behind cover. They then rushed the old man and beat him to death with boomerangs, yam sticks and tomahawks. He then scraped in the sand and handed me cakes of dry blood which he stated had bled from the old man, and had been covered with sand by natives. He then showed me to the burrow where they had buried the body. He also scraped in the sand and showed me some dry blood which had bled from the body whilst they were preparing the grave.

This was a pretty compelling story. Having acquired a list of suspects, Murray rushed over to the murder scene and arrested one of the named men, who then immediately confessed and showed the diligent police officer the damning forensic evidence. It was passing strange that, apart from this deposition to the magistrate when he was trying to get a committal for murder, Murray never saw fit to re-tell the story in anything like the same way again. It was, for sure, a fiction, invented under oath to secure an easy committal.

As 16 August dawned, the whole party was present at Coniston and two prisoners, one already dying from an untreated gunshot wound, were chained to a tree.

———

Murray was armed with a posse, two eyewitnesses (Skipper and Dodger), two suspects who the witnesses had positively identified, a list of twenty suspects in total and a report that the whole gang of killers was still camped at Yurrkuru, 14 miles west of Coniston. Murray told the Board of Enquiry that Padygar and Willingar volunteered to show him where the other murderers were, and led them some 12 to 14 miles west to their camp. The exact location of this first stopping point of the hunting party is unknown, but it wasn't Yurrkuru, where Brooks had died.[7]

The party now consisted of Murray, Stafford, Briscoe, Saxby, Wilson, Paddy, Major, Dodger and the two prisoners Padygar and Willingar, all on horseback except the last three. The prisoners were kept chained. How Willingar managed to walk at all, let alone keep up, is a mystery given that he had been shot in the head the day before and had received no medical treatment at all. Presumably this is why it took until mid-afternoon for the party to cover the short distance to its first destination.

This was an Aboriginal camp, containing an unrecorded number of members of an unidentified group (most likely Warlpiri as this was still squarely within their territory). On nearing the camp, Murray supposedly issued explicit instructions to everyone that there was to be no shooting (except in 'self-defence' or 'unless absolutely necessary', according to various recollections), because Murray wanted to make arrests of all the suspects, and that women and children were not to be harmed.[8]

Murray now set his tactical approach to the camp. The country here was flat but covered in quite dense scrub and therefore with poor lines of visibility. Major and Dodger were ordered to stay behind with the packhorses, while Paddy kept watch on the two prisoners. The rest of the party Murray arranged in 'extended order' – a military formation used for skirmishing, where the soldiers are spread as widely apart as the circumstances and terrain will permit. According to Briscoe, the men were spread out at intervals of approximately 150 yards, Briscoe on the extreme right, then Wilson to his left and Murray in the centre. Saxby said he was on Murray's left, and Stafford claimed to have taken up 'a position on the extreme South to prevent natives escaping'. Although the men were all on horseback, they quickly lost sight of each other in the scrub after Murray gave the order to advance.

The party moved in towards the camp, giving no warning that they were coming. Murray sighted the camp first. He immediately kicked his horse into a gallop and rushed towards it, still silent apart from the sound of his charge. Saxby said that he saw this and attempted to follow, but lost Murray almost immediately. Briscoe then saw Murray jump off his horse.

What Murray's plan was, assuming he acted as he later claimed, is not easy to follow. Charging headlong into an encampment of unsuspecting Aboriginal men, women and children, on a horse and clearly heavily armed, was objectively unlikely to produce a passive response. Still, that is what he said he did. As he came close, Murray said he noticed the natives gathering together and moving to meet him; 'they took up their position in the grass amongst some low bushes'. Murray went on:

Only one native appeared to be armed. I dismounted with a view to disarming the native. Immediately I stepped to the ground, the whole of the native party rushed me with weapons in their hands – they having had them concealed in the grass. I seized one native and threw him. The others then commenced to strike me with their weapons. As the position appeared serious and I could not see any of my party in sight I drew my revolver and fired two shots.

This was Murray's evidence to the Board of Enquiry. He gave no indication of whether his shots had hit anyone. However, in a deposition to the Coroner a few days after that appearance, he was more forthcoming:

As I could not see any of my party in sight to render me assistance I realised that I would be overpowered and badly injured if not killed. I drew my revolver and fired two shots at natives who were actually in holts [fighting] with me. The two natives were shot dead.

In the commotion, Murray's horse had bolted back to where the packhorses were being held by the trackers. The other members of his party told differing versions of what happened next.

Saxby said he had lost sight of Murray in the scrub. He heard a lot of shouting and rattling of spears, so he rode back to where he had last seen Murray, but only saw Murray's horse bolting. For some reason he now dismounted and ran to where he thought Murray might be. Arriving on the scene, he saw about thirty Aboriginal people, all naked, all armed with sticks, spears and boomerangs, rushing at Murray. He heard Murray's two shots, and this caused the attackers to go harder, so Saxby fired three shots with his rifle into the mob from about 50 yards. Whether he hit anyone he couldn't tell. He heard two other guns go off from another direction but couldn't identify the shooters. At this point the attackers 'stampeded away'.

Briscoe, by contrast, had eyes on Murray right until he was attacked, although he was further away from him than Saxby. He saw Murray gallop ahead and jump off his horse, and 'try to arrest a native'. The 'natives' then attacked, rushing Murray. 'The lubras ran around him with nulla nullas and yam sticks.' Briscoe yelled at Wilson, who was presumably closest, to 'get in there and help Mr Murray'. Briscoe himself, he claimed, did not do the same; 'I heard a noise in the scrub and thought it was natives escaping. I galloped round the scrub in that direction to see if there were any. I did not see any.' While doing this, he heard four or five shots, and made his way back to where Murray was.

Stafford also saw Murray gallop towards the camp, and said that he heard Murray calling to the inhabitants 'to stop in English. I don't suppose the blacks understood but there was no other way of speaking to them.' Stafford had now lost sight of Murray and everyone else, and decided to gallop 'for the back of the camp to prevent them escaping'. He heard some shots fired, figured that Murray must be under attack and rode back towards the scene.

When everyone had reassembled, they found four Aboriginal people dead on the ground: three men and a woman. A second woman was badly wounded, and died shortly afterwards. Everyone agreed with this death toll of five, but nobody could say who had fired the fatal shots. None of the party had been injured, whether by the thirty or so supposed attackers with their spears, boomerangs and clubs, or by crossfire – quite fortunate, given the confusion, the lack of visibility and the fact that the group had converged on the scene more or less simultaneously and from every direction. Equally surprising was the absence of any non-fatal injury to the multitude of men, women and children at the camp. At least, neither Murray nor his party mentioned any.

Murray now reasserted order, which he said had been his intended aim from the outset.

> The natives were instructed by myself to sit down and remain quiet. Myself assisted by Mr. Stafford then disarmed the natives. We collected 23 spears which were concealed in the grass and bushes, apparently in readiness for an attack; also a number of boomerangs, nulla nullas and yamsticks. The weapons were destroyed by fire and the camp searched. A quantity of property was recovered and identified by Stafford as the property of Fred Brooks deceased – consisting of coat, shirt, singlets, quart pot, blanket, calico, knives, tobacco.

It was a detailed list, and not one which Stafford or Murray could have been expected to commit to memory for recitation to the inquiry four months later. For, in his original report to Noblet, Murray had not mentioned the quart pot but had said that the property identified as belonging to Brooks included – critically, because they would have conclusively identified the property's owner – his wallet and papers. Perhaps the inconsistency was the result of mere sloppiness, but it ought to have interested the Board of Enquiry (it didn't). None of the items, it appears, was retained as evidence, because none was presented at the subsequent committal and trial of the suspected killers.

To complicate matters further, although Murray said that Stafford had identified Brooks' property, Stafford didn't say so; but Briscoe in his evidence claimed that it was he who had recognised the items (again, a slightly different list from Murray's, and not including a wallet or papers) as belonging to Brooks.

Stafford, who was anxious to affirm that he had personally fired no shots in the incident, added to his later evidence an additional piece of news that had obviously high significance, but which Murray never mentioned. Stafford recalled that, after the shooting, Major had ridden up to the scene, 'pointed to the blackfellow who was dead and said "That's the one wanten killem you"'. Major then also identified the fatally wounded woman as 'the one that held Brooks while the blacks came up and killed him'.

Major, of course, had not been at Yurrkuru when Brooks was killed, but at Coniston, so he couldn't identify anyone. Indeed nobody had claimed to have witnessed Brooks' actual murder. By contrast, Murray told the Board of Enquiry that it was Dodger who came up after the shooting and recognised the four dead Aboriginal people 'as being the natives who were camped in the vicinity of Brooks camp'. Even if true, this wasn't evidence of any culpability for Brooks' death.

When Murray gave an interview to the journalist Ernestine Hill in 1933, he recalled this first incident differently. There was an ambush, and Murray was attacked when he dismounted. But, 'The firing broke out – I don't know who started it, but the whole 17 were dead when it finished'.[9] Was that a lazy compression of several incidents into one? It seems not, because Murray went on to tell Hill about several other shootings during the same expedition, including more deaths. His comment has attracted little historical attention, but it strongly suggests that Murray's very first encounter with Aboriginal people during the hunt had resulted in not just five deaths but a wholesale massacre. If so, what else was to come?

Murray now ordered Briscoe to make the surviving Aboriginal people move down the creek and camp there for the night. Meanwhile, Murray and Stafford buried the dead and the party made camp, as it was getting dark. Establishing a pattern that he would consistently follow, Murray had no thought of suspending or ending his expedition to deal with the legal consequences that should have followed the shooting of five civilians (if that was the true count), whether in self-defence or not. There was to be no independent investigation or inquest into this incident or any of those which followed, and no attempt to preserve evidence, not even a report to headquarters, until Murray had completed his hunt and returned to Alice Springs.

During the night came a further incident. Murray and Wilson went out into the long grass that night about 100 yards from the Aboriginal camp. Murray was expecting that some male members of the camp would have been out hunting and would try to return in the darkness, and he wanted to intercept them.

> Within half an hour a slight noise was heard in the scrub and within a few minutes three objects were seen approaching. Myself and Wilson remained silent having instructed him to allow them to get between us and the natives who were camped. Then we would rush them. The three objects passed within a few yards of where we were lying. I could see that they were weehis [Aboriginal children]. Two of them ran and sat down among the other natives. The third one hesitated. We sprang to our feet and the third one made off in the darkness. I followed him and brought him back. Wilson having detained the other two.

The three little boys told Murray that a group of adult males was waiting out in the scrub and had sent them in to find out what had happened at the camp. Nobody else was seen approaching that night. In the morning, the captive boys 'volunteered' to show the party the tracks back to where the missing men had been. The whole day was spent fruitlessly searching for these tracks. That evening, Murray decided to keep one of the boys, called Lala, and let the rest of the original camp members go. He instructed them to move to a spring 4 miles away, telling them they would 'not be interfered with' there.

On 17 and 18 August, two further days of unsuccessful hunting for tracks followed. Murray gave no details of where the party went but, according to Briscoe, they rode about 20 miles to Cockatoo Spring. During those days, Briscoe said he heard a rifle report in the hills but told nobody about it, and later on Murray came into the camp with 'one old blackfellow and two lubras'. Briscoe didn't say what happened to them.

On 19 August, the party retraced its steps back to Coniston. The stories diverge somewhat here, as Stafford told the Board of Enquiry that he had left the others on the morning of 17 August, the day after the first shooting. He said he went to the White Stone, about 12 miles away, 'to see if there were any blacks there'. There were not, so he rode back to Coniston and claimed that he never went out with Murray's expedition again.

The other members of the party had Stafford remaining with them until they all got back to Coniston together on the 19th. Murray reported to Noblet that 'from enquiries I ascertained that some of the murderers were camped about forty five miles north west'. He did not indicate with whom these enquiries had been made. Already by this date, the news that a white man's punitive expedition was on the warpath had spread well up the Lander valley, and Aboriginal groups were starting to disperse to get out of its way.

The party camped overnight at Coniston, and Stafford remained behind the next day when they headed off. The two prisoners, Padygar and Willingar (the latter still carrying his untreated head wound but, amazingly, clinging to life), as well as the captured child, Lala, were also left behind. Murray said that 'Tracker Jack' from Alice Springs had by then arrived at Coniston, and Murray instructed him to keep close watch on Lala and the prisoners.[10]

The party could move more rapidly now, unencumbered by the two prisoners on foot. The riders headed roughly north-west, following the dried-up Lander. They camped at Boundary Soak, where they encountered some Aboriginal people who told them that 'the alleged murderers were at the 6 mile soak'. The Six Mile Soak was some 32 miles north-west of Coniston; when they arrived there, the party found tracks heading towards the south-west. Leaving Major and Dodger behind with the packhorses, the party followed the tracks for some 10 miles until they came upon another camp comprising, according to Murray, six men and about twenty-three women and children.

Murray again placed his men in extended order, with the intention of surrounding and surprising the camp inhabitants. The disastrous outcome which this tactic had produced a few days earlier (at least, in terms of Murray's stated desire of capturing suspects, not shooting them) did not apparently deter Murray from repeating it.

As they approached the camp, Murray and his men were sighted and six adult males stood up, armed with spears and boomerangs. Murray told Noblet that the Aboriginal men were warning his party to leave. Murray said he remained mounted 'and cautioned them of the consequences should they attempt to escape'. As Briscoe put it, 'Alex Wilson yabbered to these natives and told them to put their weapons down.' The stand-off continued for some time, before – according to the whites – the Aboriginal men ended it by starting to throw their boomerangs and spears. Briscoe said they were about 80 yards away at this point. Murray reported:

> My tracker [Paddy] narrowly avoided being struck by a boomerang. The position again appeared serious and I ordered one of my party to fire at the shield in a native's hand. The bullet split the shield and it fell to the ground. The infuriated natives attacked in earnest. Three were killed and three wounded.

To the Board of Enquiry, Murray revealed additionally that he had, on this occasion as with the first, decided to dismount in the midst of the hostile Aboriginal men

> and the six natives immediately rushed me. I received several blows from boomerangs and yamsticks and was compelled to use my revolver. I fired four shots also heard shots from other directions.

Briscoe claimed to have been 100 yards away from the fighting and that he didn't shoot anyone. Saxby said he had worked his way around to the back of the camp, furthest away from Murray. He heard but didn't see Murray telling the men to drop their weapons, and galloped in that direction. As he came into view, he had to dodge several spears. Jumping off his horse, he fired four or five shots. He couldn't tell (again) whether he had hit anyone but, as he said, 'I certainly tried.' What part Wilson and Paddy played, again, none of the witnesses mentioned.

Now 'order was restored' and three Aboriginal men lay dead. Three others had gunshot wounds, but Murray said they 'did not appear to be seriously wounded in my opinion'. They received no medical aid, not that Murray was really in a position to offer any. None of his party had been injured, notwithstanding that Murray himself reported that he had again taken several blows from Aboriginal weapons at close range and, clearly, there had been a lot of shooting.

The 'battle' had been fought at about 5 pm. Murray rounded up the three wounded men and the women and children at the camp, and marched them back to the Six Mile Soak, arriving about midnight. The whole party camped there.

At this point, Murray testified to the Board of Enquiry, 'the three wounded prisoners were identified as the alleged murderers of Brooks'. By whom, he did not say. Dodger was still with his party and might have identified them as among those who had camped at Yurrkuru when Brooks was there, but not as his killers.

Three days later, Murray swore a quite different version of events to the Coroner: in fact, he said, even before hostilities commenced, Paddy had identified all six of the Aboriginal men who were confronting the party, 'by name and description'. This would have been quite remarkable, since Paddy had no connection to the Warlpiri or Kaytetye people. In any event, after the shooting had died down, Murray claimed, the three wounded men positively identified themselves as well as the three dead men as having been 'implicated in the murder of Brooks'. That must have come as a pleasantly convenient surprise.

In the morning, Murray found that two of the wounded prisoners had died during the night. The women and children were left unmolested at the Six Mile Soak, while the party headed for Briscoe's camp at Boundary Soak some 6 miles away, with the remaining shooting victim in tow. Murray, concerned for his welfare, 'endeavoured to persuade the prisoner to ride a horse but he refused to do so'. So, presumably, he walked. On arrival at Briscoe's camp, the prisoner died and was buried there. The party headed south, arriving around sunset back at the camp where Murray had sent the survivors of the first shooting incident, four days earlier. The site was empty.

Now Murray decided to change things up. He had already killed by his own count eleven suspects, of whom nine had been identified as being among Brooks' murderers, and he was still also holding two confessed murderers prisoner back at Coniston – meaning that he had now captured a total of eleven killers either dead or alive. But perhaps the pace of the hunt was still too sedate. The action now shifted to the west, into the rocky hills stretching towards the Western Australian border 300 miles away. This was territory foreign to everyone in the hunting party, and traversed to that date by no more than a few intrepid white explorers.

On the morning of 22 August, Murray split his party up, sending each man in a different direction on horseback to look for tracks. Only Dodger remained behind. Murray immediately found tracks leading away from the campsite, 'many more bucks' tracks there than could have been made by the party we had left there'. The men reassembled and followed these tracks to the foot of the hills, where it was too rough for the horses. Murray told Paddy and Major to keep following the tracks into the rocks. When they came down at midday, they reported that the tracks continued westerly along the range. The rest of the day was spent following the tracks, finding water and setting up camp for the night. No Aboriginal people were sighted.

Early on the 23rd, Murray told the Board of Enquiry, 'several natives were noticed up on the ranges probably two miles distant'. He again split his party, sending Briscoe, Saxby and Wilson each to a different spring to wait for any prey who Murray was able to flush out, 'as the natives must certainly go straight to water'. Major and Paddy went on foot towards where the Aboriginal men had been sighted, and Murray followed on horseback as far as he could.

> I then dismounted and very soon sighted some natives in the valley. I waited then noticed my two trackers coming up behind the natives. The trackers overtook the natives before I could reach them. When I arrived on the scene, I found that Paddy had two male natives handcuffed together with the one handcuff. Two lubras and one old blackfellow were sitting down. A number of boomerangs and yamsticks were lying close handy. I questioned the two prisoners. They admitted having been at Stafford Spring and had assisted to kill Brooks.

As Wilson was not present and there is no indication that Paddy or Major spoke the relevant language, how exactly Murray obtained this confession is unexplained. That is quite apart from the yet again extraordinary coincidence that just about every Aboriginal person Murray ran into turned out to have been one of Brooks' murderers.

However, these prisoners were not so quiescent. While Murray was momentarily distracted,

I noticed that the prisoners had slipped the handcuff and were making off down the hill. They were called on to stop several times but it had no effect. I drew my revolver and fired several shots over their heads. It had no effect. I then fired at the native closest to me who was then at least 150 yards distant. He fell. I considered the second one out of revolver range and called on my tracker to get the rifle. Two shots were fired and the fleeing native fell having been hit through the head. Both natives were dead.

What is most immediately obvious about this incident is that it could in no sense be said to fall within Murray's proscription that nobody was to be shot at except in self-defence. More significantly still, as with many aspects of his own accounts of these events, Murray told this story in a number of markedly different ways over the following months. In his initial report to Noblet, Murray made no mention of an initial capture or the men escaping his custody:

Myself and one tracker dismounted...and got within close quarters of the natives (two males and two females). They refused to be captured made off over the rocks. We followed for some distance repeatedly called on them to stop, then fired. Both males were shot dead. The lubras stated that both males had assisted in killing Brooks. The dead had some of Brooks' property in their possession.

Murray was questioned on this discrepancy by the Board of Enquiry. He explained that he didn't mention the handcuffing of the two men in his initial report 'because I did not actually see them handcuffed'. He also clarified a critical point:

> Tracker Paddy shot the fleeing native with a rifle. I did not report that Paddy an aboriginal shot a native with a rifle. I mentioned the fact that natives were killed but I did not think it necessary to say who killed them.

The board did not query why Murray had testified before it that the two dead men had confessed to Brooks' murder before they escaped, when his original report to Noblet had them being identified only postmortem by the two women who were with them; or why the number of people present, both hunters and hunted, differed between his two versions; or why he had felt it appropriate to shoot at the fleeing men at all, rather than continue to pursue and attempt to recapture them. Maintaining his rigorous application of correct policing procedure, frontier-style, Murray said that he questioned the surviving old man and two women, satisfied himself that they had not been involved in Brooks' murder, and let them go.

This was 23 August. The date is significant, because eight more days were to elapse before Murray and his party turned up back at Coniston on 31 August, the next ascertainable date in the chronology. Murray, in none of his statements, gave particulars of this period any more specific than a reference to 'several days' in his first report to Noblet. All previous historical accounts of Coniston gloss over Murray's compression of these eight days out in the wilderness into what sounds more like the activity of two or three days.

What Murray did tell Noblet was that, having killed the two escapees among the hills, he 'ascertained that a party of the murderers had made for the Western Australian border' (he didn't reveal from whom he heard this). He elaborated to the Board of Enquiry that the party found tracks and followed them west for about 36 miles.

> We sighted a number of blacks who were apparently sitting in the shade under some cliffs. Immediately they sighted us they took up their position amongst some boulders and in caves. At times we could see them. They were instructed by the trackers but they replied that they would fight us if we came near them. I instructed my party to spread out and get around the hills to avoid any escaping. Myself dismounted and went on foot searching for the natives amongst boulders and caves. After some little time two natives rushed out of a cave as I was passing. I received several blows from yamsticks. Having my rifle in hand in readiness, I fired and shot one native dead. The other native disappeared amongst the rocks.

Later the same day, Murray encountered an Aboriginal man with a number of women and children. He captured the man and brought him back to the camp, where everyone else except Wilson had already assembled. Two other prisoners had also been brought in by Paddy and Major, both with serious gunshot wounds. Typical of his prosaic manner of reporting death, Murray recorded these events thus:

> I examined the prisoners and found that they were very seriously wounded. I also informed the rest of the party of their condition. We then had lunch. The two

wounded died during our lunch hour. We then returned
to Cockatoo Spring.

Briscoe and Saxby had little to say about this period in the
rocky hills. Briscoe told the Board of Enquiry that, after the
party split up and he was sent to block any escape, he saw some
Aboriginal people making their way across the rocks, and he fired
some warning shots but 'did not try to hit them. The result was
a jeering laugh from the blacks. They went on through the rocks
and got away.'

Briscoe heard several shots before the party reassembled, but
didn't know who had fired or what else had happened. He certainly hadn't shot anyone. All Saxby said was that the party had
spent several days ranging towards the Western Australian border
following their quarry, who he occasionally saw in the distance.
He also heard some shots but, as in all the previous encounters,
did not kill anyone himself.

Thus were eight days filled. According to Murray, Briscoe and
Saxby, it was spent mostly in fruitless chases across the rocks and
cliffs of the no-man's land west of Cockatoo Spring. Only three
small groups of fugitives were physically encountered, resulting in
a further five deaths and the capture of one live prisoner.

It is a story which beggars belief. It would have made no sense
to occupy so much time in pursuing random Aboriginal people
over this country way past the outer edge of white civilisation,
with no rational basis for even hoping that the actual suspected
killers of Brooks might be encountered (and, again, bearing in
mind that Murray had already supposedly accounted for eleven of
them one way or another). Apart from anything else, there was
precious little water to be found out here (moreover, nobody in
the party was familiar with where it might be found) and no food;

no relief for the party's horses, who had already been going for a week before this phase of the hunt began; and the men themselves must have been close to exhaustion. Whatever they were doing in these eight days, it wasn't chasing after Aboriginal shadows.

But finally, the first manhunt was over. Murray's party returned to Coniston on 31 August with one prisoner, whose name was Akirkra. In his deposition at Akirkra's committal hearing in early September, but in none of his other statements, Murray claimed he had taken Akirkra to the scene of Brooks' murder, presumably on the way back to Coniston. This repeated the pattern with the earlier arrest of Padygar, who had also allegedly confessed at the murder scene, according to Murray's deposition.

> [Akirkra] showed me where Brooks had been camped and uncovered dry blood from the sand, which he stated had come from the old man. He then showed me the spot where the body was buried, also uncovered traces of blood within a few yards of the burial place.
>
> I then formally arrested the two prisoners Padygar and Akirkra, charged them with the murder of Fred Brooks and brought them into Alice Springs.

Willingar, the prisoner who Murray had shot in the head back on 15 August, had lingered on under Tracker Tommy's guard, but died on the 31st after Murray's return to Coniston. After a one-night stay, Murray headed back to Alice Springs, taking Paddy, Tommy, the two surviving prisoners Padygar and Akirkra, and the little witness Lala.

So went the story of what had gone on out in the scrub and the hills during those first two weeks of police investigation into the murder of Fred Brooks, according to Murray and his white compadres. It wasn't the only available version, then or now, although it was the only one that mattered.

———

Paddy, the unofficial tracker, was the only Aboriginal witness called to give evidence to the Board of Enquiry. His two statements are remarkable for the relative clarity of the chronology they laid out; and for the almost total inconsistency between that chronology and the one given by Murray and the other white members of the hunting party.

Paddy's narrative contains no dates, but presumably begins on 15 or 16 August. He departs immediately from Murray's version of events, which started with the arrest of Padygar and Willingar at the Coniston homestead. According to Paddy, that incident took place some five days later, and a lot had happened in the intervening time.

The first thing Murray's party did, according to Paddy, was to go to the scene of Brooks' murder at Yurrkuru. That would have seemed the most logical initial step in the police investigation. Paddy said he saw Brooks' body lying on its back on the ground. The party reburied the corpse, which would have been in an advanced state of decomposition by now, over a week after his death, and certainly would have been unrecognisable. They then returned to Coniston.

The next day (probably 16 August, as per Murray's version), the party headed west again. Paddy's narrative does not have them taking Padygar and Willingar along, as in his story they had not yet been encountered. That night, two 'weehis' were spotted coming in from the bush by Paddy and Wilson (contradicting Murray's claim that there were three weehis and that they were spotted and detained by him and Wilson).

> I told Alex Wilson I wanted to talk to these two when they come up. I asked them which way all about black fellow. He said we been leave them longa bush and pointed with his finger. I said to the little boy you stay here till daylight. I spoke in Aboriginal language. The boy said all right me camp longa you. The two sat down in the camp.

Paddy had somehow managed to overlook the small matter of the ambush of an Aboriginal camp and shooting of five Aboriginal people, which according to Murray had taken place that same day. Fortunately, the Board of Enquiry gave him the opportunity to rectify this gap in his evidence when it recalled him the next day.[11] Memory suitably refreshed, Paddy told the story:

> We then spread out riding through the country looking for the blacks. Constable Murray and I in the middle, Briscoe Saxby and others on each side of us. I was riding behind Mr. Murray. I saw a picanniny standing under a tree. Mr. Murray rode up quickly. He tried to take a boomerang and a yamstick from a black fellow. He was off his horse. The gins and black fellows were gathering all around him. The picanninies and some of the blacks scattered. I galloped around the outside to head them off. When I got back near Mr. Murray again I saw a gin with a yamstick hit at Mr. Murray. The blacks and gins were all hitting at him. Mr. Murray had hold of a

yamstick trying to pull it away from a black fellow. They
were pulling one against the other. I had to head off
the runaways again. When I came back I saw two dead
blackfellows. I don't know who shot them.

The next morning, 17 August, one of the little boys who had
come in the night before went out with Paddy to look for the
tracks of the men the boys had been with out in the scrub, with
no luck. The whole party, everyone on horseback except the
two little boys, who walked, then headed west and Paddy found
some more tracks to follow. They found a small soakage and
camped overnight.

The 18th of August brought some action. The party mounted
up, leaving Stafford behind with the two little boys. Paddy
recorded that they reached the hills this day, which would have
placed them a long way further west than Murray had them at the
same time. He said they dismounted and walked up the hill, but
found no Aboriginal tracks. They returned to the camp. Then it
got interesting.

The boys then said they saw a big mob of blackfellows
on the hill. I left my horse in the camp. I got handcuffs
from Constable Murray and went across to the hill and
on to another and saw a lot of blacks. I hid myself. The
blacks all had spears, boomerangs and shields. I made
them stop and arrested two and put handcuffs on them –
one on each.

Murray now arrived on the scene. One of the two captives
slipped his handcuffs and ran off. The other stayed put. Murray
fired twice at the escapee, missing both times. Paddy chased him

over a couple of hills and shot him dead. The other captured male and two Aboriginal women were then taken back to the main camp, where they were released later in the day. Oddly, according to Paddy, 'Constable Murray did not ask the old man or lubras who killed Brooks' before he let them go. This incident is clearly the same as that related by Murray involving the escape and shooting down of two prisoners in the hills; but Murray had this occurring on 23 August at the outset of the long far-western hunt, five days later in the chronology than Paddy placed it.

Paddy now had the party returning to Coniston, probably arriving on the evening of 18 August but possibly a day later (it isn't clear from his testimony whether they camped at a spring along the way). The next afternoon is when Paddy brings Padygar and Willingar into the story.

Paddy recorded that the two 'bush natives' walked into the native camp at the station carrying boomerangs, spears and shields. Paddy and Major walked down from the motor-car shed, where they had been resting, to see who they were. As we've already seen, the ensuing fight resulted in Willingar being shot above the eye and both him and Padygar being chained to a tree.

Murray had the party leaving Coniston again on the 20th, so that is probably the right date for Paddy having them depart as well. Stafford and the two prisoners, by both their accounts, were left behind.

This day involved a lot of tracking and no finding. The party followed various tracks up and down the creek beds, with Major and Dodger identifying their owners variously as 'Ungarra and Padygar', 'Alatjagatanyee' or 'Camaltjiburga'. At one point Paddy recorded that he 'saw Ungarra chasing a bullock' and followed his track for a while without success. They eventually turned back to a soakage and camped the night.

The next day, the party rode to Six Mile Soak (Murray's narrative skipped the previous day of unsuccessful tracking, so he had this day as 20 August, putting him a day behind Paddy at this point). Paddy proceeded on foot, and came across six Aboriginal women near Briscoe's camp at Boundary Soak. He said he spoke to them in his own lingo, which they spoke too (this seems highly unlikely). Paddy brought them back to 6 mile, noticing a lot of fresh tracks along the way. Murray, Briscoe and Saxby had gone out separately, so Paddy and Wilson followed some tracks into the 'spinifex country' until they came across a 'big mob' of tracks made by men, women and children.

Now Paddy and Wilson had an encounter which bears no similarity to anything recorded by Murray. Paddy told it so:

> [It] was close to sundown. I heard a picanny [sic] cry in the scrub. Alex Wilson went one way and I went another. Later Alex Wilson sang out 'Look out Paddy Big mob blackfellows there'. He sang out in English. I got into an open space and saw all the blacks jump up with boomerangs. Every one had a boomerang. Alex Wilson sang out 'Sit down they're chucking boomerangs.' I and Alex Wilson had rifles. A boy called Yarragula threw a boomerang at Alex Wilson and just missed his head. It was nearly dark. I was a little bit frightened. I sang out to the blacks to leave their boomerangs. I called in blacks language (Arunta language) but they couldn't understand me because they were Illparra blacks.

Paddy fired his revolver three times into the air, and Wilson fired his rifle twice. They ran towards the Aboriginal men, who were still holding their boomerangs and shields.

> Alex Wilson threw the boomerang to one side and I arrested Yarragula and Camalatjiburga and Canatjiburga. We handcuffed the three and picked out the picaninnies and lubras and all and made them walk straight…We then went back to the water. All the blacks came too. The boomerangs were left behind.

Murray and the others came into camp later, and everyone spent the night together. Now it got interesting. As Paddy told it, he went out in the morning to get the horses and pack up the camp. All the Aboriginal people, including the three handcuffed prisoners, were present. Paddy headed off with Major and Dodger and the packhorses, carrying Yaragula on one of them. The women and children 'went back', presumably towards Boundary Soak, whereas

> The other two blacks who were handcuffed were left at the soakage and I did not see them again. The other blacks were at the soakage when I got up but I don't know what became of them. I did not hear any shots fired. About dinner time Constable Murray, Wilson, Saxby, Briscoe caught me up. There were no prisoners.

The remaining prisoner, Yaragula, was sick, telling Paddy, 'I got something no good inside'. Paddy left him in the shade near the well, and went ahead again with Major and Dodger.

We left Yaragula sitting near the well and Constable Murray Saxby Alex Wilson and Briscoe stayed at the well. Constable Murray told me to go with the packhorses. I don't know whether he told me to leave Yaragula behind. When I came back from filling the canteen I said to Constable Murray 'What about that boy' meaning Yaragula. He said 'He is bit crook leave him behind.' I did not see Yaragula since. We went on with the packhorses and Constable Murray and the others caught us up again at Dinner time.

Nothing came of Paddy's evidence, of course – the Board of Enquiry basically ignored it – but it's hard to read the above passage in any light other than that Paddy was quietly seeking to throw Murray under a bus. These three named captives, according to him, had not been wounded during their capture. They did not attempt to escape. When he last saw them, they were in Murray's custody. And then they disappeared. This stands out as the only, albeit implied, allegation made by anyone against Murray's party of murdering identified individuals. Of all people, it came from Paddy.

Anyway, the hunt continued. Over the following three days, Paddy followed numerous tracks with Major's assistance, travelling mostly west but apparently not going a lot further out than Cockatoo Spring. They saw no Aboriginal people at all.

Eventually – this was probably 26 August – moderate success came in the form of Akirkra. According to Paddy, Akirkra was alone when they found him, and did not resist arrest.

Contrary to Murray's report, Paddy had the party stopping off at Yurrkuru on the way back to Coniston. Paddy helpfully recalled the particulars of Akirkra's on-site confession:

Constable Murray asked Arkirkra where Brooks had camped and Arkirkra showed him. Constable Murray then asked Arkirkra where he had camped and Arkirkra showed him the place close up. Arkirkra said we came along and old Fred Brooks was sitting down here and we been kill him. Constable Murray asked him where you been hit him and Arkirkra said 'we been hit him right here' and pointed to the back of his head. Constable said Where did he fall down and Arkirkra said he been fall down here indicating the place. Constable Murray then said 'Where you been bury Fred Brooks' and Arkirkra then showed him the place.

Paddy's testimony wrapped up with his assurance that he had shot only one person during the hunt – the one he chased over the hills. Otherwise, he could not help much as he hadn't seen anyone else being shot.

Paddy's narrative of the two-week hunt, taken as a whole, was at least as coherent and plausible as the competing versions given by Murray and the other whites. In some respects, it was better, as Paddy included considerable detail regarding identified individual Aborigines who the party was hunting. That, of course, might reflect the lack of importance which the white men attached to positively distinguishing one Aboriginal person from another.

It is impossible to choose between the versions of Murray and Paddy. A number of observations can be made, however. First, the fact that Murray's statements were largely corroborated by Briscoe, Saxby and Stafford can be safely disregarded; they obviously colluded for the purpose of the Board of Enquiry's proceedings. Second, Murray contradicted his own testimony in many material particulars between his various reports and depositions. Third, Paddy had nothing to gain and plenty to lose from pointing the finger at Murray in respect of three apparent murders of Aboriginal prisoners, when he could have just as easily omitted to mention their existence altogether. Finally, and most importantly, the simple fact that two of the primary actors in the punitive expedition managed to recall its detail, a few months later, in such dramatically different terms, suggests strongly that neither should be believed at all.

At the very end of the transcript of Paddy's testimony, after members of the Board of Enquiry had questioned him, there is a note of almost transcendent irony:

> By Constable Murray – I do not desire to ask any ques-
> tion [of Paddy] because in order to get a concerted story
> from witness I would have to ask leading questions
> and by asking leading questions I could get witness to
> corroborate every detail of the occurrence.

Quite.

———

As the shooting progressed during August, the machinery of officialdom started to slowly grind its gears. On 11 August, the day Acting Sergeant Noblet had received Stafford's call from Ti Tree Well reporting Fred Brooks' death, Government Resident Cawood sent a telegram on to the Department of Home and Territories in Canberra noting that Brooks had been 'murdered by blacks'.[12]

This seems to have elicited no reaction, but official anxieties were soon enough raised when the *Sydney Morning Herald* report of Brooks' death landed on the departmental doorstep on the 14th. J. A. Carrodus, of the department, noted by hand next to the newspaper clipping the following day: 'Have we had any advice from Govt Resident re this matter! If not, inquire by *lettergram*.'[13] A mere five days later, a telegram made its way to Cawood in Alice Springs: 'Yours eleventh glad receive first mail full particulars regarding reported murder Frederick Brooks.'[14]

While Cawood was contemplating his reply, some more news arrived at police headquarters with a pair of prospectors called Young and Carter, who had just come in from a surveying expedition for the Mid Australia Exploration Company in the country around Coniston. Their travels around the area coincided with Murray's first punitive expedition, but they gave no indication that they were aware of his party's existence.

Young and Carter reported to Noblet (in his capacity as Warden for Mines, as he noted to Cawood) on 25 August:

> Nearly all the Station owners we met out west are complaining bitterly of the destruction of their stock by the Natives, they are killing cattle, sheep and Goats wholesale, and on our arrival we learned that a prospector named Brooks had been killed by the Natives...If some severe steps are not taken they will drive the Pastoralists out of the country as it is impossible for the few Police to cope with them.[15]

Noblet passed these comments on to Cawood by official letter, which judging from the records was an unusually diligent step for him to take. Of course, both Noblet and Cawood knew that Murray was at that moment out in the same district, carrying whatever explicit or tacit instructions they had given him or allowed him to assume, but had chosen not to record. Young and Carter's contemporaneous report of Aboriginal mayhem falling into their laps was, if nothing else, serendipitous.

Cawood responded finally to the department's request for a report on 30 August, a day before Murray rolled back into Alice Springs.[16] In his report, Cawood advised that he had despatched Murray to Coniston to 'carry out the investigation' into Brooks' murder. He added, 'Complaints are continually being received from outlying settlers as to the depredations by bush blacks'. However, the under-resourced police were finding it 'impossible to give the necessary relief'. It was by this letter that Cawood forwarded the note from Chapman to Stafford reporting Brooks' death, and the statement which Stafford had supposedly dictated to Purvis filling in the details of the murder.

This material arrived in Canberra with the mail on 7 September. On the same day, a report arrived at Alice Springs that there had been a fresh development that would make things even worse for the already beleaguered targets of Murray's revenge: another white settler had been violently attacked.

Chapter 5

SEPTEMBER

Three weeks after Fred Brooks' death, the Warlpiri made their second assault. The victim this time was William 'Nugget' Morton.

If Randal Stafford was by reputation the most benign of the sparsely scattered white pastoralists in the hard lands of the Lander River country, then Nugget was unquestionably the meanest. Not a kind word seems to have been recorded anywhere about this man, including by himself.

Morton was not, like many of his contemporaries, a long-term resident of Central Australia. He had come into the region in about 1923, from Melbourne, initially taking up a pastoral lease on the Lander which he called Broadmeadows. He later shifted to another adjacent property with his partner, Bruce Sandford, called Anningie Station, and was stocking cattle there in 1928. This was Warlpiri land.[1]

Strehlow recorded an eye-opening interview with Morton during his travels through the Centre in 1932, sitting around his camp on 44-gallon drums in the red dust.[2] Morton set the scene:

'You know', he remarked...'I've been in this damn country only a few years, but I've had more than my share of trouble with these dirty, thieving, treacherous, stinking bastards.'

He wasn't referring to his white neighbours. Strehlow graphically described Morton's appearance:

> Nugget was a short, heavily-built man, stocky of stature. A strong bull-like neck supported a cannon-ball type of head, whose round shape was revealed clearly by a fast-receding hairline. He looked as tough and as nuggety as his name implied. In bush language, he was 'just a bloody ball of muscle'.

White attitudes to Aboriginal people at this period of Central Australian history ranged widely, although paternalistic sympathy rather than equality-based empathy tended to be the most positive disposition in evidence. Regardless, Nugget Morton was at the far opposite end of the scale: he was an active hater. None of the southern hand-wringing about dispossession for him; his attitude to the question of land rights was straightforward enough, as he was happy to explain to Strehlow.

> The old niggers reckoned we were sitting down in *their* country, and they started frightening our stock boys by telling them that they'd start shoving spears into them if they didn't go back to their own country and take their cattle back too. They reckoned that there wasn't enough grass or water in the country for our cattle and their damn kangaroos, for us and for them. We, of course, told our boys to take no notice of any talk by any dirty myall niggers. They might have lived in this country before us, but they'd never done anything with it, had they? We had to look after our cattle; and anyway, this

country would be better off if it got rid of all those thieving black bastards.

Still, Morton did have uses for Aboriginal people, at least some of the young female ones. It appears to have been widely known that he was in the habit of forcibly taking young Aboriginal women and girls and raping them; in one instance, he was said to have murdered an albino Warlpiri woman who resisted his advances.[3] In another story related to Strehlow and confirmed by Morton himself, he kidnapped a girl from the Top End while he was up there buying cattle, and dragged her all the way back to Anningie.[4]

The reality about Morton, if the accounts are accepted, is that the life he was leading out on the fringe was not one of knockabout pioneering harshness with hefty doses of rough frontier justice, but one of base depravity. This was starkly illustrated by a further encounter Strehlow had with him in 1937, when he was officially investigating Morton's conduct towards Aboriginal people:

'Nugget' Morton was keeping a West Australian lubra there for his stockwork: she had tried to run away – as well as some of the girl victims mentioned below – but Morton got her back (and the other two) each time and inflicted a severe hiding as a deterrent against further attempts to run away. 'Nugget' was since employing as 'stockmen' (he has no male abos working for him) one or two other little native girls, 9 or 10 years of age, whom he had raped. Another little girl he had given to his nephew 'Shrimp', who was about 17 years of age. Ben Nicker, who was working for Nugget was similarly using a little girl, and both Ben and the girl were suffering from gonorrhoea.[5]

Enough said about Nugget Morton's character, but it remains to explore how he came so close to suffering an identical fate to that of Fred Brooks on 28 August 1928.

That day, Morton was camped at Boomerang Waterhole (Jangan-kurlangu in the local language). He had been shifting his location between the few remaining water sources as the drought worsened, as had the other cattlemen in the region. The Lander was dry, and the waterholes were depleting; the competition for precious water between the white men's cattle and the increasingly desperate Aboriginal people was turning deadly. According to Aboriginal stories of the time, Boomerang was the last spot with decent water.[6]

Morton told the story in much the same way:

> It all started in the Big Drought. All the stations around here were eaten out bare, and all the cattle men had to shift their cattle out to the Lander River. There was nothing on the Lander River then, excepting a few myall nigger that had scarcely seen a white man up to that time. We, young Harry Tilmouth from Napperby Station and me were the two who were furthest out on the Lander; and we had a pretty tough time getting enough water for our cattle, and enough feed for them too, though we were camped a good many miles apart. At first we thought we were doing well, and then these bloody black devils started getting cheeky.

The result was the attempted murder of Morton by a group of Warlpiri men. Unlike the story of Brooks' killing, there is not much dispute about the details of the attack on Morton; he survived to tell a tale that pretty much concurs with how Aboriginal stories recorded it. As to why he was attacked, of course, there isn't quite the same level of agreement.

For Morton, the assault on him was simply the natural instinct of 'thieving, murdering niggers' in action. There was nothing more to understand about it. However, Aboriginal tradition indicates that, as with Brooks, his treatment of their women may have been a trigger. Jimmy Jungarrayi told the Reads that a big mob of Warlpiri were near Boomerang Waterhole at the same time as Morton (who had come up there a couple of days earlier from his main camp at Mud Hut). Morton had several Aboriginal women with him at the time. The Warlpiri plotted to attack and kill him: 'Well, that our people bin thinkin, "What about we killem Nugget Morton, because they come and take our women?"'[7] An alternative version was told to Territory historian Dick Kimber by William Brown Jampitjinpa, who said he had visited Morton's camp shortly before the attack. Morton was cleaning and oiling his rifle, and told Jampitjinpa that he was heading out to shoot a bullock, but Jampitjinpa believed that he was 'getting the rifle ready to shoot some blackfellows'. He then met up with the Warlpiri men who were making their own plan: to kill Morton before he could start shooting.[8]

Either way, there's no doubt that the attempt on Morton's life which unfolded on 28 August lacked an immediately proximate provocation; whatever the Warlpiri's motive was, its roots were deep. And they certainly weren't aiming to miss.

As Morton told the story to Strehlow, the attack came in the early morning as he was sitting by his camp fire. As the sky started to brighten, a few men from the Warlpiri mob came near to him.

> One of them points to some meat alongside of me, and I cut off a piece and hand it to him. The old devil grabs my hand, not the piece of meat. And then the others rush up, and they all jump on top of me.[9]

What followed, according to Morton, was an absolute frenzy of fists and weapons as the mob tried to bring him down and Morton fought back with superhuman strength and an impressive instinct for survival. He was hit numerous times by weapons, including a boomerang 'cracking me under the jaw and just about laying me out'. As Morton saw it, what saved him in fact was the sheer number of attackers – 'they couldn't get a proper lash at me for fear of hitting their own stinking cobbers'. One of them was even brandishing a steel tomahawk:

> if the others had just let me go instead of struggling with me, he would have finished me. He did get a weak blow in on the back of my skull. But when he tried to have a second go at me, I managed to push my arm out at the last minute and bowl him over; and the tomahawk just skimmed down along my bare arm. Well, there were up to fifteen of them bloody tar-pots trying to do me in; but in the end I managed to crack that big woolly-headed bastard one a fair bloody stinger right on the jaw, and down he went, and then I knocked out another with a hefty whacking upper-cut.

That was that; the attackers scrambled to get away as Morton recovered his wits and went for his gun on the far side of the fire.

Actually that wasn't quite it: Morton neglected to mention to Strehlow that, in fact, the attack had been ended not by his fists but by his gun. He told the Board of Enquiry that he had fired several shots at his attackers, killing one of them.[10]

Morton was extremely lucky to survive this assault, which was certainly intended to be lethal. He was badly injured, nevertheless, and not out of trouble yet. Fortunately for him, the Warlpiri had had enough and made no further attack. Morton managed to bandage his wounds, collect his horses and gear and make it back to his main camp and his partner, Bruce Sandford. Sandford got him to Ti Tree Well, then on to the hospital at Alice Springs.[11]

While at Ti Tree on 30 August, Morton made his report to the police by a letter which he dictated to Sandford (he was too badly injured to write). Giving the basic details of the attack (but not his shooting of one of the attackers), Morton included his prescription: 'I would like you to send out a party to arrest the culprits. If you decide to send one, they will want camels, as horses will be no good.'[12]

There is no indication why, but Morton's report took eight days to get to Sergeant Noblet, who recorded its receipt on 7 September.[13] Cawood passed on the news to Canberra by telegram on the 8th,[14] following it with a letter forwarding Morton's statement and reminding his superiors that 'Strong indignation is expressed by the residents of Central Australia at the inadequacy of the police patrol. My repeated requests for an extra mounted constable have not even been met by the courtesy of a reply.'[15] Perhaps to underline the point, no attempt to investigate the attack was initiated for another week.

Murray had arrived back at Alice Springs on 1 September, to a presumably delighted Noblet, whose permanent appointment as Sergeant of Police had been confirmed the day before.[16] Murray got straight on to writing up his report, which he delivered to Noblet on the 2nd.[17]

Meanwhile, it appears that Murray's departure had not necessarily put an end to the quest to avenge Brooks' murder back at Coniston. On 1 September, Michael Terry pulled in to Stafford's homestead, coming down from the north-west (in the direction of Briscoe's camp). He was greeted by Stafford and Saxby.

Stafford told Terry that he and Saxby had been out that day hunting for 'blacks involved in Brooks' murder'. They had come across several Aboriginal men busily grilling part of a freshly killed bullock, but the suspects heard the horses approaching and escaped their grasp. What Stafford and Saxby had been planning to do if they had caught up with these men they didn't say. Whatever ostensible protection of the law they may have had while riding with Murray had certainly expired with his departure for Alice Springs.[18]

Murray was not destined to enjoy a long rest at Alice Springs after his exertions over the previous fortnight. On 4 September he was despatched again, along with Paddy, to head back to Coniston following up on a complaint (from an unidentified informant) that Brooks' killers were still at large and killing cattle.[19]

At this point, the evidence trail stops dead, reviving again only on 13 September when the Alice Springs Police Station Day Journal records that Murray and Paddy arrived back at the station 'from Stafford's, Moar's and Turner's, with two prisoners Ned & Barney, re killing of Moar's cattle'. Alex Wilson was with them.[20]

This and one other document form the only surviving record of what happened during the nine days between 4 and 13 September. Murray tendered to the Board of Enquiry in January 1929 a handwritten page listing his movements between May and October 1928 to justify the 'brevity' of his official reports to his superior, which had apparently caused some comment from the board. For the period between 4 and 13 September, the list noted only that Murray had 'left Alice Springs to investigate alleged cattle killings at "Pine Hill" and "Coniston Stn"', that he 'returned with two prisoners' and that he had travelled 395 miles. That is, an average of some 44 miles per day.[21]

Dick Kimber was certain that the various Aboriginal oral histories of the whole Coniston period (roughly August to October 1928) provided sufficient basis to conclude that, during those nine days, Murray went on another punitive expedition looking to shoot any Aboriginal people he could find. Kimber identified seven possible encounters as Murray and Paddy made their way north along the Hanson and Lander rivers and then back down to Coniston again, before returning to Alice Springs with the two unfortunate (or perhaps exceedingly lucky) prisoners.[22] It's likely there were other volunteers with them; it certainly wouldn't have been surprising to find Saxby or Briscoe, at least, coming along for another ride, and it is clear that Murray picked up Alex Wilson again at some point along the way.

It's difficult to be confident about this, because the recorded Aboriginal histories carry no timelines and were told as stories, not chronological history. That doesn't affect their veracity, but it makes it almost impossible to nail any particular incident to a point in time.[23]

Nevertheless, some tentative conclusions can be drawn on the dark period in the Coniston story from 4 to 13 September.

Murray had just returned from his first, clearly punitive expedition, during which, on his account, at least seventeen Aboriginal people had been shot by him or his party. The latter part of that hunt had included a lengthy lapse of time, about eight days, which his otherwise detailed accounting simply glossed over.

Then there was this mysterious hiatus, after which, as we shall see, Murray went out hunting yet again, with equally bloody results for the Aboriginal people he encountered. And so, sandwiched in between these two periods of acknowledged hunting and killing was this strangely tranquil week and a half which Murray supposedly spent doing nothing more than tracking down and peacefully apprehending two Aboriginal men suspected of cattle killing – in the exact area where both of the officially recorded killing sprees occurred.

History has swallowed whole what happened in that time. There is no more evidence to be found. Constable Murray was off the leash in those nine days, and it's difficult to accept that he used this opportunity to do anything other than continue the killing – killing that he happily admitted to doing in the periods immediately before and immediately after. The carnage, surely, did not abate.

Whatever Murray had been up to, Cawood was already somewhat occupied by the early stages of the coming minor furore over the death toll from his first manhunt, which Murray had casually reported on 2 September. Cawood's bureaucratic instincts quickly kicked in, as he sent a telegram to Canberra on the 3rd:

Police arrived Alice Springs Saturday evening first September with two prisoners murder Frederick Brookes. Others concerned in outrage died from wounds in fight with police and civilians while resisting capture. Posting full report.[24]

The question this report immediately raised was asked by a clearly alarmed department in its unusually rapid and terse response: 'Yours third what were number of fatalities.'[25] Cawood replied the next day with the missing body count and an urgent misdirection:

17 casualties. Urgent request from settler Stafford near scene last murder asking protection. Sending police patrol today. Cannot approval be given my request of March last for extra mounted constable.[26]

Murray was indeed despatched that day to search for those who were allegedly killing Stafford's and Moar's cattle. Cawood now forwarded Murray's report of 2 September on to Canberra, where it arrived on the 12th.[27]

The lost week and a half of 4–13 September, while Murray was out 'on patrol', passed in torpid inaction at police headquarters, interrupted only by Morton's report of his assault and the formal arraignment of Padygar and Akirkra on the 7th for Brooks' murder. The proceedings took place in the Alice Springs Police Court before the town's sole judicial officer, Ernest Allchurch. Allchurch was another local institution with more than twenty years in Central Australia; in fact, his death notice in *The Advertiser* in 1932 headlined him as the 'King of Central Australia'. He was the Postmaster and Chief Telegraphist at Alice Springs, as well as Justice of the Peace and Special Magistrate (the 'Special' indicating that he was not actually a lawyer). So far as the majesty of the law was physically present in the Territory of Central Australia in 1928, Ernest Allchurch was the start and finish of it.[28]

The Information and Complaint presented by Murray and purportedly signed by him on 7 September (which it definitely was not) charged that Padygar and Akirkra, 'Aboriginals of Central Australia…did Feloniously, wilfully, and of his malice aforethought, did kill and murder one Frederick Brooks'.[29]

The charge raised – murder – was brought under section 5 of the *Criminal Law Consolidation Act no. 38 of 1876*, which prescribed the death penalty; but, being a South Australian law, it had had no application whatsoever in Central Australia since its annexation by the Commonwealth in 1911. Not that the accused were likely to notice or care about the difference, as they spoke no English and were unrepresented by lawyers. Since the case couldn't proceed without Murray anyway, Allchurch adjourned it until his return and the prisoners were remanded to the custody of Noblet.[30]

Proceedings resumed on 15 September, with the two prisoners again legally unrepresented but with Sergeant Noblet, in his capacity as Protector of Aborigines, ludicrously present on their behalf. Sworn evidence was received from the two prosecution witnesses, Murray and Lala. Murray's brief exposition on his investigation, capture of Padygar and Akirkra and their separate murder scene confessions to him we have already explored, along with how much of the detail that he included in this evidence differed materially from what he had reported to Noblet a few days earlier, and from what he would tell the Board of Enquiry some months later. In any event, Murray was clearly aware of the evidentiary force of a voluntary confession, particularly in the absence of any forensic evidence or even a corpse.[31]

Lala's statement was crucial; here at last was direct sworn evidence from an actual eyewitness to the killing:

Lala (Native Cautioned, through Half-caste Intepreter Alick Wilson) I know the two Prisoners, Padygar and Akirkra, I was Camped at the Spring where Fred Brookes was camped. I seen from some distance off the two prisoners help to kill Fred Brookes, they used Yam Sticks and Akirkra used a Tomahawk. I also seen them assist to carry the Body away, they placed a Bag over him and covered him up in a Rabbit hole, they then took Brookes Rations Flour Tea Sugar and other rations out of his Boxes, also one shirt, also one blanket. They hunted the Camels away the night previous so Brookes boys would be out longer hunting for them, the following morning, when the two Boys of Brookes did return the next morning the Natives helped to put the Packs on and sent them into Coniston Station, having previously stripped the two boys Dodger and Skipper, of their clothing and blankets. Previous to murdering Fred Brookes a Lubra was sent to his Camp and held him whilst the Natives killed him, the Lubras name was Marunali, this Lubra has visited the Missionarys Camp on the Woodforde many times, this was the Lubra that was shot at the first Camp.[32]

A shakily hand-drawn cross on the typed deposition apparently represents Lala's mark. His evidence was certainly clear, if nothing else, in its close similarity to the story of Brooks' killing which had appeared in the Adelaide newspapers well before Lala had encountered Murray or any other white man and had a chance to tell them. Of course, if it was all true, that would make sense.

The Crown case having been presented, Allchurch moved to the next phase of the proceeding with all due formality:

thereupon the defendants being asked by me whether he wishes to plead to the said charge and the defendants signifying a desire to do so and the said charge being read and explained by a Interpreter to them and I having said to them 'Are you guilty or not guilty of the offence with which you are charged' the defendants thereupon pleads guilty.[33]

The Advertiser's correspondent, who was in the court, reported the guilty plea thus: 'Through an interpreter they practically admitted their guilt, but did not seem in the least concerned about their position.'[34] Having played his part, Allchurch committed the defendants for sentencing by the Supreme Court and in the meantime sent them back to gaol, as provided by the *Justices Act 1921* – another South Australian law with no application in Central Australia. Padygar and Akirkra would remain in the Alice Springs prison until November.

It was a busy day at Police Court; Ned and Barney, the alleged cattle killers Murray had brought back with him a couple of days earlier, also pleaded guilty and were given a six-month term in the Alice Springs gaol for unlawful possession of part of a cow's carcass.[35]

Chapter 6

'A DISGUSTING CREATURE'

They are the most degraded of the human race, and never seem to wish to change their habits and manner of life.[1]

As events were rapidly and violently unfolding in the desert and being digested at leisure in Alice Springs and eventually Canberra, another storm was beginning to brew through August and September that would ultimately engulf all the main players.

The Adelaide newspapers had broken the colourful detail of the Brooks murder on 14 August. On the 16th, *The Register* ran another scoop. J. Hutson Edgar, it reported, had just returned from a lengthy expedition all through the Central Australian territory, and he had some controversial things to say regarding its inhabitants with direct relevance to the Brooks incident.[2]

Edgar was a missionary who had spent many years in China and Tibet and had been invited by the Aborigines' Friends Association to travel with a local missionary, Ernest Kramer, to Central Australia to investigate mission work among the Aboriginal people there. They arrived at Alice Springs on 6 June and headed south-west to the South Australian border, then circled west towards Western Australia and back around to Alice Springs via Uluru and the Hermannsburg Mission station. They covered some 1,000 miles.

Edgar's travels did not intersect with any of the main Coniston events, and it does not appear that they took him into the Lander River country. However, his reports were to play an outsized role in the forming of public opinion as (some of) the facts began to emerge.

Edgar certainly was not one to hold back his opinions. His principal impression of the Central Australian Aboriginal people he had encountered, as he told *The Register*, was unambiguous:

> Mr Edgar formed a low estimate of their qualities. They were wild and nude savages. Men, women and children had no clothing and seemed to have no idea of using the skins of animals for even warmth by making them into blankets. These aborigines were a disgusting crowd.

This crowd, Edgar said, was a tribe of some 120 people he had met at Lake Wilson. Speaking with confidence and absolutely no proof, he went on:

> That, said Mr Edgar, was part of the tribe whom Dr Basedow believed to have murdered Prospector Bruce [sic]. It was easy to believe that murder would not be abhorrent to them, for during the stay at Lake Wilson Mr Edgar saw many of their hateful practices.

The witness nominated by Edgar was Dr Herbert Basedow, who was about to engage in a lengthy and increasingly vituperative slanging match with the missionary through the letters pages of *The Register*. At issue was the Aboriginal 'problem' à la 1920s Central Australia.

Edgar had plenty more to say, and *The Register* was delighted to run it.[3]

> Mr Edgar said…that the Australian aborigine was a disgusting creature. His habits were abhorrent and cruel, and from what he had seen any white man who could contaminate him must be extraordinarily degraded. The wild native was a blot on Australia.

This wasn't much of a hopeful foundation, but Edgar had worked out both the problem and the solution.

> The aborigine…was a nomad. He had no system of conserving game, and when he settled temporarily at one waterhole he quickly frightened all the game away to another. Then he moved on also. He was a menace to pastoralists by killing stock, for which the owner had no redress. Lonely travelers were also in danger from him.

However, Edgar had been greatly impressed by the way the outback station owners were dealing with the Aboriginal people on their stations, enjoying great success in civilising them and turning them into useful station workers. His prescription was 'an extension of stations in all directions' which, by providing work and food to the 'wild natives', would convert them from their nomadic ways. Missionaries could then look after the remaining business of saving their souls.

The answer was obvious, and the need urgent:

> Something must be done by the Government to rescue the natives from their present degradation. In other

countries it had been necessary to impress on savages the requirements of English law, and it could be done with the Australian aborigine.

Even for 1928, these were incendiary words. Not the notion that Aboriginal people were living in degradation or that they were generally pretty disgusting – most white people agreed on that – but the correct direction of the finger of blame was hotly disputed. The letters pages duly erupted. A writer called 'White Australian' posited that the real 'blot on Australia' was the way Aboriginal people had been treated:

> I would be more inclined to use the appellation 'disgusting creature' to some whites supposed to have heard the teaching of Christ, rather than to the primitive unclothed black who has his own system of ethics which should not offend us until we show him something better.[4]

That didn't go down well. 'Angipena' was horrified: 'When "White Australia" [sic] suggests that contact with the whites has made for degradation among the aborigines, he makes thoughtful people wonder exactly what he means.' Quite apart from which, there was the awful reality to consider:

> Is the Government going to continue to leave them alone to eat their babies and torture their women; to cut off the heads of solitary whites, and stuff them into rabbit burrows; to spear cattle and generally menace the settler?[5]

In fact, not quite everyone readily accepted that Aboriginal people had nothing useful to contribute to the debate. Dr Basedow stirred on 21 August, archly asking in the South Australian Parliament (of which he was then briefly a member) if the Minister would place Mr Edgar's comments under the notice of the Chief Protector of Aborigines, and 'request him to deal with the matter in the way that it deserved?' He added that he had been requested to raise this by 'two aborigines, who were civilized, and had read the report'.[6]

Now it was on for young and old, as Edgar and Basedow traded blows via *The Register* in increasingly long and tedious verbiage. *The Register*'s editorial writer was drawn in, coming down solidly on Basedow's side of the argument, although not as to the merits of Aboriginal people as people – 'the black man, of course is very foolish', observed the editor in passing – but on the messy and irreconcilable dispute as to, really, whether they'd have been better left alone.[7]

Basedow, for his part, continued to voice an exceptionally nuanced view for his times. Quoting from his own book, *The Australian Aborigines*, which he had published in 1927 after extensive anthropological studies in Central Australia, he made his case succinctly enough:

> Although under ordinary circumstances the aboriginal of Australia is a peaceable, placid individual...yet, being human, there are naturally extenuating circumstances, which might thrust the obligation upon his shoulders to pick up arms and fight for the sake of his individual honour or his tribe's safety.
>
> The methods he resorts to cannot be regarded as more degrading in his case than in our own, because we

as civilized peoples made use of worse during the late European war.[8]

But, of course, the argument about Aboriginal society can never be held down to the specifics of cause and effect, at least not in the minds of those whites who view Aboriginal people with perpetually jaundiced frustration. Edgar was certainly one of these, and he was adamant that it be accepted that his subjects were literally disgusting. On and on he went, jumping from wife-beating to infanticide to cannibalism, with frequent delicate allusions to 'sexual' practices of which he dared not freely speak.[9] The debate was quickly heading off the rails.

Just in time, the abstract debate over Aboriginal degeneration was overtaken by events, as Murray's return to Alice Springs on 1 September brought to the newspapers an avalanche of new 'facts' regarding Brooks' murder. *The Advertiser* and *The Register* jumped over each other in their eagerness to report every salacious detail of the killing. The obvious source for this new information was Murray himself, but no doubt the Alice rumour mill had gone into overdrive, taking any semblance of editorial circumspection with it.[10]

The story the papers ran with was not inconsistent with Murray's official report to Noblet, but they included a ton of detail which he had not mentioned. It was commonly agreed that Brooks had fallen victim to his own generosity and the grasping hands of a treacherous lubra, who held him so that the men of her tribe could rush him and beat him to death in a wild and bloody assault. Their number was twenty-one or fifty, depending on which paper you read, and they had come from a place about 70 miles west of Coniston. Brooks had caught them with a freshly slaughtered bullock of Stafford's, and they killed him so he couldn't tell.

The news of Brooks' death, in these new versions, was conveyed to Stafford by an 'old lubra'. Murray turned up and his party headed straight to the scene of the murder, where the killers had remained. In one version, there was a big fight at the scene; in another, Murray and his men had to pursue the killers all over the countryside. No direct mention of Aboriginal deaths was made, although *The Register* recorded the result of the assault on the Aboriginal camp as being that 'it was only possible to disperse them' − 'dispersal' being the recognised code word throughout frontier Australia for mass killing of Aboriginal people. *The Advertiser* was a little less subtle, reporting that Murray had been forced to resort to 'extreme measures', which wasn't really code at all.

Murray told *The Advertiser* that 'this tribe is very cheeky' − another conscious use of frontier code, as when white men called Aboriginal people 'cheeky' they meant that they didn't know their place.

Murray headed back into the killing fields on his mysterious 4–13 September expedition while the fiery debate, which he had just effectively stoked, raged on in print. Dr Basedow was freshly aroused, giving *The Register* on 5 September the benefit of his considered (and, in contrast to almost everyone else, well-informed) opinion as to what exactly was going on.

Referring to the messages from Alice Springs concerning the killing of Mr Brooks, Dr H Basedow on Tuesday said the opposition by natives to the white man in those particular localities had been pronounced ever since the white man had gone there. On his first visit to Central Australia, particularly the north-west ranges, Ernest Giles met with opposition, and he had referred to this in his journal. He said the natives objected to him coming into their tribal country, and they endeavoured to send him out of it.

Dr Basedow said that…he could recall cases where travellers had been molested by the aborigines, but it seemed that these attacks were actuated by interference with the native women. In all probability, therefore, the native tribes in the country to the west of the ranges had inherited a hatred of the white man.

[Referring to the report of 'extreme measures'] he took it that most of the natives were shot on sight, as happened in nine out of 10 such cases. Consequently, the latest advices received, that the natives were again attacking Stafford's and other stations west, would indicate an avenging party…Having seen some of their members fall, it was only natural, and in accordance with tribal law, that such cases should be avenged.

'The cause of the trouble is undoubtedly the killing of cattle by the natives', Dr Basedow added, 'but they are doing it in all conscientiousness, believing themselves justly entitled to do so, seeing that the white man never hesitates to help himself to the native's game. Most of the tribes are more or less communistic in their ideas and sentiments, and would look upon such an act as merely a reciprocal one and not in any degree criminal. Furthermore, the aborigines are very dignified individuals and resent an insult by a stranger, such as a white man, as much as a white man would resent it himself.'[11]

The news of the attack on Nugget Morton hit the Adelaide papers on 8 September, adding fresh impetus to the growing sense that Central Australia was out of control.[12] On the same day, *The Register* carried a dire warning of coming bloodshed (which was in reality already well underway). Charles Young, who had been prospecting in the Centre for some time, was visiting Adelaide and was happy to share his concerns. Unlike J. Hutson Edgar, who had fingered the 'wild natives' as the cause of trouble, Young said that the 'myalls' caused no problems at all. Instead:

> it was the semi-educated natives from the mission stations who were becoming a menace, as they were cunning, treacherous, and thoroughly bad. They stole everything they could lay their hands on, and were continually driving off and killing stock. At Conniston Station hundreds of goats had been killed and the blacks were now spearing cattle.

The problem was the lack of police. If this wasn't fixed, Young knew what would happen:

> Similar troubles with the natives had developed many years ago both in Western Australia and in New Guinea, and there the settlers had taken matters into their own hands and shot any of the blacks who had interfered with them. Similar measures might be necessary in Central Australia, if more adequate police protection were not forthcoming.[13]

Given what Mounted Constable Murray was then in the middle of undertaking in the name of 'police protection', we can fairly speculate what more of the same might have meant for the

Aboriginal people of Central Australia. As it was, Murray was doing a more than adequate job of executing the kind of 'measures' which Young had in mind.

Whatever the solution might have been, the alarm bells were being rung more and more loudly. On 11 September, Young's warnings were amplified with a near-hysterical edge by another (unnamed) Central Australian resident, under the screaming headline 'BELLICOSE BLACKS – SETTLERS IN ARMS – A MENACING POSITION'. According to this correspondent, the settlers had already taken matters into their own hands, as the situation had spiralled out of control. He noted that 'the blacks are becoming boastful and aggressive', and that seventeen of them had been shot and killed already.

This man was sure the aggressors were the 'myall blacks' from out west, but the cause of their hostility was the teaching on the mission stations:

> There the natives were taught to believe that all men were equal in the sight of God, and the native mission bucks were openly strutting round, and saying that they were as good as the white station owners…Those natives, many of whom belonged to the same tribes as the wild blacks, were going out west to meet the uncivilized aborigines, and advise them to kill the white men's cattle, and the white men if they could.

Ominously, 'it was reported that a few of the young men were making a systematic hunt of the blacks, and there was bound to be bloodshed'.[14]

One can imagine the editor of *The Register*, observing the flow of unreliable reportage and alarmist opinion-making which he had been putting in print through August and early September with apparent even-handedness, musing over when might be the right moment to draw the threads together and deliver his editorial judgement on the whole mess. On 12 September, he did just that.

Noting that 'a sort of guerilla warfare is in danger of breaking out in Central Australia between the settlers and the Aborigines', he pointed to the devastating drought as the proximate cause of tensions, as it had dried up the waterholes and crystallised the competition for water between people and animals. The consequences had already been disastrous, and the rumours 'that an unofficial expedition has gone out to avenge one murder with an indiscriminate massacre' demanded immediate government action to prevent the situation from getting any worse.

The editor went to the practical, if not empathic, heart of the problem:

> there is an inevitable conflict between the fundamental rights of the black man, on the one hand, and the white man, on the other. Both have the right to live – whatever the members of the reported punitive expedition may believe to the contrary – and the resources of the country are probably not so abundant as to permit of the survival of one, except to the prejudice of the other.
>
> Our responsibility, as a nation, for the just and even generous treatment of the aborigine whose country we have annexed, sits too lightly upon us.

Rising to the full height of righteous indignation, the editor concluded:

The white man, instead of offering the black man flour and blankets, has taken a gun in his hand, to drive the wretched savage back into a waterless wilderness. The individual station owner, fighting for his livelihood, if not for his life, in circumstances which defy the imagination of the city dweller, will be condemned with a very bad grace by a community whose sustained indifference and neglect have thus placed settler and savage at enmity. Australians in general will be disgraced afresh, if something is not done quickly to give to the aborigines, in the drought-stricken areas of the far north, something better than a choice between death by starvation, and death by shooting.[15]

He was right, and it was already too late.

Chapter 7

OCTOBER

You might think thirty-four niggers to be a fair enough bag.
Who knows? There might have been some more.[1]

So Nugget Morton reflected, sitting around the fire with T. G. H. Strehlow at his camp in 1932, on the last of the punitive expeditions led by Mounted Constable Murray in the Lander River region, between 24 September and 15 October 1928. Morton was the cause of, the co-participant with Murray in, and subsequently the most forthcoming about what happened during this final episode. And he didn't have that much to say about it, at least not much we can safely believe.

Murray had left Alice Springs on 16 September, heading to his station at Barrow Creek. He was back in Alice Springs on the 19th, for reasons which are unrecorded, and the next day he and Alex Wilson (who had been in town to interpret for Padygar and Akirkra at their committal hearing) left again, this time for Morton's place.[2] Given that Noblet had received Morton's letter reporting the attack on him on 7 September, there is no obvious explanation as to why Murray hadn't been sent to investigate earlier.

Murray arrived at Morton's station on 24 September. On the way, he had had to investigate yet another incident involving an alleged attack on a white station owner.

The victim this time was Henry Edward 'Harry' Tilmouth, part-owner (with Tom Turner) of Napperby Station. Strehlow, who spent time with Tilmouth during his legendary trip in 1932, described him as having 'the spare but powerful build of the typical bushman of Australian cartoonists. He looked every inch a son of the local soil.'[3] Tilmouth's attitude to the Aboriginal people with whom he was sharing the Napperby land was also spare, and brutal – 'bloody useless bush niggers' was how he summarised their characteristics.[4]

Tilmouth was a long-term Central Australian, nephew of another, more legendary, Harry Tilmouth, who had been the local camel-postman for many years.[5] Tilmouth Jnr and Turner had stocked Napperby Station, which was south of Coniston, back towards Alice Springs, in about 1915.[6] In 1928, the drought had forced Tilmouth to take cattle north up the Lander in search of the remaining waterholes, and he was camped at White Stone (roughly halfway between the two soaks where Brooks and Morton respectively were attacked) with 1,500 bullocks by August 1928.[7]

The local Aboriginal people were, quite unfairly, as it seemed to Tilmouth, not particularly pleased by his presence.[8] In late August, he said, he was confronted by a 'nigger' who 'threatened me with the boomerang and told me I would have to get out of the country. I fired two shots to frighten him.'[9]

On the night of 10 September, as Tilmouth reported, two Aboriginal men crept up near his camp but were chased away by his dogs and a shot from his rifle. Tilmouth, on his own admission feeling quite frightened about the insecurity of his position,[10] had his 'working boy', called Peter, issue warnings to the local people to keep away, but 'they got sulky' and continued to scare his cattle.

Matters came to a head for Tilmouth on 16 September. As he told the story, a solitary Aboriginal man sneaked into his camp. Peter warned Tilmouth, who got up and fired a shot at the intruder. His rifle then jammed, and it took him ten minutes to get it working again. Apparently, while he was so vulnerable, his putative attacker patiently waited. Rifle ready once more, Tilmouth ended the proceedings:

> I could see the nigger coming up on the other side. I called on him to stop. As soon as I spoke he raised his boomerang to throw it...I fired at him to stop him. The bullet entered his body over the heart. I had no further trouble with the blacks.[11]

The dead man was called Wangaridge.

Murray turned up at White Stone on 23 September, on his way further north to meet up with Morton. There is no indication that Tilmouth had reported the attacks on him or his shooting of Wangaridge, so Murray's arrival may have been coincidental. In any event, Tilmouth told Murray what had happened, which Murray put in writing for Noblet on 19 October when he was finally back in Alice Springs again. Tilmouth said he had buried Wangaridge's body; Murray didn't inspect it and no official action was taken to investigate his death until the following January.[12]

On to Broadmeadows Station Morton and Murray went, still accompanied by Wilson. We now enter the last of the dark periods of the Coniston story, a particularly long one, running from 24 September when Murray and Morton met up to 15 October when Murray said he was back at Mount Barkly checking in on Tilmouth (on his way back to Alice Springs, where he arrived on the 18th). From the white side, the events in this period are evidenced mainly by various statements and depositions given by Murray and Morton, supplemented only by snippets of later conversation which hinted at a far bloodier trail than their sworn evidence had admitted.[13]

It is impossible to reconstruct the chronology of this twenty-two days with anything like the accuracy which we can apply to the earlier Brooks hunt, because neither Murray nor Morton bothered to record any dates in their evidence and they were vague as to their exact movements. What we know for sure are three things: the hunting party on this occasion was small, consisting of Murray, Morton, Wilson and a small Aboriginal boy who seems to have been brought along just to mind the packhorses; the party took no prisoners; and the official toll of dead Aboriginal people this time was fourteen.

Morton had been attacked by about fifteen men, on his account, and he claimed to know all of them because they had worked for him. This set the agenda for the hunt: he and Murray would track down their quarry for Morton to identify them on sight and Murray to then arrest them for attempted murder.

The expedition began with an incident which neither Murray nor Morton referred to in any of their statements, but about which Murray was happy to tell Ernestine Hill when she interviewed him in 1933. Most likely, their reticence at the time was due to the absolute illegality of what they did. Basically, they kidnapped three innocent young Aboriginal boys, held them captive and forced them to act as trackers. Why Murray had not brought a police tracker with him is unknown.

Murray told Hill the story.

> Morton and I rode out together, secured three boys who were innocent, and demanded that they guide us to the

guilty group. For three days those boys fooled us, leading us miles to wurlies long abandoned and to dry soaks.
They were young initiates and dare not disclose the
secrets of the older men. During the night they actually burned their feet to raw blisters and pounded their
toes to pulp so that they could not walk. We covered
their feet with bags and made them go on – but to no
purpose. At last I resorted to a ruse. Taking one of them
out of sight, I fired twice into the dust. The other in
quivering fright agreed at once to track the offenders.[14]

There is no record of what happened to the boys when their
usefulness had been expended.

In their evidence to the Board of Enquiry the following
January, Murray and Morton were utterly consistent; they
had obviously colluded in preparing their statements, to the
extent that much of the language is practically identical. They
admitted to three incidents during their three-week hunt in
which they encountered groups of Aboriginal people and killed
some of them.

The first such incident took place at Tomahawk Waterhole, 40
or 50 miles north-west of Morton's main camp. The men claimed
to have followed native tracks from the scene of the attack on
Morton, a month earlier. Four adult Aboriginal men were shot
dead here.

The party then headed back up the Lander to Boomerang
Waterhole, and followed more tracks north-east to Circle Well,
where they found a second group of Aboriginal men and killed
two of them.

Finally, on the lower Hanson River, Murray and Morton
came upon a large group of forty or so Aboriginal people, with

the result that eight more men died. The total death toll was fourteen. No prisoners were taken and there was no mention of anyone being wounded but not killed. Murray's party reported no injury to themselves.

Since their evidence was so obviously concocted, there is little point to a detailed recitation of how Murray and Morton said the incidents played out. What is interesting, however, is Murray's claim that he set about repeating the well-worn pattern of behaviour that he had established during the first manhunt, with the same consequences.

Each time, Wilson and the Aboriginal boy were instructed to keep back with the packhorses. Each time, Murray and Morton separated with the intention of surrounding the Aboriginal camp and surprising them. Each time, on reaching the middle of the camp, Murray dismounted. And each time, to his surprise...

[At Tomahawk Waterhole] I dismounted and the natives immediately attacked me.

[At Circle Well] I decided to dismount. Immediately I stepped to the ground the two of them jumped on top of me.

[At Hanson River] I then decided to dismount. As soon as I did quite a number of the natives rushed me and attacked with their sticks and boomerangs.

The same thing had happened to Murray three times during the Brooks hunt, but he supposedly never changed his approach. Certainly, the practice of giving up the obvious advantage which being on horseback gave him was guaranteed to increase the risk that he would be attacked; equally certainly, being attacked gave him a ready justification for acting in self-defence.

The need to shoot was, on Murray's evidence, desperately urgent in every case. That he survived all these close shaves, let alone uninjured, was a miracle. This was the stuff of *Boy's Own*:

> I threw them aside and got possession of a tomahawk from one of them. He then attacked me with his boomerang. I used the tomahawk to defend myself. The second blow struck him on the head and he fell dead. The second native was in the act of driving a spear through me from about two yards distance. I drew my revolver. Both Morton and I fired at the same instant and the native was killed.

And this:

> Two natives rushed to get the one spear that was standing upright in a bush. I noticed their movement and I also grabbed for the spear. Myself and a native got hold of the spear together. I wrenched it from him. It broke and left the small end in his hand while I had the strong end. The natives were then so close around me I felt that I could not get my revolver in time so I drove the spear right through a natives chest; then jumped back drew my revolver and fired.

Fortunately, according to the claims of Murray and Morton, all fourteen dead natives were guilty. At Cockatoo Spring, after four men had been killed, Morton said he 'looked at the natives who were shot and recognized them as being four of the natives who attacked me'. At Circle Well, a group of eight Aboriginal men were instructed to 'sit down' by Morton in their own language.

All but two did, and those two attacked Murray and were killed. Morton: 'I knew those two natives as amongst the ones that attacked me.' The other six were allowed to go, as 'they had nothing to do with the attack on me'.

Finally, at Hanson River, forty or so Aboriginal people were rounded up, including nine men, and 'most of the nine were among the aboriginals who attacked me'. Two minutes later, eight of them were dead. That was that; the killing was finally over. Murray left Morton to his own devices and returned south, dropping in on Tilmouth, who confirmed that he had had 'no further trouble from the natives' since shooting Wangaridge.[15]

So much for the official record; but Murray and Morton each added a little extra colour a few years later. Murray told Ernestine Hill, referring to the Morton hunt, that 'this time we took no prisoners'. He went on: 'It was a drastic case and it called for a drastic remedy. There are times when the natives understand nothing else, as history will show you.'[16] Morton was equally coy with Strehlow:

> Young Shrimp [Nugget Morton's nephew] suddenly sat up. His eyes gleamed with excitement. 'And now tell them, uncle', he grinned, 'just how you paid those damn myall niggers back in their own coin when you felt alright again.'
>
> 'Well there's no need to waste much time about that', replied Nugget, giving a pleased laugh. 'You've heard it all about a dozen times already; and these southern city chaps mightn't want to hear much more about the whole bloody business. But you know how it is, don't you?' He added for our benefit. 'Shrimp here is my own nephew, and he thinks the world of his old uncle, and I

like the kid and want to make a good bushman out of him: can't start them off too young when training them to be tough with these nigger bastards.'

Morton went on, disclosing perhaps more than he intended:

'But both of you probably know what happened anyway; all the southern papers splashed the news about for weeks afterwards. The police hadn't done their job half well enough for my liking; for the Government is always frightened of what the city folks will say when someone wants to teach these bush myalls a decent sort of a lesson.

'The official evidence showed that Murray's party had shot seventeen niggers at one soak on the Lander "when they were resisting lawful arrest", and another seventeen niggers at another soak some time later.'

Nugget paused. A hard scowl of unrelating hate settled like a cloud on his broad face, and he added grimly – 'You might think thirty-four niggers to be a fair enough bag. Who knows? There might have been some more. But I'm not satisfied yet by a long way. I was a member of one of these parties when some of those murdering myalls were knocked over – in fact, I managed to square my account with one of the bastards that had nearly got me. But one is not enough. I did not see any of the others there, and I know that that big woolly-headed devil with the steel tomahawk is still alive, hiding himself somewhere. I'm still on the look-out for him. Some day I must ride out to the Lander again; and then I shan't be satisfied unless I see his face through the sights of my rifle.'[17]

How this admission – that 'I did not see any of the others there' – might be reconciled with Morton's earlier insistence that he had positively identified all of the fourteen men who he and Murray acknowledged killing as being among his attackers, is an interesting question. His tally of the dead – thirty-four – was a few more than the official total from all the hunts of thirty-one, but of course there 'might have been some more' on top of that.

Safely back in Alice Springs, Murray filed his reports regarding Morton and Tilmouth on 19 October.[18] His report of how he had spent the previous three weeks was brief, providing scant details of the various incidents and reporting that 'unfortunately a number of natives were killed', but giving no indication of how many.

Again, there was to be no rest for Mounted Constable Murray. The next day he departed Alice Springs, with the prisoners Padygar and Akirkra and the witness Lala, heading for Barrow Creek and then on to Darwin for their date with the Supreme Court.[19]

––––

The killing was over, and the unfortunate thirty-one deaths which Murray had recorded give us the starting point for assessing what had really happened between 16 August and 15 October.

Aboriginal accounts of these events are, as is traditional, oral and not particularly fixed in terms of time. No serious attempt to record these stories was made by historians before the 1970s, by which time there were few survivors still alive. It is impossible to reconstruct any kind of certain chronology from the available sources, but many of the recollections are definite as to place and all are compelling in their raw sincerity.

It would be wrong to accept as objective truth what the Aboriginal tradition recalls and to wholly reject what the white men claimed, just as much as would be the reverse. All of the evidence must be given a fair hearing, all the more so because no such attempt was made by the official government inquiry at the time. Then we can draw some tentative conclusions and accept that the remaining gaps will in all probability never be filled.

A fair starting point for comparison is geography. The various white accounts of the expeditions (excluding Murray's movements between 4 and 13 September, about which we know nothing) say that Murray's parties travelled to and encountered Aboriginal people in the following places.

First expedition (Brooks hunt):
- a camp 12–14 miles west of Coniston (somewhere near Yurrkuru)
- Cockatoo Spring, further west of Coniston
- Boundary Soak, up the Lander River from Coniston
- Six Mile Soak, 32 miles north-west of Coniston, also on the Lander River
- a camp 10 miles south-west of Six Mile
- out in the ranges to the west of Cockatoo Spring, towards the Western Australian border.

Second expedition (Morton hunt):
- Tomahawk Waterhole and Boomerang Waterhole (roughly 120 miles north-west of Coniston, up the Lander River)
- Circle Well (on the Hanson River, about 120 miles north-east of Coniston)
- other places on the Hanson River, unspecified.

On the basis of these reports, the two expeditions can be placed in two rough circles. The Brooks hunt ran up the Lander River from Coniston as far as White Stone and then out west past Cockatoo Spring into the ranges towards the Western Australia border, then back to Coniston; an area perhaps 100 miles east to west and perhaps a little less north to south.

The Morton hunt also ran up the Lander, but with White Stone as its southern starting point, north to Tomahawk Waterhole, then east across to the Hanson River. Its area would therefore be somewhat smaller than that of the first hunt, focused heavily on the remaining soaks in the two dry rivers.

The Aboriginal stories provide corroboration that this description of the areas of operation was correct; they say that the hunting parties went to most of these places and killed Aboriginal people there. However, they say two other things as well: first, there were other places where Aboriginal people died which the whites did not mention, extending the area considerably; and, second, the hunts were not nearly so linear as the white record suggests.

Instead, the Aboriginal stories leave the distinct impression that Murray and his parties travelled up and down the Lander and Hanson valleys many times between August and October, covering the same ground repeatedly and hunting incessantly for any Aboriginal people they could find. Rather than a targeted investigative expedition diligently following leads left by suspects, it begins to look more like a random and opportunistic trawl through the countryside seeking out such prey as might be on offer.

Specifically, Aboriginal tradition identifies that killings took place at White Stone and Warlawurrukurlangu on the Lander, north of Willowra, and at Curlew and Dingo waterholes another 50 or so miles further north up the Lander from Tomahawk, way up near Lake Surprise. Several additional sites are named along the Hanson River, including a major massacre at Baxter's Well (Wajinpulungk), just south of Circle Well. Killings are also recorded as taking place at Tipinpa, a soak on the Patirlirri Creek north-west of White Stone, at Rabbit Bore and at Mount Theo, in the wilderness way out to the west from White Stone. Finally, a massacre was reported at Mission Creek, west of Coniston near Yuendumu.

Tim Japangardi gave a relatively detailed account of the first (Brooks) expedition in 1978 to George Jampijinpa, who translated it.

[The hunters] split up into two parties; one went south and the other west. There was a camp to the south where the ones responsible for killing the white man had been camping. The whites coming from the north were then ready to attack towards the south. They shot all the people they found. They attacked in the late evening. Many people ran away to hide during the fighting.

Some people were camped near a soakage called Yarlalinji near Yajampiyi (Mt Denison). A lot of old men walking around south of there were all shot. Many others travelled at night and some were shot as they arrived exhausted at the watering place. These were drinking when they were shot. There were a lot of people camped at Ngarntampi, all of whom were shot by the whites.

The whites then came further west to Yipirri (Mission Creek) and shot people camped there. As the whites turned back from there to return east they came across another lot of people and shot them all.

Other whites returned to Alice Springs to get more bullets. They then came back in search of other Warlpiris. They shot people they found around their camp fires.

Some Warlpiris had made a bush fire to the north and when the whites saw it they headed that way to attack whoever might be there. A lot of Warlpiris were camped by a waterhole. The whites came there and shot them all. There were really a lot of people living in that camp. They didn't even know about the trouble and the killing of the white man.

After that the whites headed further north to Ngunurlurru to shoot more people before returning to Yimpampi (Coniston). They looked around for some more Warlpiris but didn't find any.[20]

D. M. Jakamarra also spoke of a massacre at Mission Creek:

Murray went right up past Wakurlpu…He killed everybody. There was nobody left at Mission Creek, you know, to the west. No-one again was left of groups of people returning from ceremonies who Murray met up with, none of them survived either.

Well, that was the first expedition. Then he went away on the other side, still killing all the people. He went over there killing all the people.[21]

Jampijinpa told the Reads about a mass killing by Murray and Morton at Tipinpa. Jampijinpa was then a little boy, and his father was one of the victims:

I seen him. I seen him. Murray, Murray grab me then and he's hold me on the shoulder. When I was little feller.

There was big camp there, makinem, they was gettem em all the bush tucker you know, but he shot at about ten o'clock in the morning, ah, eight o'clock in the morning, shot at.

They yardem round, bringem to one mob, see, make it one heap. And they shottit. Two or three shotgun is goin', people is goin'. Nugget. Whatsaname was there too, Jack Murray. They shottit, and the travellin' this way.

Well they come round with the horses this way, and this way. Yardem. Yeah. Roundem up. Just like cattle we roundem up. And bringem one mob this way. Just suddenly. And just shottit there.[22]

Tim Japangardi's family was caught up in the Morton hunt as well, having headed north and west of the Lander after the first expedition. This was when Murray was based around Mud Hut and ranging up and down the Lander:

[Murray] bin turn back, come back after shoot two man. They bin followem [the Lander] now. All the girl bin carting water from bush, longa dry camp. They bin followem and findem there longa bush. Girl and kid and all. They bin finishem again, whole lot. Finishem, to come back again.[23]

Rosie Nungarrayi was a young Warlpiri girl living near White Stone (Briscoe's campsite).

the policemen came to Liirlpari (Whitestone). Again the policemen killed some people there. Then the police-men travelled west to Patirlirri (Rabbit Bore) looking for people. Again they killed a lot more of our people... For a whole day they went around shooting at people. They shot them just like bullocks. They shot the young men coming out from bush camp where they'd been initiated. People were shot digging for rabbits in our country, Muranjayi. They were getting yakajirri berries, yams and wanakiji tomatoes. Those people they shot had nothing to do with it. The policemen shot them for nothing. Again they killed a lot of men there. No-one breathed. All were dead. Women were alive. They let the women go alive and killed the men.

Nungarrayi said that Murray's party then went to Boomerang Waterhole and further north towards Lake Surprise, as far as Curlew Waterhole, killing whoever they found.

The whitefellas then travelled east to Warlawurrukurlangu, where they found Molly Napangardi's father's eldest brother, a Japanangka, who had two wives, two Napurrulas. The whitefellas sent them away and then fired after them, shooting them like dogs. Half of the men and women were shot. The wives tried to protect the men by standing in front of them and blocking the bullets, but they were shot too. My husband's father, Jampijinpa, was one of them.

On it went, east towards Barrow Creek.

[Murray] continued on to Barrow Creek. He went backwards and forwards over the same tracks, looking for people and their hiding places. Back over the tracks, looking for people who had come back after the shooting. Even then he shot more people.

Nungarrayi added a note of interest:

Another group of white people were travelling from the west, bringing bullocks and wagons with them, and these people also started shooting our people. Molly and I were only young girls. We used to run away frightened when we saw the whitefellas come up. Frightened, we'd hide. We'd dig a hole in the wet sand to make ourselves cool and sleep there until dark.[24]

If the news of Murray's handiwork had inspired other whites out in the wilderness to join the fun, that would hardly be surprising. Since the only police officer in the region was actively leading the shooting, there could be nothing to fear in terms of consequences if a few (or few dozen) more Aboriginal people fell to the bullets.

The massacre that took place at Baxter's Well on the Hanson River during the Morton hunt appears to have been particularly vicious. Johnny Nelson Jupurrula, a Warlpiri, was there. His family was part of a large group gathered at Baxter's Well, a sacred site, for a corroboree. They knew nothing about the troubles until a mob from the Lander region came running, escaping Murray's party.

Jupurrula's father was captured by Murray, put in chains and forced to show where his mob was. He was then shot and the killing began.

They coming there now, chasem round now, some all run away. Right, prisonem whole lot, everyone. Tiem up longa trees. All little boys, oh, lotta tracker, some stockmans too. And shootem whole lot, some feller, shootem, heapem up.

Tie'em up whole lot. And shootem in the morning. That's the last one they bin shootem all along, Wajinpulungk, Hanson Creek. That's where my father got shot there too.[25]

The corroboree at Baxter's Well appears to have been a particularly large one, involving Warlpiri and Kaytetye people and perhaps others. Kaytetye women Ivy Apenangke, Daisy Akemarre and Katie Ampetyane were little girls at the time and also witnessed the massacre.[26]

Tommy Thompson Kngwarraye spoke of the same incident:

They had gathered for an Itharte ceremony. Poor things, they were unaware of what was going on. They were dancing an Itharte ceremony there at Athimpelengkwe (Baxters Well). The two Kemarres [Major and Skipper] brought the police to where the old men were. The police saw them.

The poor old men got painted up with [feathers] and everything, unaware. So the men danced in the daytime. The police came around on horseback with their guns. Then they started shooting everyone. They circled around the Itharte camp, all the people in the middle. They were killed there at Athimpelengkwe.[27]

The first importance of the Aboriginal accounts, only some of which are quoted here, is of course their capacity to humanise the story; they give some sense of the confusion and terror among the Warlpiri and Kaytetye people as the shootings unfolded and they desperately tried to get away from the white men on horseback who, from their perspective, seemed intent on hunting them all down.

However, the stories also have strong forensic significance, for all the imprecision and probable confusion between specific events as to time and place. Most importantly, they provide a coherent solution to the main problem presented by the 'white' evidence: the fact that the hunters spent a lot more time out in the country than their chronological accounts of where they went and what they did would suggest. That is, there are big gaps in the white narrative, and the Aboriginal stories credibly fill them in.

The fairest conclusions which I feel can be drawn are that Murray and his parties ranged considerably more widely than he acknowledged; that the killings of Aboriginal people occurred at numerous more locations and times than he admitted; and that the hunters paid no more than lip service to the pretence that they were searching out particular identified targets. Rather, it is unarguably clear, they were hunting Aboriginal people per se.

The final question is the big one: how many died? Was it the thirty-one claimed by Murray and accepted by official history?

I have already pointed to later comments made by Murray and Morton which suggested that the tally was considerably understated. They were best placed to know. There is precious little recorded discussion among white people of the true tally, but Alice Springs local Ada Wade, who lived her whole life in the Centre, gave a clue in an interview in 1981, saying that 200 had died and adding this:

Walter, my brother, seen it afterwards; he seen it with his own eyes; he said they were like pineapples and water melons, scattered everywhere. Just shot them, little kids and all.[28]

If the general thrust of the Aboriginal stories is accepted, then thirty-one must be a gross underestimate. Not including the 4–13 September period, Murray was out hunting for a total of five weeks of nonstop effort. There is ample evidence of indiscriminate shooting involving large numbers of victims, and at least several major individual massacres.

All things considered, Murray and his colleagues almost certainly killed over 100 Aboriginal people;[29] taking into account the estimated population of the area of operations, it may have been as many as 200. Whatever the true tally was, the Coniston events constitute one of the largest mass killings in Australian history. That is a fact, and a fact largely unknown.[30]

Chapter 8

HEAT ON THE HOME FRONT

The shooting was over. Now, as white tempers out on the frontier cooled and black mourning began, the simmering was just getting started in the more 'civilised' rooms of media and government. The question was: would it boil over, or could it be contained?

A warning of the scale of trouble ahead was sounded on 13 September, when George Yates, a federal MP, asked the Labor Party Conference to condemn the Federal Government for its inaction in protecting the Aboriginal people of North Australia and failure to prevent 'the unofficial punitive expedition and the possible massacre of natives taking place'.[1]

In Canberra, following the brief flurry on 3 September when the department had urgently asked Cawood to confirm how many Aboriginal people Murray's first party had killed and been given the number of seventeen, the normal pace of activity resumed. On 18 September, J. A. Carrodus finally created the first departmental record of events, drawn from Murray's original report and adding some critical editorial content. Noting that all seventeen victims had been shot in self-defence, Carrodus added:

> Definite evidence of the implication of the aboriginals in the murder of Frederick Brooks was established before action for their arrest was taken by the Police, and in all the camps articles belonging to Brooks were found.[2]

Not a word of that sentence was true, and it was in fact contradicted by Murray's report of 2 September, then the only document constituting any evidence of the relevant events. The government was showing its hand already.

The Minister for Home and Territories saw the departmental memo on 21 September and issued his instructions, which were conveyed to Cawood on the 28th.[3] Cawood was directed to provide a report 'containing your personal observations on the circumstances connected with the investigations of this murder, and in particular your own views on the actions of the Police party and the results of such actions'. He was also to obtain statements from 'as many of the white members of the Police party as possible'. Finally, it was 'assumed' that the proceedings of the coronial inquest into Brooks' death would be forwarded in due course.

Deciphering the bureaucratic code used by civil servants having an eye to the future public record, this note expressed some considerable ministerial anxiety. Responsibility was being sheeted to Cawood, along with a heads-up that he had better move quickly to shore up the official line. As for the Brooks inquest, had one even taken place? The department was astute enough to give Cawood a big hint in that direction.

The last point was somewhat awkward. Brooks' body had not been recovered or medically examined. As Cawood knew, there had been no inquest and there was no death certificate. He ignored the department's hint but, after another follow-up two months later,[4] Cawood finally produced the Coroner's hand-written certification that he had made enquiries into Brooks' death and confirmed his opinion that a coronial inquest would not be required. Consequently, Brooks' body could be buried without further ado. The author of this document was H. B. Mackington.[5] Cawood forwarded it to the department on 19 December 1928.[6]

In handwriting on the back of the certificate is a note also signed by Mackington: 'From evidence of B Chapman and native La La Brooks met his death by being murdered by natives at near Coniston Station Central Australia.' The certificate is dated 7 August 1928. This is of course impossible, as is it also impossible that Mackington had taken any evidence from either Chapman (who wasn't capable of giving a statement between his return to Alice Springs in early September and his death a few days later) or Lala (who wasn't captured until sometime later and who Mackington could not have encountered at all before 1 September, when he was taken to Alice Springs by Murray). Even if Mackington did eventually get to talk to Lala, Brooks' remains had long since deteriorated well past the point of any useful forensic examination. In the interim, no attempt or suggestion had been made by anyone in Alice Springs that Brooks' corpse should be preserved or moved.

The Coroner's certificate was a patent fabrication, procured by Cawood in November or December in response to the department's demands. If the department noticed this (Cawood had hardly made the fraud difficult to detect), it elected to say nothing. Since nobody in either Alice Springs or Canberra cared about the actuality of due process, as opposed to its appearance, a doctored death certificate would suffice.

On 20 October, Cawood forwarded to Canberra Murray's brief report on his expedition with Nugget Morton. He followed this on the 25th with his detailed response to the department's note of 28 September, which Cawood said had taken a month to reach him.[7]

Cawood had been instructed to take statements from the white members of Murray's party from the first hunt back in August. He reported that he would endeavour to do so, but it would take some weeks. However, he had not been idle: 'I have had interviews with various settlers on the incidents leading up to and following' Brooks' murder. This expedient, he went on to explain, had provided all the answers the government would really need to any questions it might be contemplating.

The starting point for Cawood was, as always, the lack of adequate police resources. This had caused delays in investigating complaints from settlers into the unspecified 'depradations of the blacks', which delays had been 'accepted by the natives as a sign of weakness on the part of the administration of law and order, consequently the natives have adopted a cheeky attitude...and have made threats to wipe out the white settlers'.

The 'civilised natives' were not the problem, because they submitted to authority. The 'myalls', however, had 'no respect for the sanctity of human life' and 'very little idea of the deadly effect of firearms'. Their 'attitude when called upon to surrender is one of immediate hostility'. The results were predictable as police were forced to defend themselves.

Still, Cawood said, the police and settlers were 'anxious to avoid bloodshed'.

No one regrets the shooting of the blacks more than I do, but if the Government throws open country in the isolated interior, it is incumbent on the local authorities to afford the necessary protection against such unprovoked attacks as the white settlers in Central Australia have been subjected to.

In the opinion of old residents of this part, trouble has been brewing for some time, and the safety of the white man could only be assured by drastic action on the part of the authorities. In their opinion the only other alternative was to hand the country back to the blacks.

But the latest news was good:

> I am firmly of the opinion that the result of recent action by the police will have the right effect upon the natives, and while regretting the necessity for extreme measures, the fact remains that the natives brought the trouble on themselves.

If the desire in Canberra was for this whole unfortunate business to quietly go away, Cawood wasn't helping. 'Drastic action' and 'extreme measures' was not the kind of language the Minister would be keen to read. Even the most somnolent mandarin at the department could not fail to pick up on the unsubtle meaning behind Cawood's words.

Cawood's report landed on 2 November, prompting the department to immediately send him a telegram asking whether the Aboriginal deaths had been reported to the Coroner and an inquest held into them.[8] Once more, Cawood was being given the broadest of hints as to the bureaucratic measures he needed to take so that the mess could be properly papered over and forgotten.

However, spot fires were now starting to spark all over the place, although the department was doing its best to keep them contained. Two federal MPs from South Australia – Norman Makin and Walter Langdon Parsons – wrote to the Minister in October seeking information about the reported killing of Aboriginal people.[9] Each received a prompt reply acknowledging that seventeen people had been killed (only the Brooks expedition had been reported so far) but repeating the unsupported claims that Brooks had been attacked by twenty or more people, that his possessions had been found at each camp where shootings had occurred, and that 'the reports indicate' that the deaths had been an unfortunate consequence of attempted arrests.

The Minister told Parsons that, while the evidence to hand indicated that the killings were justified by self-defence, 'further inquiries are being made with a view of obtaining all particulars necessary to place the matter beyond doubt'. The conclusion was already in place; all that was needed was the evidence to justify it. The conventional purpose of official inquiries – finding out what had actually happened – clearly wasn't in contemplation.[10]

On 15 October, the department had also received a telegram from J. W. Bleakley, the Chief Protector of Aborigines in Queensland, who had recently completed an inquiry for the Federal Government into native affairs in North and Central Australia, and was still in the region. He had spoken with Annie Lock, the missionary who had been at Harding Soak (about halfway between Alice Springs and Coniston) during the killings, and passed on her report from local Aboriginal people 'that police party including 6 civilians surrounded camp when making arrest and shot number of natives and several women and children were killed'.[11]

The department forwarded Bleakley's note to Cawood on 5 November along with a hurry-up for him to 'take any action practicable in the direction of expediting the information which has been requested. The killing of the aboriginals has been the subject of a number of communications to this Department'.[12]

Now the department was made aware of the Morton hunt and more shootings, and official panic (if one can imagine a sedentary form of panic) was starting to set in. A longer letter was sent to Cawood on 9 November, with more than one sting in its tail.

[After quoting Murray's report of an unspecified number of Aboriginal deaths] It is hardly necessary to comment on the serious aspect of the killing of aboriginals by Government parties…

Full particulars should be furnished as to the number of aboriginals killed, the circumstances in which they were killed, whether the killing was reported to the Coroner, and, if so, the action taken by the Coroner in regard to such reports. Confirmation should be obtained, wherever possible, of the statements made by officers or persons connected with parties responsible for the killing of aboriginals.

Statements such as those quoted from the report by Constable Murray are of too indefinite a nature to be of any assistance to the Minister.

Cawood was given a particular bollocking for just passing on Murray's reports without his own commentary:

You will, of course, recognise that, as the representative of the Government in Central Australia, the Minister would naturally look to the Government Resident for advice and authentic information regarding all important happenings in the Territory.

Cawood was told to get moving and send in full reports on the Morton and Tilmouth cases, including statements from them. And, in case he still wasn't getting what was going on here:

This Department is at a loss to understand the sudden change in the attitude of the aboriginals of Central

Australia towards white men. Unusual circumstances appear to be attached to the cases of the attacks on Brookes, Morton and Tilmouth, in that they have all been reported by Constable Murray, and have occurred recently and within a comparatively short time, while nothing of a similar nature had been previously reported for some years.

If you are aware of the reasons for the apparent sudden outbreak of hostility on the part of the aboriginals, they might be quoted.[13]

The letter rounded off with an explanation for this sudden burst of hostility on the part of the department, including the content of two telegrams it had received that very day from missionary groups calling for an official inquiry. These groups had been alarmed by fresh developments in Darwin which had just played out in public view and would ensure that the lid was going to blow.

The law, of the courts rather than the gun, had intervened with decisive force. In Darwin, Brooks' alleged murderers had had their day in court.

Constable Murray arrived in Darwin in late October with Padygar and Akirkra for their Supreme Court trial. He had also brought with him the witness Lala. The hearing was set for 7 November. As the prisoners had pleaded guilty before Magistrate Allchurch in Alice Springs, the expectation was that the trial should be a formality. The police and prosecutors had not bothered with such things as forensic evidence or witnesses, other than Lala.

The case was presided over by Justice R. I. D. Mallam, the sole judge of the Supreme Court of the Northern Territory.

English born and trained but with twenty-five years in Australia and fifteen of those in Darwin, Mallam was as experienced a criminal lawyer as one could find in the Territory, reportedly having defended twenty murder trials as a barrister and having run some successful appeals in the High Court of Australia. He had taken up the judgeship in May 1928.[14]

Mr Asche appeared for the Crown to prosecute Padygar and Akirkra, and Mr Foster appeared for their defence.[15] Alex Wilson was also there, acting again as interpreter for the prisoners and Lala. Given his direct involvement in the series of events which included the prisoners' arrest, it was completely inappropriate for him to participate in the trial. No objection was raised, and Mallam would not have known the background; otherwise, he would certainly have prevented it.

An all-white, all-male jury was empanelled, after a minor distraction caused by a putative juror who told the judge that he could not sit on the jury as he knew nothing of Aboriginal customs or language, was therefore not a peer of the accused and that to include him would offend *Magna Carta*. Justice Mallam commented that he didn't understand what the man was talking about, but wisely excused him anyway. One more item of house-keeping had to be dealt with: the jury foreman asked if everyone could remove their coats in the heat. The judge agreed.[16]

The charges were read, and the prosecution case opened with Lala's testimony, given through Wilson. Lala told the court that he lived on Coniston, as did the two accused. Padygar, he said, was his uncle but Akirkra was not a relation. Lala said he had witnessed the murder of Brooks, from a distance of about 100 yards. He saw a woman called Lulka or Barunali hold Brooks' arms while a number of men including Padygar and Akirkra attacked him, Padygar hitting him with a yam stick and Akirkra striking him a number of times with a tomahawk. The men had discussed killing Brooks the night before, their motive being to steal his food and possessions. Their pre-planning included sending his camels further away so that Brooks' two boys would have to go out to retrieve them, allowing time to kill him. This all sounded credible; Lala even positively identified a knife which was exhibited in court, saying it belonged to Brooks and had been taken by one of the killers other than the two accused.

Under cross-examination by the defence barrister, Foster, Lala's evidence became somewhat less certain. Prompted to name names, he rattled off those of nine men other than Padygar and Akirkra, all of whom he said had attacked Brooks. Conveniently, he testified, all of them other than the two accused were now dead. He didn't say how he knew. He did however assure the court that he had not been coached in his evidence by Murray.

Now Murray gave evidence, and introduced for the first time some evidentiary details that he had not mentioned previously. He produced two knives, which he said he had taken from two Aboriginal men, Idgiewarra and Ladygynunda, during the hunt. He didn't say what had happened to them; presumably they were among the seventeen dead.

The court adjourned for lunch; on returning to the bench, Justice Mallam said that the Sheriff had reported to him that one of the jurors had gone home for lunch. The result, the judge said, was that the trial must be aborted. Then it turned out that a second juror was missing as well, and Mallam was not happy: 'How a policeman could count twelve when there were only ten was more than he could say. The whole thing was regrettable.' The rest of the jury was discharged and everyone joined the missing jurors, going home for the day.

A new trial kicked off the next morning, with an all-new, still all-white and all-male jury.[17] Lala gave his evidence again, which was mostly the same as the day before except that now he said he was not related to either Padygar or Akirkra and that they were from a different tribe from his. He was cross-examined once more by Foster, and this time his evidence collapsed in an unruly heap. According to the newspaper reports, he gave wildly contradictory responses compared to what he had said a day earlier, including identifying one of the killers as his father and confusing everyone as to how Brooks had been killed.

Murray gave his evidence and, from the prosecution's perspective, things only got worse. He was questioned in detail about the supposed confessions made by Padygar and Akirkra after he had arrested them, conceding that they had been chained by the neck, had witnessed other Aboriginal men being shot by Murray, and had at no time been cautioned. More importantly, their confessions had supposedly been made to Major and then translated for Murray, who spoke nothing of their language; but Major had not been called as a witness.

Now Justice Mallam got stuck in, interrogating Murray about the bizarre proceedings before Magistrate Allchurch in Alice Springs. While Padygar and Akirkra had reportedly made admissions of guilt there, no written record of these statements had been brought to Darwin.

Justice Mallam ruled that none of the statements allegedly made by the accused could be admitted into evidence. Whatever they had supposedly told Major and he had passed on to Murray was clearly not given voluntarily, in view of the 'violent circumstances' of their detention and the absence of any caution. As for the Allchurch proceedings, Mallam was scathing of the Special Magistrate and his apparent ignorance that Central Australia was not governed by South Australian law and had not been since 1911. Padygar and Akirkra, if they were guilty, would have to be convicted by evidence other than their own words.

Murray went on with his evidence. He said, presumably with a straight face, that when he arrested Akirkra '[I] immediately looked at his feet to see if there were any peculiarities about him. [I] compared his footprints with those followed from Stafford Springs and found it identical in every way.'

During the incident when Akirkra was captured, Murray said that his party had come upon six adult Aboriginal men. Four of them ran away; Murray shot at them and

[I] shot to kill every time. If [I] had shot to hit in the leg what was [I] to do with a wounded blackfellow away out there in the bush?[18]

Justice Mallam had some more questions for Murray, leading to this memorable exchange:

All those who were shot died. In one instance a bullet had passed through one abo and after killing him, passed on and killed another one. He could tell because the hole made was a big one. ('Mowed them down wholesale!' was His Honor's remark.)

It would be fair to say that the judge was not one for hiding his disdain, which in this case was reserved entirely for the prosecution. Whether his dim view of what had been presented affected the jury we don't know, but they certainly shared it. In a remarkable exception to the usual outcome of cases where black men stood accused of killing whites, the jury took only fifteen minutes (according to one report; forty-five minutes according to another) to come back with an acquittal of both accused. Padygar and Akirkra were free men.

Of course, they were a long way from their home. Murray still had responsibility for getting them safely there, and he left Darwin with the two men and Lala by train on 13 November. At Mataranka, they switched to his car, camping for a night at Warlock Waterhole. Murray reported to Cawood on his return to Alice Springs that, when he awoke the following morning, Padygar and Akirkra had disappeared. He left them to their own devices and continued on home.[19] Tempting as it may be to suspect Murray of dispensing some frontier justice, it seems that they had run off and eventually returned home, living until the 1950s at the Aboriginal settlement at Yuendumu.[20]

The proceedings in Darwin had been a complete debacle. After all the shooting and with seventeen Aboriginal deaths officially acknowledged (news of the toll from the Morton hunt still hadn't reached the public), the case against the two supposed captured killers had been kicked out of court with a resounding thud. No justice had been obtained, so far, for anyone.

Reports appeared in the capital city newspapers, highlighting Murray's casual admissions of extreme violence and Justice Mallam's disgusted reaction.[21] The Melbourne *Argus* also carried an ominous report from a Methodist missionary, Athol McGregor, who had just returned from the Coniston region and would be one of the loudest voices demanding an inquiry into the killings exposed by the Darwin trial. McGregor had some very pointed things to say:

> At Barrow Creek I was literally chased by the blacks
> begging food. This does not excuse the murders, but

explains it. My objection is not to constitutional justice, but to the shooting of 17 men and women by the police. No circumstances can justify the shooting of such a number, and was ever a battle fought in which 17 were hit and all died? So many settlers prefer a dead black to a live one that we must ask ourselves what did really happen. Common sense tells us that one cannot call on a black to stand in the name of the King, as English to them is only noise. I do earnestly ask for an inquiry into the stewardship of the police in this affair and into our land settlement system which makes such tragedies inevitable. The day is coming when the isolated settler must either see his cattle killed around him, be murdered himself for remonstrating, or burden his conscience with the murder of natives.[22]

Unsurprisingly, the Department of Home and Territories went into meltdown. An urgent coded telegram was despatched to Cawood on 9 November:

Press reports indicate acquittal followed upon Judges direction to Jury that evidence was without corroboration. Absence of trackers and Brookes two boys left Crown little evidence support case. Immediate report desired showing what evidence was relied upon and explanation why supporting evidence mentioned by Judge was not available.[23]

If Cawood was at last registering just how panicked his superiors were becoming and how this might impact his future career prospects, he still wasn't showing it. He did not reply to this latest urgent demand for two weeks. Meanwhile, the department was madly backfilling; another telegram to Cawood on 12 November asked whether the shooting of Wangaridge by Tilmouth had been reported to the Coroner.[24] (The answer was no; an inquest wasn't held until the following January.[25]) On the 17th, yet another telegram asked Cawood to obtain a report by the 'Protector of Aboriginals' regarding the shootings. This was patently ridiculous; as the department knew, the Protector was Sergeant Noblet.[26]

On 21 November, Cawood sent a telegram to the department responding to its request of the 17th, which had mentioned the long memorandum of 9 November then making its slow way to Alice Springs. Cawood asked if he should wait for its arrival instead of 'leaving for investigation recent killing Twenty Eighth'. Which killing he was referring to isn't at all obvious, nor how he was planning to investigate it. By return, the department told him not to go, rather to await its memorandum.

In the meantime, Cawood was informed, the government was considering the 'possibility' of holding a 'special investigation'.[27]

Cawood finally handed in his report on what had gone wrong in Darwin on 22 November. He explained to the department that there were no eyewitnesses to Brooks' murder other than Lala, and the only white man who had seen Brooks' body was the since-deceased Bruce Chapman. In any event, the guilty pleas entered by Padygar and Akirkra at the Alice Springs court hearing had made it unnecessary to worry about witnesses other than Lala and Murray. Unfortunately, Justice Mallam had got in the way.

Cawood added a gratuitous note of self-protection: the 'whole of the evidence taken in the lower court at Alice Springs was forwarded to the Attorney-General'.[28] Actually, it hadn't been; Cawood had sent the material to the department in September with a request that it be forwarded on, but the department had decided that that was unnecessary.[29]

An inquiry was already politically inevitable; the government was being hit by an avalanche of adverse press and direct demands for action. During November and into December, calls for a full inquiry were made to the department and the Prime Minister by many groups, mainly the churches and missionary societies. These included Methodist Inland Mission, Association for the Protection of the Native Races of Australasia and Polynesia (headed by the indomitable Rev. W. Morley, who would prove as unrelenting as Athol McGregor), Women's Non-Party Association, Australian Theosophical Order of Service, Australian Women's National League, Society of Friends, Australian Board of Missions, Australian Aborigines Mission, Australian Natives' Association, and Council of Churches.[30]

The newspapers were giving the government just as much trouble. An example is a report carried by the *Northern Territory Times* of a powerful sermon delivered by the Rev. Stanley Jarvis in Darwin:

> People want to know if any others were killed. It appears impossible for all those bands of natives to be associated with the murder of Brooks and it looks as if they were shot down at different places just to teach them and others a lesson. The Federal Government is being asked to appoint a Commission of Inquiry. These tragedies and horrors make the natives bitter towards white men and they wait their time to retaliate, yes, the police party shot to kill and seventeen were slain, and all for what?[31]

The Sydney Morning Herald summarised the general sentiment of the press, in an article headed 'MURDER OF BLACKS. GENERAL DENUNCIATION. OF POLICE BRUTALITY':

> Press, pulpit, and the general public unanimously agree with the jury's verdict in the aboriginal murder trial, and are shocked by the candid admissions of the police that they shot to kill on sight all the male aboriginals they came across, admittedly 17, but locally believed to greatly exceed that number.[32]

The letters pages were lighting up as well. *The Register* on 15 November carried three typical examples. 'Nudis Verbis' expressed the shame of 'every right-thinking Australian' at the photograph of Padygar and Akirkra, which many papers had published, half naked and chained together by neck cuffs in Darwin. By contrast, 'Centralian Rattler' called on his twenty years of experience in Central Australia to explain that he had 'never seen a civilized black' there; that they were completely out of control, mainly because they had been mistaught by the missionaries and not handled with enough severity. He went on:

> The Australian aborigine will never be civilized; he is the same as the dingo – liable to turn and snap you at any time, no matter what his treatment. A lot of people talk of the poor blacks being turned out of their hunting grounds, and that through the coming of the whites they are becoming extinct. No one seems to consider whether the aborigines are dying out the same as other prehistoric races, but that is my opinion, and they are only going a little faster than was intended by Nature.

You will never turn a stone-age man into a
twentieth century man in a few years, but make him do
as he is told and Central Australia will become a good
place to live in. Until the blacks are under control the
country will never be properly developed.[33]

The *Northern Territory Times* published a long letter on
16 November written by Annie Lock, the missionary who had
just returned to Darwin after months in the desert at Harding
Soak fruitlessly trying to keep a rag-bag group of sick and starving
Aboriginal people alive with almost no resources. She explained
the problem, as she saw it, succinctly. Having asserted that Brooks'
killers had come from 'far out west', she went on:

The Central Australia is in a terrible state with the
drought, and these natives find it very hard to get food
and water. The squatters have such a lot of stock on their
stations, and are compelled to see that they are watered,
and so have to use the big water holes that have been
the property or camping ground of these wild tribe
natives, and now they have been driven from them and
made go to their rock holes in the hills or other small
holes, and through the drought these are getting dry. At
these big water holes the wild animals come for water,
and the natives wait for their prey. Now they are not
allowed to camp there, for they disturb the cattle and
keep them from the water. The natives are very angry
at being hunted from place to place and unable to get
water and food.

I applied to the Government for help during the
drought for them, and the Government refused, so now

all around for 100 miles they are killing the stock for
food and threatening the lives of these squatters if they
hunt them from the water holes.[34]

Political pressure was growing as well. Francis Forde, Member
of Parliament and future Prime Minister (for eight days, in 1945),
wrote to the Minister for Home and Territories asking for assurance
that a 'searching inquiry into the whole matter' would be held.[35]

The Minister, for the moment, was Major General The Hon.
Sir Neville Howse, VC, KCB, KCMG. He had been in the
post since earlier that year. Sir Neville was seriously eminent; a
surgeon by training, he had joined the Army and fought in the
Boer War, becoming the first recipient of a Victoria Cross given
to a soldier in Australian service. He later took charge of the
Australian Army's medical services during World War I, and was
knighted along the way. He entered Federal Parliament in 1922
for the conservative Nationalist Party.

What Sir Neville thought, if he thought much at all, about the
Aboriginal people of Central Australia for whom he was directly
responsible history has not recorded. Nor is there an indication
from the archives whether he had a particular view on the events
around Coniston or the need for an inquiry. It likely made no
difference; the Prime Minister's office was being bombarded just
as much as Sir Neville's own department, and it appears that the
ultimate decision came from the highest level.

On 15 November, *The Sydney Morning Herald* carried
the first public comment on the issue by the Prime Minister,
Stanley Bruce:[36]

The Government fully realises the seriousness of the
reports with regard to the shooting of aborigines in

Central Australia. I have requested the Minister for
Home and Territories to obtain a report on the matter
as soon as possible, and when this is received I shall
consider what further course of action will be taken.[37]

To *The Age* on the same day, Bruce added the flourish that 'the
whole matter will be sifted to the bottom'.[38]

This was the last thing that Bruce needed just now. The
Prime Minister was literally two days away from a federal election, which was looking like a difficult one for him to win. The
significance of that political reality should not be overstated; the
treatment of Aboriginal people was not then (nor indeed at any
time since) a major vote-turning issue and, although the Coniston
massacres story was getting a solid run in the press with some
fairly eye-catching headlines, it was hardly dominating the front
pages. Still, it was a distraction and the government wanted it
cleaned up fast.

Bruce was at the time Australia's longest serving Prime
Minister, having been in office since 1923. His government was
conservative, a coalition of the Nationalist Party, which he led,
and Earle Page's Country Party. Bruce's pedigree was pure: born
in Melbourne, educated at Melbourne Grammar and Cambridge
University, he had come home to run the family business and then
served with distinction in the Gallipoli campaign. Following the
war, he was recruited by the Nationalist Party, then led by Billy
Hughes; he became Prime Minister after the 1922 election forced
his party into a coalition that Page refused to join unless Hughes
stepped down. Bruce consolidated power effectively, and was
re-elected with a much-increased majority in 1925.

Bruce and his government pursued an archly conservative
course. His major concern was with the need to vastly increase the

population, from the six million or so when he took office to many times that number, so that the untapped resources of the continent could be fully exploited. His vision was nationalist in part, but imperialist in whole. A lifelong Anglophile, he had chosen to serve in the British rather than the Australian Army during the Great War; after politics he would serve as High Commissioner in London for many years, ultimately being elevated Viscount Melbourne and taking his seat in the House of Lords.

For Bruce, like most of his contemporaries, Australia's future was white and British. He implemented policies designed to encourage mass immigration to Australia from Great Britain, with modest success. He was equally uncontroversial in his attitude to Aboriginal Australians: so far as the public record discloses, he never spared them a thought. There is, it appears, no sign of him ever having made a public statement on Aboriginal affairs.

Bruce's general position on race was straightforward, as he assured the crowd at his campaign launch for the 1925 election: 'We are for the Empire; for an adequate measure of defence; for the maintenance and protection of a White Australia.'[39] In this two-hour speech, Bruce mentioned Aboriginal affairs not once. This was not unusual; Australia's political class had been obsessed by 'race' questions since well before Federation in 1901, but the consistent issue of overwhelming concern was non-white immigration (particularly from Asia); Aboriginal Australians had rarely been more than a footnote to the conversation.

By the late 1920s, the popular wisdom regarding Aboriginal Australians, which had prevailed around the turn of the century, was no longer in vogue. That widely held assumption was that Australia's preferred destiny as a wholly white nation would not continue to be impeded by the inconvenient presence of a pre-existing black population, for the simple reason that they were in the process of dying out. Alfred Deakin, Australia's first Attorney-General and future Prime Minister, laid this out explicitly in 1901:

Little more than a hundred years ago Australia was a Dark Continent in every sense of the term. There was not a white man within its borders. In another century the probability is that Australia will be a White Continent with not a black or even a dark skin amongst its inhabitants. The aboriginal race has died out in the South and is dying fast in the North and West even where most gently treated.[40]

During the following thirty years, Aboriginal people had obligingly continued to diminish in numbers, but in 1928 there were still some 60,000 of them living in Australia, along with growing numbers of the product of interracial couplings. Only the most ardently optimistic racial purist was still refusing to give up on the promise of their total demise. In political circles, the question had become how to deal with the persistent residue of the country's first peoples in a way that would least disturb national (white) progress.[41]

This was the political context in which the Coniston killings landed. How Bruce's government ended up handling the fallout was with textbook amoral expediency.

It appears that serious consideration of an official inquiry had begun in early November. On the 13th, the Department of Home and Territories had asked G. M. Wilson, the Commonwealth Public Service Inspector in Adelaide, to make some discreet enquiries with the South Australian Police Commissioner, Brigadier General Leane, as to a suitable person whom the South Australian Government might be able to offer up to head such an inquiry.[42] Leane had strongly recommended Police Inspector Percival Giles, then in charge of police in the northern part of South Australia, for the post, notwithstanding the obvious criticism which his appointment would attract.

As the external pressure on the government mounted, on 19 November J. A. Carrodus produced a departmental memorandum reporting on everything the government then knew about the attacks on Brooks, Morton and Tilmouth, and the reprisal killings led by Murray. It was relatively anodyne, setting out in detail Murray's reports, the department's attempts to get information out of Cawood, and Cawood's comprehensive but evidence-free dissertations on what had gone wrong in Central Australia. It also repeated without comment the details of Brooks' murder which had been circulating since early August and remained unsupported by any evidence (and had, if anything, been completely discredited by the outcome of the trial in Darwin – an event which Carrodus did not see fit to mention in his report).[43]

The department followed up on 23 November with another, utterly extraordinary, document of uncertain authorship. A handwritten annotation on the document describes it as 'notes made by the Home Dept a summary of the position'. It was provided to and apparently considered by the subsequent Board of Enquiry, and can fairly be taken as a statement of the government's official view as at November 1928.[44]

The statement begins with an extensive quote from the report of the missionary J. Hutson Edgar on his recent visit to Central Australia, describing it as 'comprehensive and interesting'. Edgar's opinions on the Aboriginal people, of whom he admits he met 'only a few scores', are repeated in their full glory, including that the wild black in the regions visited by us is in some respects a disgusting, useless creature, living a crude, animal, anti-social existence.

But this is not all, they have just killed Brookes.

The departmental statement takes up the story from there:

It appears evident that the blacks who have been con-cerned in the recent tragedies are of the class described in the report. They are believed to have been strangers to the district and to have arrived there from the Western Australian border.

The murder of Brooks is recited, again with all the usual detail but this time stated as uncontroverted fact rather than unproved allegation. The same is repeated for the attacks on Morton and Tilmouth.

In each of the cases mentioned, there was not the slightest evidence of provocation, and the police report contains definite statements indicating that the hostility of the natives could not have been due to a shortage of food.

After summarising the results of Murray's 'investigations', the department delivered its verdict:

The information so far available indicates that the blacks received no provocation, either in relation to the dep-redations on the station stock, or in attacks on the white men. There is no evidence that they were short of native food. On the contrary the police report, if accurate, completely refutes any assertion of that nature. The reports further indicate that there is little doubt that the natives who were shot in the endeavours to arrest the murderers of Brookes, were directly implicated in the murder.

A feature of the comments which have been made on the matter is that, while there have been abundant expressions of sympathy for the blacks, none has been expressed for the white man who was murdered, or the man who was terribly battered and only escaped by a miracle, or for those isolated settlers who have suffered the loss of their stock and have been living in fear of their lives.

In reality, as at 23 November, the department could be certain of the following facts:
- Brooks was dead, killed by Aboriginal people.
- Morton had been attacked by other Aboriginal people and killed at least one of them.
- Tilmouth had killed another Aboriginal man, possibly in self-defence.
- At least nineteen Aboriginal people, but probably more than that, had been shot dead during the two expeditions led by Murray.

Everything else was speculation. There was no warrant for accepting as fact anything Murray had said in his reports, for the obvious and uncontroversial reason that a police officer cannot give conclusive evidence of his own actions. There was, at this stage, no evidence in existence from any other member of the hunting parties, nor the results of any coronial inquests (as none had been held). The evidence of Lala had been totally discredited, and Murray had already been severely criticised by Justice Mallam during the trial in Darwin (again, not mentioned in the 23 November statement).

As to the motivations or provocations for the attacks on Brooks and Morton, the department had nothing in its possession which would support even a tentative opinion, let alone the conclusions drawn in its statement. What was needed, as the department had already decided, was a full inquiry to investigate and determine all these questions. Why exactly did it feel the need to pre-empt that process in such unequivocal terms?

We can only speculate on the government's internal dialogue, as none of it was recorded. The fact that the department was prepared to go out on such a limb in asserting so many speculative opinions as if they were incontrovertible fact gives a pretty strong hint that the overriding desire in Canberra was to bury this whole unfortunate mess as quickly and neatly as possible. The department was seeking to help by tying off the loose ends with some bold assertions which, if repeated often enough, might just become fact.

By 26 November, the government was seriously canvassing who should be appointed to run its inquiry. General Leane's suggestion of Inspector Giles had been taken up and was being pushed by the department. Accepting that this appointment may be 'questioned', the idea of a two-man commission was also under discussion, and the department's secretary, W. J. Clemens, seriously proposed that J. Hutson Edgar be considered. As Clemens noted, 'his appointment should ensure that the investigation will be conducted without giving ground for allegation that the information obtained will be viewed from an administration standpoint'.

A pre-judged ignorantly racist standpoint, on the other hand, would presumably not present a problem.[45]

The Federal Cabinet met on 27 November, and the next day *The Sydney Morning Herald* was reporting the Prime Minister as saying that it had been decided to appoint an 'independent board' to investigate the killings of Aboriginal people.[46] Its composition was not yet known.

One possible candidate for membership of the inquiry whose name had not been considered or discussed at all, so far as the official record discloses, received notification out of the blue on 28 November of his imminent appointment. This surprise selection was Cawood, the Government Resident in Central Australia. The department informed him that it would be appointing three members to a tribunal to investigate the shootings, and he would be included.[47]

The absolute impropriety of Cawood's participation in a government inquiry into the shootings of Aboriginal people by parties led by a police officer under his direct command as Police Commissioner, in which events he had had a direct personal involvement, would have been as obvious in 1928 as it is today. Cawood was hopelessly conflicted: he was ultimately responsible for all actions of the police force which he led; he had issued instructions to Murray to conduct the investigations which led to the shootings; he personally knew all of the white men involved in the killings; he had even spoken with Bruce Chapman, the only white person to have seen Brooks' corpse; he had written numerous reports which pre-judged the issues the inquiry would have to determine; and he had been roundly criticised by the department for his lax responses to its demands for information and failure to obtain properly detailed reports from Murray. In short, not many people had more reasons to conduct a less than impartial interrogation of the relevant events than Cawood.

All of this was known to the government; the absence from its records of any trace of how and why Cawood came to be appointed speaks volumes. The fix was already in.

Before the formal public announcement of the official inquiry and its members, some remaining details needed to be cleared up. On 6 December, Cawood finally replied to the department's urgent question from a month earlier as to whether a coronial inquest had been held into the deaths of seventeen Aboriginal people which Murray had reported on 2 November. Cawood replied that he had intended that it should happen but, since the government was going to be having a proper investigation soon, the Coroner might as well conduct his inquest at the same time.[48] This suggestion was taken up.

Cawood wrote again, the same day, responding indignantly to the department's loaded comment about the 'sudden change in attitude' of the Aboriginal people that had supposedly caused this outburst of violence. Cawood was at pains to refute any such suggestion – in fact, he said, the settlers had been complaining about the 'depredations of the blacks' ever since he arrived a year earlier, and the overcrowded prison at Alice Springs attested to this. Even the local missionaries were calling for 'a return to the old Police methods of flogging the natives' as a more effective deterrent than imprisonment.[49]

In the most basic terms, the battle that Cawood and the department were politely fighting was this: the department wanted it on the record that it had been taken by surprise by the outbreak of violence, while Cawood insisted that he had done all he could to warn that it was coming.

159

The department had also asked for a report from the Chief Protector of Aboriginals – Sergeant Noblet – and on 8 December he obliged.[50] Obviously he had at front of mind his onerous statutory obligations as Chief Protector, under the *Northern Territory Aborigines Act 1910* and the Aborigines Ordinance 1911, which made him the personal guardian of every Aboriginal child in Central Australia and any Aboriginal adult who he decided in his absolute discretion should be under his control. He was responsible, in law, for them in the same way that any parent is responsible for their child.

So, Noblet explained how he had acquitted his responsibilities in respect of the Aboriginal people his sub-Protector, Constable Murray, had shot dead. Knowing that an inquiry was coming, he was as keen as Cawood had been to get his opinions on the record. First and most importantly, he deplored the murder of the 'very old inoffensive man' he had known well, Fred Brooks. His killers' motive was obviously that he had caught them killing stock. They had taken his food, but:

> I am sure this was not because they were starving as the natives in the North West and right down the Western side of Alice Springs are always fat and native foods of all descriptions are plentiful.

Noblet mirrored Cawood's view: there were simply not enough police. He went further in his prescriptions:

> Gaol punishment does not appear to have the proper effect with the evil doers that it should have. I think, in the early days when a little cat o'nine tails was used in addition to the sentence, it had a better effect.

Obviously, the dead Aboriginal people were killed in self-defence; Murray had said so. Anyway:

> I deplore the killing of the natives as much as anyone but, at times, it cannot be avoided and the same thing has happened in the settling of all new countries. Lessons must be taught to people who murder others. My experience in nineteen years of out back life is that the settlers are very fair to the natives but stock and natives do not and will not thrive together and it can be seen at a glance by the restlessness and tucked-up look of the cattle when they are together.

This was, admittedly, new evidence – even the cattle were eyeing the former owners of their land with instinctive suspicion.

Chapter 9

THE BOARD OF ENQUIRY

justice should not only be done, but should manifestly and undoubtedly be seen to be done.[1]

The Cabinet having decided that some form of inquiry would have to be commissioned, the governmental boffins turned their minds to exactly what that meant. The Department of Home and Territories had realised by mid-November that there was actually no law in force in Central Australia under which an investigative body could be empowered to subpoena witnesses and take evidence on oath, leaving two options: either make a special law for this inquiry, or appoint a Royal Commission. The choice was so important that the Prime Minister himself scribbled a note on the departmental memorandum: 'Ordinance to be drafted by A.G. Dept!'[2] And so it was.

While the legal drafting was in process, the membership of the inquiry was also being settled. Cawood was in place; the suggestion of Inspector Giles of the South Australian police was also taken up, notwithstanding the knowledge that appointing a serving police officer to investigate fellow police officers potentially implicated in mass murder might attract criticism. Of course, compared to Cawood's appointment, Giles' was hardly controversial at all.

Percival Aldridge Giles was fifty-one years old; according to his boss General Leane, he had thirty years' service as a police officer, multitasking also as a clerk of the courts and prosecutor in the remote areas where he had been mostly stationed. He was then in charge of the whole northern part of South Australia, bound by the borders with Western Australia, Central Australia and Queensland. His territory had included Central Australia as well, before the Commonwealth takeover in 1911. Leane commended Giles as 'a well educated, fearless man, with a sound well-balanced mind who thoroughly understands the natives and their conditions of life'.[3]

The final member, and Chairman, of the inquiry team would be Arthur Henry O'Kelly, a Stipendiary Magistrate in Cairns, Queensland. He was, at least, a judicial officer rather than a serving policeman like his fellow inquiry members. The Premiers of Queensland and South Australia graciously consented to the loan of O'Kelly and Giles for what the Prime Minister's office was estimating would be a two- to three-month period.

The news of the full appointments broke on 30 November.[4] This was met with dismay by some advocacy groups, particularly the Association for the Protection of Native Races, which had been pushing for one of its members to be part of the panel and had been assured that the Prime Minister would consider this favourably. Furious protests were lodged, to no avail, the Prime Minister noting how difficult it was to find men 'with experience of aborigines'.[5] The association pressed on, demanding that the government at least provide funding for legal representation for the Aboriginal side of the case.[6] That also fell on deaf ears. The Board of Enquiry would hear nothing from the Aboriginal populace, either in person or by proxy.

Logistics were next. O'Kelly had to get from Cairns, and Giles from Adelaide, to Oodnadatta. Cawood would collect them from there and drive them to Alice Springs. O'Kelly was directed to detour first via Canberra, however, 'for the purpose of perusing [the] Department's file of papers relating to the matter to be inquired into'.[7] There is no record of his visit or any instructions issued to him.

The cost of the inquiry had to be requested specially from Treasury, as the department had no provision for such an adventure in its budget. Each member was to be paid £21 per day while in Central Australia and £25 per day outside it. Train fares were calculated at an exact £59 6s 4d for O'Kelly and £14 10s 4d for Giles. With a contingency of £95, the total cost of the affair was to be £800 1s 8d, the equivalent of about $60,000 today.[8]

While all this was being sorted out, there had been a reshuffle in the federal ministry. Howse was out, the Department of Home and Territories had been renamed the Department of Home Affairs, and a new Minister, C. L. A. (Aubrey) Abbott, had been appointed. It would be his job to shepherd the Board of Enquiry through its work and defend the results when they emerged.

And there had been another attack on a white settler in the Centre. On 15 December, Mounted Constable Johnson, who had taken over at Barrow Creek from Murray, received a report that Harry Henty had been murdered on his station at Frew River.[9] The story, according to the 'half-caste' Jack Spratt, was that he and Henty had been at Hatches Creek, the station run by George Masters. They stopped near a hut owned by Masters, and encountered an Aboriginal man named Willaberta Jack. Henty called out, 'Where is my boy?', referring to a worker he was looking for. Willaberta Jack took exception to something and challenged Henty to a fight. Henty dismounted and approached the hut to which Willaberta Jack had repaired, when without warning Willaberta Jack shot him through a crack in the door with a rifle.

Henty was hit in the face and died instantly. Spratt rode off in a panic and reported the shooting.[10]

With this killing, unusually, an actual inquest of sorts was held. Johnson was joined by Donald Campbell, the Stock Inspector at Alice Springs who also acted as Coroner. They located Henty's body on the 20th and Johnson conducted a cursory examination of the badly decomposed corpse, which was then reburied. Having examined Spratt, the only eyewitness, Campbell made his formal findings:

> That the said Harry Henty was shot dead by an Aboriginal named Willaberta Jack, and that, at that time, the said Harry Henty did not provoke or make a quarrel with Willaberta Jack, but that the said Willaberta Jack shot the said Harry Henty dead from a distance of about Ten feet from a concealed position, without warning, or threatening the said Harry Henty with a firearm.[11]

Campbell had overreached his function as a coroner, which should have been limited to determining the cause of Henty's death and, if there was sufficient evidence, identifying Willaberta Jack as the likely killer. Factual findings as to whether he really did shoot Henty and if there was any available defence, such as provocation or self-defence, were matters for a criminal trial. Not that it was surprising that Campbell had no real understanding of his role. There still not a single qualified lawyer in Central Australia.

Two local men were deputised to help Johnson search for Willaberta Jack, but he had disappeared. He would re-emerge and his story intertwine with Murray's in an intriguing postscript, some months later. For now, his killing of Henty just added extra urgency to the need for the Board of Enquiry to be established.

That job was finally completed in a rush on 13 December 1928, when the Governor-General, Lord Stonehaven, gave royal assent to Ordinance no. 30 of 1928, Relating to Boards of Enquiry (the law which had to be passed to allow for the board to be established), and signed the formal document appointing O'Kelly, Giles and Cawood to constitute the Board of Enquiry into the Coniston affair.[12]

The Board of Enquiry's instructions were 'to enquire into the following matters':

(a) The circumstances attaching to the shooting of aboriginals by Mounted Constable Murray and party in connection with the arrest of aboriginals implicated in the murder of Frederick Brookes, and whether the shooting of such aboriginals was justified.

(b) The circumstances attaching to the shooting of aboriginals by Mounted Constable Murray and party in connection with the arrest of aboriginals implicated in the attack upon W. Morton, and whether the shooting of such aboriginals was justified.

(c) The circumstances attaching to the shooting of an aboriginal by H. Tilmouth and whether the shooting of such aboriginal was justified.

(d) Whether on the part of the settlers in the districts concerned, or in any other direction, any provocation had been given which could reasonably account for the recent depredations by the aborigines and

their attacks on white men in Central Australia. If
not what, in the opinion of the Board, were the
reasons for the aboriginals' actions.

Much could have been said about these terms of reference, but they
were not publicised and the media appeared satisfied by the fact
that an inquiry had been announced. Mr O'Kelly was recorded
making one public statement as he passed through Melbourne
on his way to Adelaide, that the inquiry 'would not be a mere
white-washing one'.[13]

Item (c) of the board's terms of reference was straightforward
enough: to determine whether Harry Tilmouth had really been
acting in self-defence when he shot Wangaridge dead (the only
possible legal justification he could have had). However, it was
also entirely out of place. The Tilmouth matter required a coronial
inquest and, if justified, a criminal trial (of Tilmouth, for murder
or manslaughter), not a special inquiry. Its inclusion was in one
sense obvious, but at second glance quite curious.

The first two instructions presupposed a critical matter: that
the shootings of Aboriginal people by Murray and his party were
in any way connected with the arrest of suspected criminals. A
threshold question was skipped over: what exactly were Murray
and his crew doing out in the scrub during all those long days
which, when the board was appointed, remained largely unac-
counted for? All that was known for certain was that a lot of people
were dead, spread over a wide area and a long period of time; the
only explanations so far proffered were Murray's brief reports and
a large pile of speculation generated by Cawood and Noblet in
support. The assumption that these deaths were necessarily a consequence of any kind of proper police action was entirely unsafe.

This fatal flaw in the drafting could only infect the conduct of the inquiry.

There was more. The board was tasked with determining whether the shootings in all three cases of Aboriginal people were 'justified'. This was extremely peculiar, for two fundamental reasons. First, the proper function of an inquisitorial body in a case of this sort was to hunt out all of the available evidence surrounding the shootings, work out as best it could what had happened, and determine whether there was a basis for anyone to be charged with criminal offences. If so, that would then be a matter for the appropriate prosecutorial body and the criminal courts.

Second, to make that determination would require ascertaining who shot who, and the circumstances of those killings. Everyone involved was subject to the criminal laws of Central Australia; there was no difference in the eyes of the law between a white and black victim or killer. Therefore, the killing of one person by another could only ever be 'justified' if the killer was able to access one of the grounds of absolute defence to a charge of murder; and relevantly this could only mean the ground of self-defence. The use of the broad and non-legal term 'justified' was extremely telling.

The final instruction was a discreditable piece of drafting. It was appropriate and necessary that the board conduct a broad-ranging inquiry into what was going on in Central Australia which had led to this outbreak of violence on both sides; not much would be achieved if it was restricted to only the specific incidents in question. But the context was not limited to the possibility of provocation; the question should have been far more widely framed. The drafting again presupposed facts which should have been in issue: that there had been 'depredations by aborigines' at all, and whether their 'attacks on white men' were properly so described. It is uncontroversial in the light of all we now know that Brooks was murdered and Morton almost murdered by Aboriginal people, and that these were not acts of self-defence (under Australian law). But at the time, these matters had become accepted as fact only by repetition. The other side of the story had not been heard at all.

More importantly, the inquiry should have been established as one which would go wherever the evidence led it. This required an open examination of all aspects of black–white relations in Central Australia, and fair contemplation of fault on either side.

Bad drafting is always the result of either incompetence or design. If the government's desire was for a whitewash, of the kind which O'Kelly had promised his inquiry would not produce, then the terms of reference were perfectly suited to that end.

O'Kelly and Giles made their slow way to Alice Springs to join Cawood for the Board of Enquiry's proceedings. They began their hearings at 11 am on Sunday 30 December 1928, in the administrative offices in Alice Springs.

The Chairman opened by tabling the Ordinance and formal instructions that had established the Board of Enquiry, then immediately set about breaching one of the fundamental principles of the law governing administrative tribunals with this ruling:

> The Commission at this stage through the Chairman intimates that it might be desirable for Constable Murray to be present during the whole of the proceedings and the Commission will allow him to ask any questions through the Board of any witness and further to produce for the Board's examination any witness whom he thinks can be of any benefit in the matter of throwing any light on the subject matter of the Commission.[14]

A knowledge of administrative law is not necessary to understand why this was wrong. The primary job of the board was to determine the facts relating to the shootings of Aboriginal people by the parties led by Constable Murray. In that matter, Murray was a vitally interested party. He was at least a material witness and person of interest; potentially, he was the principal suspect in multiple cases of unlawful killing.

The board would be (or should have been) hearing evidence from witnesses who had something relevant to say in relation to the killings. Investing Murray with the right to sit through every witness's testimony and question them like a de facto member of the board itself or at least some kind of assisting counsel, and giving him a wideranging power to introduce any witnesses or evidence he liked, was an outrageously improper thing for O'Kelly to do. The main witnesses would be the members of the parties that Murray had led; this was analogous to the police allowing a Mafia boss to sit in on the interrogations of his own underlings, and even participate in their questioning!

In legal terms, it was fatal to the entire process. The board's proceedings would be infected by Murray's presence with an abject failure of procedural fairness so profound that it could not be overcome. It wasn't a promising beginning.

An example of Murray's interference in the proceedings occurred during the testimony of his tracker Paddy. Paddy was telling the story of how Padygar and Willingar had been detained at the Coniston homestead, during which process Willingar was shot by Murray. He said that Dodger had then identified the two prisoners:

> I asked Dodga in blacks language what were their names. Dodga said Padygar. I have forgotten the name of the

other one. The name of the other black as supplied by
Constable Murray is Willingar.

The only record on the transcript is of what Paddy said. Obviously,
he had forgotten Willingar's name, or never knew it, and Murray
interrupted his testimony to provide him with that name. Apart
from rendering Paddy's evidence on this particular factual issue
valueless, it undermined his entire testimony. This example is
glaringly obvious from the record; it isn't possible to determine
on how many other occasions during the hearings Murray used
his privileged position to prompt witnesses with answers to the
questions they were being asked.

Putting aside these structural flaws, there was a practical job
to be done and the board got on with it. Between 30 December
and 18 January, when it concluded its work, the board held hearings on thirteen days. It presumably spent most of the other days
travelling, because it covered some 1,500 miles by motor car over
some of the worst roads in the world.[15]

Starting in Alice Springs, where a large number of witnesses
were heard from during the first four days, the party travelled
to Hermannsburg Mission, some 85 miles west of Alice Springs,
north to several pastoral stations as far as 160 miles away, back to
the Alice, north-west again through Harry Tilmouth's station at
Napperby, White Stone on the Lander and back to Coniston, then
back to Alice Springs for some final hearings to wrap things up.

Funny things can happen on the road. A Territory old-timer,
George Birt, related a story that Murray had told him about the
trip to Coniston:

well Murray told me that he wanted to very anxiously
to get on, he was driving the Magistrate [O'Kelly]

around. He went in his Ford car and he was followed by Mr Carrington driving the Magistrate. He desperately wanted to get to Singleton Station to tell the station owner, Randall Stafford, what to say. So he arranged with Carrington to pretend to get stuck in the sandy bed of the creek while he went on ahead to see Randall Stafford, apparently not knowing that the Magistrate and Carrington were stuck in the creek. He desperately wanted to get there to tell him what evidence to give, so that made me a bit suspicious about the inquiry…Murray didn't know what my sympathies were at the time.[16]

The briefest inspection of the statements made to the Board of Enquiry by Murray, Stafford and their other white hunting companions makes it clear that Murray had succeeded in arranging for their evidence to be, at the least, coordinated.

The board took sworn testimony from thirty witnesses. Apart from Murray and his companions Stafford, Saxby, Briscoe, Paddy and Morton, as well as Tilmouth, these were a quite random mix of station owners, officials, Alice Springs residents and a few itinerant prospectors, drovers and the like. The only variation came in the form of several missionaries, including Annie Lock. Their evidence was taken in no apparent order.[17]

A number of important observations can be made regarding the proceedings and evidence at the outset. All of the testimony was recorded in typed form, apparently by Victor Carrington, who accompanied the board everywhere as official secretary. Every witness statement was signed, and witnessed by all three board members.

First, there is the order of evidence. The board's first priority was, or should have been, to find the evidence which would enable it to determine whether the shootings of Aboriginal people by Murray's two parties and by Tilmouth were 'justified' – which, as we have seen, could only mean 'in self-defence'. The obvious starting point for this inquiry was to get the evidence of the men who had done the shooting: Murray and his colleagues. They were all either in Alice Springs or around Coniston; and there had in any event been plenty of time for Cawood to arrange their availability. Instead these men were the very last witnesses seen by the board, after it had completed its travels.

This begs the second question: where the board chose to go. It travelled widely outside of Alice Springs, to eight different remote stations. Where it did not go was to any location where the shootings of Aboriginal people were reported to have occurred, or even to the places where Brooks and Morton had been attacked.

For an inquiry team which was evidently not afraid of travel, this was a strange choice. Even without the statements of the shooting parties, the board had available to it Murray's reports to Noblet, which identified at least some of the places where deaths had occurred. The board's hearings were still soon enough after the events to make a physical inspection of the scenes potentially highly relevant. For one thing, if mass killings had taken place, the board might expect to find the landscape in some places littered with the bones of the dead. Or not, which would be equally important a thing to know. It is not unreasonable to suspect that there were plenty of things that the board did not want to know.

The next problematic aspect of the evidence is its form. Each statement was typed, as if every word spoken was recorded. The opening part of each is a first-person monologue by the witness, as if they were speaking without interruption. This is followed by a series of what appear to be answers to specific questions, identifying the questioner (e.g. 'Ins. Giles') but never the actual question.

When reading the statements, it becomes immediately obvious that each records one side of an interrogation – not just the latter parts where the questioners are identified, but the whole thing. The content and tone of each statement is discursive, and they often jump rapidly between multiple subjects. Critically, the same subjects keep coming up in statement after statement, indicating that the witnesses were being prompted, from a standard list of questions, as to what they should talk about.

There is no difficulty with the prompting; the board was inquisitorial in nature and its job was to ask questions and direct proceedings to get to the answers it was seeking. That entitled and obliged it to interrogate the witnesses who appeared before it.

However, the record discloses only one side of the conversation. In considering an answer that a witness has given, it is essential to know what question they were asked. Otherwise there is no context and no way of knowing whether the question was misleading, laden with pretext or in some other way designed to produce a particular response. The board knew what it had asked, and was not handicapped as anyone later reviewing its findings is by this omission. However, the absence of the questions from the record was another significant procedural failure. To dissect their evidence, we have to guess at the questions that the witnesses were asked.

Then there is the absence of a key witness: Alex Wilson. The board dealt with this omission in its final report:

> It was found impracticable to examine the witness Alick [sic] Wilson. He was ill in the hospital at Darwin when the Inquiry opened and it was ascertained one week before the conclusion of same that it would be six

weeks before he could arrive at Alice Springs. Constable Murray intimated that he did not desire his presence so the Board dispensed with his evidence. In any case, he was, on most occasions, in charge of the packhorses back from the shooting.[18]

More detail about Wilson was recorded by the board during the course of its hearings. On 9 January, it noted a telegram received from Darwin advising that Wilson was fit to travel but there was no transport available until the 30th. The record goes on:

> Constable Murray was asked if the failure to call Wilson in the circumstances would prejudice him in any way or the calling of him would assist him…Constable Murray replied that the non-calling of Wilson would not prejudice him; that he was an illiterate man – a half-caste and probably his evidence would be unreliable and I don't think it would be any more reliable than Witness Paddy's.[19]

There was quite a lot going on in these two short passages of deliberation. Murray's blithe racism was a given, and was accepted without demur by the board's members. It obviously influenced the board's relaxed attitude to the importance of obtaining Wilson's evidence. The fact was that Wilson was well enough to give that evidence; he was just physically remote, 1,000 miles away in Darwin. Certainly this was a practical obstacle. There was a train line from Darwin to Mataranka, some 300 miles south, but that still left 700 miles to traverse by motor vehicle. The board's estimate of six weeks was leisurely, including as it did three weeks of waiting for the next regular transport to leave Darwin. Another possibility, that of flying Wilson down to the Alice, was evidently not considered at all.

Still, even allowing for this would have meant that the board's report might be pushed back by one month. In the scheme of things, it is hard to see the problem with that. Alternatively, the board could have commissioned an appropriate person in Darwin to take Wilson's evidence on its behalf, using questions which could have been sent up by telegraph. There were people in Darwin capable of administering an oath and doing the job.

Wilson's evidence was, after all and quite obviously, crucial. It was entirely beside the point to ask Murray whether he wanted or needed it. It was scandalous that the board asked him whether *not* calling Wilson would prejudice him, or calling Wilson would assist him, when it should have been asking itself how important Wilson's evidence might be in support of the board's quest to get to the truth. Murray had every obvious reason for not wanting Wilson's evidence obtained, particularly when he had been out of Murray's reach (unlike the other witnesses to the killings).

Major and Dodger, also, were not required:

The evidence of Tracker Major could not be taken – his services had been dispensed with, and he had gone 'bush'.

The aboriginal boy Dodger was not called as he witnessed none of the shooting – he being with the packhorses.[20]

As to what Major or Dodger had actually seen, the board had no source of knowledge apart from Murray and the other white members of his party. Nobody had suggested that they had participated in any of the shooting, meaning they might be the most impartial available witnesses to the killings of Aboriginal people. The board's uninterest in hearing from them had, no doubt, a racial component to it, but that doesn't quite suffice to explain the choice.

Of course, no consideration was given by the board to seeking or obtaining evidence from any other Aboriginal people. Apart from Paddy, every witness would be white. The landscape of Central Australia was literally full of eyewitnesses to the actions of Murray's expeditions; it would not have been hard to find a few of them.

The recorded testimony discloses one last curiosity: of the thirty witnesses, only one was subjected to any questioning by the board which might be described as hostile. This, curiously, was the hapless Sergeant Noblet, who was last to take the stand. Possibly the board members were at the end of their endurance and somewhat irritable, and certainly there was plenty of ammunition for having a go at Noblet. It appears that they roasted him slowly, and the suspicion lingers that this, too, was in accordance with a pre-written script.

Noblet had been negligent and incompetent in his handling of Constable Murray, for sure. The board forensically dissected his every failure to demand proper reports from Murray, to take any proper tally of the number of people Murray and his colleagues had shot (or any of their names), or to even bother finding out whether they were male or female. Noblet, at points, helpfully confirmed that, if the victims had been white, he certainly would have taken all these steps. He couldn't assist the board in understanding why he had not done so for the Aboriginal dead. One passage in particular gives an idea of how hard a time the board was giving him:

> I can't say that I remember whether Wilson and party brought in two natives who subsequently died. I may have read and I may not have read it. I do trouble whether I read it or not.

There would have been no doubt in the mind of an objective observer: Noblet was going to be the fall guy. Not that any objective observers were present.

Once it got going, the board set about its work with considerable speed, completing its task in three weeks flat. On 18 January 1929, it took its last piece of testimony, and handed in its final, four-page report.[21] The report contained four sets of findings, directly answering the questions it had been asked: as to whether during each of the hunts that followed the attacks on Brooks and Morton, and in the case of Tilmouth's shooting of his alleged attacker, the Aboriginal deaths that had occurred were 'justified'; and why the attacks on the white settlers had happened in the first place.

The board started with the seventeen deaths during the first (Brooks) hunt:

> the evidence of the following reputable settlers [Stafford, Briscoe and Saxby] corroborates the account given by Mounted Constable Murray which shortly is to the effect that, on each of four separate occasions, the pursued natives who had been identified by Tracker Major as being implicated in the murder of Brooks, after being repeatedly warned to lay down their weapons, were the

aggressors, and attacked Mounted Constable Murray who, on each such occasion, was endeavouring to effect the arrest of the guilty natives and for that purpose was on foot and his horse had galloped back to where the packhorses were camped.

Each of the witnesses was subjected to a rigorous cross examination and each of them emphatically stated that the shooting was absolutely necessary to save their own lives. After the first shooting, the Police party followed up those implicated in the murder – hence the four separate occasions when shooting occurred. Constable Murray also shot one aboriginal who had attacked him at Conniston Station.

Tracker Paddy corroborates Constable Murray's account, and here again it was essential to shoot to protect himself. Constable Murray cannot say who shot the lubras but these two lubras, with others, were amongst his attackers on the first occasion and as all the aboriginals, male and female, were mixed up, the shooting of two lubras could easily have been quite unintentional and accidental. There is no evidence to the contrary. Briscoe and Stafford state they shot no natives. Saxby says he fired eight or nine shots with a rifle and heard two other firearms discharged and we are of the opinion that he was afraid to admit he killed some of the blacks. The Board is prepared to believe the evidence of all witnesses.

These were the factual findings on which the board based its decision that the seventeen shootings were 'justified'. There are two questions to be asked in reassessing the board's work: were the factual findings sound; and, if so, did they support the ultimate finding of justification – that is, self-defence?

The board believed the evidence of all the witnesses, including Paddy. That took some doing, since their evidence was inconsistent, and Paddy's in particular was wildly different from the others'. Paddy had sworn to a materially different chronology of events, and had told the board about several Aboriginal prisoners taken during the hunt who disappeared without trace when left with Murray and the other whites. Paddy may have been lying, but if he wasn't then the others were.

The simple juxtaposition of the final two sentences quoted above illustrates the impossibility of the board's conclusion: it held the opinion that Saxby had been lying about not shooting anyone himself, but believed his evidence?

Stafford's story also differed from Murray's, and he, Saxby and Briscoe all told inconsistent versions of some of the shooting incidents. They did however corroborate Murray's story as to his habit of dismounting from his horse every time he entered an Aboriginal camp.

The board's findings regarding the actual shooting incidents recited that all the 'pursued natives' (whatever that meant) had been identified by Major – who had not been at Yurrkuru when Brooks died, had no means of identifying his killers at all, and in fact had never even pretended to do so. This was a simple error, no doubt – presumably they meant to confer the eyewitness label on Dodger – but a damning one, given the central importance of identification.

The witnesses, the board said, were all 'rigorously cross-examined'. In fact they were not cross-examined at all, as there was no counsel at the hearing representing the interests of those who had died. The board's questioning, such as it was, had clearly been anything but rigorous given the gaping holes that it allowed to be left in the evidence.

Perhaps most glaring is the total omission from the report of one of the admitted shootings which on no basis could have been called an act of self-defence. This was the shooting by Murray and/or Paddy of two Aboriginal men in the ranges who had been captured but then escaped and ran off, only to be shot down at a distance. Nobody was in danger from them, and there was simply no justifiable reason for Murray to shoot them. The board dealt with this anomaly by ignoring it altogether.

As to whether the findings could support justification, the board simply fudged. Murray's evidence of his approach to each incident – in particular repeatedly dismounting when he was every time immediately attacked – was inherently improbable; none of his party sustained any injuries in any of the life-threatening attacks on them; no Aboriginal people were wounded, other than fatally. No Aboriginal witnesses were heard from or sought out; none of the scenes of the killings was visited. Wilson, Major and Dodger were missing from the record. On no basis could a conclusive determination that all seventeen victims had been shot with legal justification be reached.

The board then turned to the fourteen killings in the Morton case:

> the evidence of Mounted Constable Murray is corrobo-rated in every detail by Mr Morton.
>
> Morton can speak the 'lingo' of that particular tribe (the Walmullas). This tribe was also implicated in the murder of Brooks. Morton swears he warned the natives repeatedly, on each occasion, to sit down and put their weapons down on the ground; that they refused;

and that, on each occasion when Constable Murray dismounted to endeavour to effect an arrest, the natives attacked with boomerangs, spears, nulla nullas and a tomahawk and it was necessary, in order to save their own lives, that the blacks should be shot.

Morton knew each of the blacks who attacked him as they had at times worked for him and he identified them on each occasion and in some instances blacks were allowed to go free as they were not implicated in the attack on him.

The Board sees no reason to doubt the evidence in this case.

Morton also shot one of the aboriginals dead when he was attacked at his camp and the Board is of the opinion he was fully justified in so doing.

The Walmullas were incorrectly identified; the Warlmala, a sub-group of the Warlpiri, ordinarily lived further north up the Lander from Morton's location and, in any event, had relocated en masse much further north to Wave Hill Station before the relevant events. As we have seen, the men who attacked Brooks and Morton were Warlpiri, but from a group local to the area. They and the Kaytetye to the north felt the force of the reprisals. Ironically, the Warlmala were physically unaffected, but were unable to return to their traditional land as a result of the killings.[22]

There was again the ridiculous notion that Murray persisted in dismounting every time he entered an Aboriginal camp, only to be set upon and then have to shoot Aboriginal people to save his own life. Further, the board blithely accepted the farcical proposition that every time during this wideranging hunt when Murray and Morton ambushed an encampment of Aboriginal people and had to shoot some of them, the victims turned out to have been part of the party which had attacked Morton.

Morton, most likely, was justified in shooting at the men who attacked him, whatever he may have done to provoke them. There was no doubt that, otherwise, he would have died. However, the board's findings regarding the victims of the subsequent hunt were based solely on two factors: an acceptance of Murray's plainly self-serving and illogical story; and Morton's corroboration of the same. Wilson, who could have told the board exactly what had happened, was left out. Again, the result was a determination that the board could not properly reach. But that's what it did.

Finally, there was Tilmouth's shooting of Wangaridge: 'the Board examined Tilmouth and an intelligent aboriginal in his employ who corroborated Tilmouth's story, and has no hesitation in finding that the shooting was justified in this case'. That was untrue. The board had taken a brief statement from Tilmouth, in which he said simply that 'it was either him or me for it and that is why I shot him'. It had not examined 'an intelligent aboriginal' at all. Victor Carrington, who was acting as secretary for the board, on 12 January also put on his hat as Coroner and conducted a brief coronial inquest into Wangaridge's death. He took sworn evidence from Peter, Tilmouth's Aboriginal worker, who said he had witnessed the shooting and corroborated Tilmouth's explanation. Peter was not, however, examined by the board.[23]

Carrington had formally found that Wangaridge had been killed by Tilmouth in self-defence (again, a finding which a coroner could not properly make). To round things out, on 19 January (the day after the board concluded its work), he conducted perfunctory inquests into the thirty-one other shootings and issued his findings that those victims, too, had all been shot in self-defence 'under reasonable fear of life or limb'.[24]

This was all for show. Carrington's proceedings were a parody of a proper coronial inquest, carried out to provide some ostensibly independent quasi-judicial corroboration for the parallel work of the Board of Enquiry. If two official inquiries, each taking sworn evidence separately from the same witnesses and examining the same killings, came independently of each other to the same conclusions, then who could say they were wrong? In reality, it was a low-grade farce.

In the end, the whole Tilmouth incident was an irrelevant distraction which should by rights have been left out of the board's terms of reference. It was a simple case of a white man shooting a black man; either he did it in self-defence, or he was a murderer. Wrapping it in with the work of the Board of Enquiry achieved nothing more than enabling Tilmouth to avoid the proper police investigation that should have taken place.

Having found all thirty-three shootings justified on the apparent grounds of self-defence, the board also had a bone to pick with those who suspected that something more untoward had happened, and elected to include a comprehensive demolition of any such suggestion in its report.

> Dealing generally with the suggestion that the shooting of the blacks by the Police Party was in the nature of a reprisal or a punitive expedition of which there is not a scintilla of evidence, the Board, in addition, would like to emphasise the following points which appear to discount such a suggestion:
> 1. If a massacre of the blacks was contemplated, would they not have shot every one at Coniston where the first encounter took place and not have allowed 23 of them to go free?

2.   Would not the Police Party, in Morton's case, have
      shot the six adult male natives who were allowed to
      go free when Morton said they were not identified
      with those who attacked him?

3.   If a massacre was intended, is it likely that Constable
      Murray would have dismounted from his horse
      on each occasion and alone gone amongst the
      natives at the risk of being killed, to effect arrests
      when all the party could have remained mounted
      and, from a distance of safety, wiped out all the
      blacks?

4.   If a massacre was intended, why tend to the wounded
      as the evidence shows was done in several cases?

      Constable Murray was candid throughout the
Inquiry. Had he desired to disguise the number of
natives killed, he could have done so in his official
reports and evidence. Furthermore, if a massacre was
intended, the Police Party could, as the evidence shows,
have killed a hundred natives.

If the members of the Board of Enquiry had decided that they
would like to be remembered by history as a pack of fools, then
including this passage in their report was a good way to go about it.
Their reductive reasoning is, at best, embarrassing. Summarised,
the board's killer argument against the idea that Murray had been
leading punitive shooting parties was to point to two things:
how easy it would have been for Murray to conceal the killings
altogether; and how much easier it would have been to kill a lot
more victims.

    Was there a 'scintilla of evidence' of reprisal killings?
Admittedly, none that the board had seen. There was in truth

a wealth of available evidence of exactly that type; certainly testimonial evidence might have been sought from the Aboriginal survivors who were then scattered in all directions from the hunting grounds. Furthermore, if there had been mass shootings, then there were certain to be mass human remains, or at least physical evidence to support or deny the claims that massacres had taken place. But the board had chosen not to seek Aboriginal evidence, and it had elected not to visit a single location where the shootings had allegedly occurred.

The board might have asked itself a second set of questions in addition to those it posed in its report: did Murray really allow twenty-three people to go free at the first encounter; did he and Morton release the six men as they claimed; was Murray really so stupid that he continued to dismount every single time knowing that he would be attacked and nearly killed; and did the wounded receive any treatment at all? The board's assumptions that underpinned its reverse logic were all dependent on the credibility of Murray and his men. They might as well have floated in on the wind, for all they were worth.

There is at least a poignant irony in the rhetorical flourish with which the board closed its case on the whole question: Murray's party could, 'as the evidence shows, have killed a hundred natives'. That was something that, indeed, the evidence had shown. They could well have killed a hundred. Or more.

The board had one last question to answer: why had Brooks and Morton been attacked? The terms of reference required it to determine whether the Aboriginal attackers had been the victims of some provocation, by the local settlers or otherwise, that could reasonably explain why they had suddenly taken on a homicidal intent. If the answer to that question was no, then what was the reason for this outbreak of violence?

For this purpose, the testimony of the twenty-one 'lay' witnesses (excluding Murray and his party, and Sergeant Noblet) was all the evidence the board collected and considered – presumably, although it did not say so, in addition to the extensive knowledge of the board's members themselves from their long experience of 'dealing' with Aboriginal people.

What the board had really collected was a grab-bag of random witnesses, including station owners, missionaries, Alice Springs residents and assorted itinerants. They did offer a fair cross-section of perspective and opinion from the tiny minority white segment of the Central Australian populace. They offered very little in the way of objective, credible evidence.

As with the police party members' evidence, all of the witnesses' statements read as a one-sided conversation. It can be deduced from reading them together that the board was in the habit of prompting each witness with a fairly set list of questions: they were evidently asked to talk about their personal experience with Aboriginal people throughout their lives; whether they had noticed the local Aboriginal people becoming more hostile in recent times; whether the Aboriginal people had been starving or having trouble accessing food or water; and what, in their opinions, had caused the 'trouble'.

It is no easy task to forensically analyse the evidence in this case, because no attempt was made by the board to distinguish between fact and opinion or to follow any kind of coherent plan for gathering a body of actually usable data. Instead, it gave the witnesses free rein to get their long-held grievances and personal opinions off their chests.

Armed with this material, the board felt able to reach definitive conclusions on the central question of why Brooks and Morton had been attacked. First, this had been clearly established:

'No provocation has been given which could reasonably account for the depredations by the aborigines and their attacks on white men in Central Australia.' The absence of any provocation had been established by the unanimous agreement of the witnesses. Those who had known Brooks were adamant that he had been a generous and good man whose name had never been mentioned 'in connection with lubras' (not that anyone other than the local Aboriginal people was suggesting such a thing, but nobody was asking them for their opinion). There were no corresponding character references for Nugget Morton, but nor was there evidence before the board of his treatment of Aboriginal people. In fact, no attempt was made by the board to investigate the events leading up to the two specific attacks.

Typical of the evidence that was led out of the witnesses on the issue of provocation was the response given to a question from the Chairman by James McDowall, a survey hand who happened to be working in the region north of Alice Springs and dropped in to the board's hearing to lend it the benefit of his opinions:

> I have never heard of blacks being driven off water holes by white settlers. I do not know of any instances where white men have taken lubras to live with them against the wishes of the tribe. I cannot give any reason for the recent actions of the blacks. In my opinion the blacks are treated very well in this country.

McDowall explained his definition of good treatment by reference to an incident a few years earlier when he said his camp had been invaded by 'blacks' trying to get at his livestock. He chased them away by firing over their heads. Asked about this by Inspector Giles, he commented:

I do not think the practice of shooting over their heads gains any respect for the white man. The other times [the Aboriginal people] came back I flogged them out of it with a stockwhip.

So that was easy: the Aboriginal violence was unprovoked. But from where then did it come? The board had ten answers to this. In its considered opinion, the reasons for the 'aboriginals' actions' were these:

(a) the advance of the Walmulla tribe on a marauding expedition from the Border of Western Australia into the Conniston country, – the tribe had threatened to wipe out the settlers and working boys, as the evidence shows;

(b) unattached Missionaries wandering from place to place, having no previous knowledge of blacks and their customs and preaching a doctrine of equality;

(c) inexperienced white settlers making free with the natives and treating them as equals;

(d) semi-civilised natives migrating and getting in touch with myalls;

(e) semi-civilised natives losing their skill for hunting wild game through lack of practice, preying on the working boys at stations;

(f) a woman Missionary living amongst naked blacks thus lowering their respect for the whites;

(g) crimes and minor offences by natives going unpunished owing to insufficient Police;

(h) insufficient Police patrols;

(i) imprisonment not being a deterrent to native offenders;

(j) escaped prisoners from Darwin not being re-arrested – wandering about in their native country and causing unrest and preaching revolt against the whites.

It was quite a list. Perhaps emboldened by having spent the past three weeks listening to the unrestrained racism of the local whites, perhaps mindful of its riding instructions from Canberra, the board did not hold back from giving full expression to the prevailing wisdom of Central Australian social theory. Here was a prescription not just for what had gone wrong at Coniston, but for the whole sweep of relations between black and white through Australian history. It is not a stretch to suggest that the board members were indulging the thought that they might just be making some of that history themselves with their ground-breaking report.

The board's ambition in diagnosing the cause of the nation's race-relations malaise calls for an examination of exactly how it found all these symptoms to exist. First, there was the invasion of the dreaded Walmullas, a tribe whose homeland the board incorrectly identified as being in the borderlands out past the ranges to the west of Coniston.

The tale, for the board's purposes, seems to have come from James McDowall, the survey hand. As he told it:

In September 1928, when our prospecting party was out in Noolan's Cave District about 200 [miles] NW of Conniston Station the king of one of the tribes told our black boy that a mob of natives were after gins and they were generally bad and not to let them get near our camp. They were killing bullocks, blackfellows and would kill us too. They were making in towards Titree and we were warned to look out for them on their return as they were travelling the same route as we were. That would bring them across the Conniston country.

Questioned further by Murray, McDowall conveniently corrected his dating of this event to July or August, and declared that he thought it was possible the tribe he had been warned about was 'the party who murdered Frederick Brooks'.

So far as corroboration for this story goes, there was William Briscoe:

The station boys told me when I first came to Napperby and Conniston that the niggers were going to come in from the west and wipe out the whites and also the working boys. I said 'what for'. They said 'I don't know. They too much cheeky.'

And also Murray:

The Walmulla tribe extends to the WA Border and as far north as Powell's Creek and roam over all the country west of the telegraph line. They have a very bad reputation as marauders, thieves, cattle killers and even murderers. The witness Lala and the two small boys who were with Brooke's informed that one of the lubras that were shot had been stolen from Woodforde by that tribe.

Dodger and Skipper told me that the wild mob
from the west were going to kill all the white men and
working boys.

Saxby had volunteered as well that he thought the attackers were
of the Walmulla tribe.

As we have seen, the main problem with the Walmulla theory
was that the tribe did not exist as such, although the Warlmala, a
sub-group of the local Warlpiri people, did. There was another
problem: compelling as the notion was of a marauding gang of
wild natives sweeping in from the western desert on a mission
to wipe out every white in Central Australia, even most of the
white witnesses gave it no credence or support. Stafford located
the Aboriginal people who had attacked Brooks as coming from
country between Coniston and Tanami, which was Warlpiri land
a long way to the east of the border.

A number of the other witnesses were sure that the attacks
had come from local 'semi-civilised' Aboriginal people who had
been corrupted by their proximity to white people and easy food,
had forgotten how to hunt wild game and had become too lazy
and indolent to bother doing anything more strenuous than beg.
For example, Charlton Young from Cockatoo Creek said he had
been prospecting near Coniston just before the troubles:

I did not have any trouble with the wild natives during
the eight months prospecting tour that I have mentioned.
When we came in close to Conniston Station we had
trouble with the natives. The first thing we noticed at
Conniston was that the niggers there seemed to be out
of control. They came round our camp and demanded

food and tobacco. They all had spears and boomerangs and were semi-civilised blacks.

Young identified them as 'Lander River niggers', not from the west. He also reported that he had encountered Fred Brooks a few days before he died.

> He asked us how we were getting on with the blacks. We said not too bad until we came in here and we have had trouble with them. He said that is a funny thing. They have been ratting my camp lately.

Apart from all that, the board itself had already said that it accepted Nugget Morton's claim that all of the fourteen Aboriginal people he and Murray had shot dead had previously worked for him and were therefore, obviously, locals.

In short, the evidence was a long way from proving the existence of the mythical marauding expedition that the board insisted had taken place and pointed more strongly towards a local source of the trouble. The fact, as all of the Aboriginal people in the whole region already knew, was that the attackers of Brooks and Morton were local Warlpiri.

Next was the influence of missionaries, specifically 'unattached missionaries wandering from place to place…and preaching a doctrine of equality'. Charles Maynard, a drover, told the board: 'The Missionaries make brothers and sisters of the aboriginals and shake hands with them.' He didn't mean this as a good thing. Maynard was quite upset about the Aboriginal people not being kept 'in their place', but actually had more of a concern with the 'instruction' of the missionaries. The board, mindful not to suggest that Christian proselytising among the heathen natives should be discouraged, politely ignored any such comments and focused its summary on the less controversial idea that teaching equality to Indigenous people was unarguably problematic.

Dudley Adamson, a telegraphist at Alice Springs, explained the issue more scientifically:

> They [the missionaries] have preached to the blacks that the white man is the black man's brother. The aboriginal does not understand the true meaning of that and expect the white man to treat them as brothers. If the white man did this he would naturally sink back to the level of the blacks. Eventually the black fellow would get on top.

The board's reference to 'unattached' missionaries was significant: it had heard from a number of missionaries who were very attached, and they were keen to preserve their patch. Herman Heinrich, from the long-established Hermannsburg Mission, south-west of Coniston, was adamant:

> no Missionary should be allowed to work amongst the natives without the sanction of the Government. By letting so many free lance missionaries of different creeds wander through the country and mix with the blacks confuses the blacks and hampers the operations of the authorised Missions. Any benefit to the natives can only be attained by continuous sustained Missions such as our own.

It wasn't just random missionaries who had been treating the 'natives' as equals; 'inexperienced white settlers' were making the same mistake. Charles Maynard described this problem precisely:

> I have heard of instances of where white man has told the blacks that white man take your country you can go and spear their cattle. The blacks really believe they are on the level of the whites and that they can go and take cattle or anything they want.

Pressed by the board for specifics, Maynard went on: 'I can give no specific instance of where white people told the blacks that they could take cattle. I am only speaking generally and from rumour.' Still, he wasn't backing down:

> It is not possible for Station work to be done satisfactorily if the white man in charge lives in a state of equality with the blacks. If the white man gives away his superior position they become cheeky and audacious.

Aaron Meyers, a saddler in Alice Springs, agreed that new whites had been coming in and putting themselves 'on a level with the blacks which has a tendency to make the blacks cheeky'. Dudley Adamson thought the same thing, adding the obvious corollary of inequality: 'The blackfellow only understands one argument that is force. I have heard the blacks talk of a white man who has treated them as equals "Him bloody fool".' There was general agreement on this point, including the need to always have a gun handy when dealing with Aboriginal people. Donald Campbell, Commonwealth Stock Inspector:

I never go amongst blacks without being armed. They are treacherous, and may do anything at any time.

In cases of disobedience, it is necessary to deal quickly and firmly with the blacks. If one were weak and undecided with the blacks it would not do. One must be firm and show superiority.

The board's conclusions on these points, to the effect that the Aboriginal people had been led astray by misguided white people who were teaching them (incorrectly) that they were equal, were indeed consistent with the views of all of the witnesses from whom it heard (except Paddy, who wasn't asked for his opinion). True, their unanimous agreement with the fundamental principle of racial inequality sounds to modern minds just so much racist tripe, but it did represent the majority view at the time.

Oddly, though, the board did not appear to notice the inconsistency between its findings. The perpetrators of the attacks on white men were 'myalls' from the far west, it said. If so, they would therefore have had no contact with missionaries or 'inexperienced white settlers' and no opportunity to have been taught misleading thoughts about their own equality. The first determination, as to who the killers were, rendered all of the subsequent ones, regarding how the 'semi-civilised natives' had been corrupted, irrelevant.

One of the board's findings sought to establish a tenuous link to explain this contradiction: that 'semi-civilised natives' had been 'migrating and getting in touch with the myalls'. What this meant wasn't explained, and there was nothing in the evidence to support it.[25] If anyone had supposedly 'migrated' it was the 'myalls' from the desert, not the 'semi-civilised' Aboriginal people who had been accused by most witnesses of being too lazy to move around much at all.

The next finding was undoubtedly the weirdest: 'a woman Missionary living amongst naked blacks thus lowering their respect for the whites' was somehow partly to blame for the troubles, according to the board's considered opinion. This was a direct accusation against Annie Lock, who had attracted considerable comment, almost universally derisory, from other witnesses.

There was a backstory to this, revealed by a report Cawood had sent to the department in November 1928. In September, Rev. Athol McGregor (who also gave evidence to the board) prevailed upon Annie Lock to give up on her hopeless situation at Harding Soak and return with him to Darwin. She took with her two little Aboriginal girls who were, she believed, orphaned and certain to die if not rescued. Word of this reached Murray, who was heading for Darwin for Padygar and Akirkra's trial.

In Darwin, there was a minor sensation when Murray took the girls away, only for Lock to march into the police station and take them back. Murray confronted her and tried to forcibly remove the children from her arms, the scene threatening to turn ugly as a crowd sympathetic to Lock started to gather. Official complaints flew in all directions, and Cawood did not miss the opportunity for some dressed-up slander. His official report on the incident included this outrageous passage:

> Miss Lock is an eccentric woman, and her ideas of Missionary work and the methods employed are certainly degrading not only to herself as a white woman but to the blacks that she has gathered around her.
>
> Investigations made at the time of the murder of Frederick Brookes proved beyond doubt that the lubra that pinned Brookes hands while he was brutally

murdered was at one time an inmate of Miss Lock's so called Missionary camp.

I have had considerable trouble since this woman started her missionary work in Central Australia, and quite recently I determined to ask her to leave the country but she evidently got word of my intentions as she left for the Katherine in company with Mr Athol McGregor.[26]

Needless to say, Cawood made no disclosure of these previous entanglements with Lock, let alone his obvious infection by bias where she was concerned, during the board's proceedings.

Even more critical of Miss Lock, however, were her fellow missionaries. Ernest Kramer, of the Aboriginal Friends Association, had visited her camp at Harding Soak before the massacres. He said he had urged the Aboriginal men there to go away:

I told the old men not to go there because I did not think it was fit for them to be there because the old men will not be ruled by a women [sic] in the first place; they would eventually impose on her and most of them had no clothing whatever. I do not think any good could result from such effort. I consider it would lessen the respect of the blacks for the whites for an unattached women [sic] to be amongst them.

Herman Heinrich from Hermannsburg Mission had also met Lock:

I came up with Miss Lock from Oodnadatta to Alice Springs about two years ago. She appeared to me to be rather eccentric. She gave me to understand that she would be quite happy to marry a native. These myalls move about in their nude state…

Robert Purvis of Woodgreen Station agreed that Lock's presence had been an unmitigated disaster:

> I have known the natives in the Woodford Creek District for many years. Until twelve months ago they were good hunters well provided for with native foods which they were capable and willing to catch. Since then a woman Missionary has established a camp near there. Her name is Miss Lock. In consequence of her association and teaching the same blacks are nothing but cadgers spongers thieves – too lazy to hunt, insufficiently fed by the Missionaries and if there are any starving blacks in Central Australia it is in the neighbourhood of Miss Locks camp.

Edward Dixon of Harper Springs Station also confirmed that there had been no trouble at all until Lock turned up; the problem, he said, was that she and other missionaries were in the habit of gathering the local Aboriginal people together but then had insufficient resources to feed them, so that they would start killing stock.

As it turned out, the only specific complaint against Lock which could not equally have been applied to other (male) missionaries was Ernest Kramer's statement that there were Aboriginal men at her camp who had no clothes, supported by Heinrich's vague assertion of general nudity. However, it was enough to trigger a moral panic in the newspapers. On 8 January, the Adelaide *Register* ran no fewer than five articles on the Annie Lock scandal, followed by a full editorial devoted to her the next day. The centrepiece was a photo of Lock with unidentified Aboriginal people, under the headline 'HAPPY TO MARRY A BLACK'. In the accompanying articles, assorted men with missionary experience lined up to support Heinrich's disapproval of women missionaries. As Pastor Albrecht, head of Hermannsburg Mission, pointed out, Jesus had not called on any women to be among his disciples; more importantly, Aboriginal men did not respect women at all, and certainly not white ones.[27]

On this basis, the board felt it appropriate and reasonable to point an accusatory finger directly at Lock for laying part of the foundation which led inevitably to the terrible events which the board was tasked with unravelling. This touch of misogyny, hardly novel for the times, at least made for a brief variation from the pervasively racist tone of the whole proceeding.

The final group of findings pointed at issues of law and order: the lack of sufficient police; imprisonment being inadequate to deter Aboriginal people from criminal behaviour; and escaped Aboriginal prisoners wandering about the countryside 'preaching revolt against the whites'. The obvious solutions: more police and harsher punishment.

Pretty much every witness said at some point that there needed to be more police patrols, because the Aboriginal people behaved better when there were. As James McDowall commented, if there were more police patrols 'there would be less cheekiness and cattle killing by natives'.

Interestingly, the argument that imprisonment was not working as a deterrent to Aboriginal offenders came exclusively from the missionary witnesses, not the pastoralists who were the principal victims of their crimes. Ernest Kramer noted that it did not lower their social standing with their peers, and in fact they tended to eat better in prison. He went on:

> I have always held the view that fatherly chastisement
> of the blacks would have a better effect on them than
> imprisonment...I believe this chastisement should be
> administered at the place of the crime in the presence of
> the tribe. I think it would have a great humiliating effect.

As to what 'chastisement' Kramer had in mind exactly, Herman Heinrich of Hermannsburg Mission was more forthcoming. Noting that corporal punishment of young Aboriginal people was still practised at his mission, he lamented that it was not being extended to adults:

> when we threatened the natives with getting the Police in
> they only laughed and said 'we not frightened of Police.
> We get good holiday at Gaol.' Under such conditions
> gaoling was not a deterrent. I think legalised corporal
> punishment would have more effect than putting the
> natives in gaol.

The most fervent advocate of violence as lawful punishment was, surprisingly, Annie Lock. She was sure that the cattle-killing problems were being caused exclusively by 'semi-civilised blacks':

> a few of them should be made a real example of and not
> be sent back after a few months of good food in prison.
> They think a spell in prison is a joke and has no good

effect on them. I don't think a little flogging would hurt
a lot of them.

A grateful board latched on to these comments, although it
elected not to explicitly call for the re-legalisation of flogging for
(Aboriginal) convicts; still, the point could hardly be missed.

As for the statement that Aboriginal prisoners were escaping
from Darwin, making their way hundreds of miles south to the
Centre, and there fomenting violent rebellion, there was literally
nothing in the evidence which remotely suggested any such thing.
Although no doubt an attractive image, in the sense that it evoked
the worst fears of the isolated frontier whites – a dark uprising – it
was in fact a pure product of the board's imagination. Nothing of
the kind had ever happened anywhere in Australia; perhaps the
board had been reading about slave rebellions in the antebellum
south of the United States.

Thus, to the board's satisfaction, were the killings of Brooks
and Morton explained. Its work was done, but it decided to end
its report with a final flourish: a conclusive repudiation of the
persistent claims that the Aboriginal people of Central Australia
had been short of food and water in the current drought and that
that had somehow been causally connected to the troubles.

Almost every witness had something to say on this subject,
no doubt prompted by the board. With a couple of exceptions,
their view was strongly unanimous: the drought was not a factor.
Their language took on a monotonous similarity: there were
no starving Aboriginal people; there was plenty, ample, abundant native food and water. Nobody was saying there hadn't
been a drought, but everyone was adamant that nobody was
going without.

At least, almost everyone; the missionary witnesses had a more nuanced perspective. Ernest Kramer claimed that the Aboriginal people throughout Central Australia were suffering from a lack of some native foods which had become scarce in the drought, and had to resort to digging for rabbits. However, even they were disappearing. While his view on this point seemed initially unequivocal, further questioning elicited a substantial backdown by Kramer, who ultimately testified that any starvation he had seen was restricted to older Aboriginal people living around the stations, not the 'myalls'.

Annie Lock was the only witness, ultimately, prepared to say that there was starvation in Central Australia:

> There were natives starving about Harding Soak, I fed them there. They came in there and were ravenously hungry. The reason I left the centre was that I couldn't stand seeing the blacks coming in hungry and starving any longer.[28]

On the evidence, it seemed there really was no problem with food or water supplies at all. The board was anxious to put the matter to rest once and for all, which it did in clear terms:

> In conclusion, the Board wishes to state that there is no evidence of any starvation of blacks in Central Australia. On the contrary, there is evidence of ample native food and water.

So what was the truth? Unlike much else, this was a matter of objective fact. The controversy had first arisen in February 1928, with a detailed report in Darwin's *Northern Standard* from Ernest Allchurch, the Chief Telegraphist at Alice Springs. According to Allchurch, the Centre was in the grip of a severe drought, and things were looking grim:

'The drought is something terrible', Mr Allchurch said, 'and is so far as I know, the worst experienced in the history of Central Australia...if rain does not fall next month, Alice Springs will be wiped off the map, so far as the raising of stock is concerned.'

For the Aboriginal people, it was particularly bad:

Animal life is extremely scarce, and hardly a kangaroo or wallaby can be seen now. This also applies to birds. The aborigines in consequence are having a hard time, and those in and about Alice Springs are being kept alive on rations supplied by the resident Commissioner... Just how the bush aborigines are eking out an existence is a puzzle.[29]

Not in doubt was the severity of the drought, which had begun back in 1925 and gotten progressively worse. At the Hermannsburg Mission, Rev. Albrecht recorded by May 1926 that the waterholes were drying up and cattle were dying.[30] The worst year of the drought was 1928: total rainfall at Alice Springs was only 61 millimetres, and 86 millimetres at Barrow Creek.[31] Late in the year, the southern newspapers were picking up reports of starvation among the Aboriginal people, providing a possible context for the recent atrocities. A small piece in *The Advertiser* on 13 December also drew the Federal Government into the picture:

The report from Mr Michael Terry that blacks in
Central Australia were suffering from want of food,
owing to the dry season, was brought under the notice
of the Minister for Home Affairs (Mr Abbott) today. Mr
Abbott said enquiries were being made, and if necessary,
steps would be taken to relieve the distress.[32]

Another report on the same day in the same newspaper, sourced
from the Victorian Anthropological Society, claimed that 'hundreds' were starving in the Centre.[33] On the 18th, *The Advertiser*
reported that the Prime Minister had intervened,[34] but also carried the 'Official Reply' from none other than J. C. Cawood,
whose reports to the Department of Home and Territories
'appear to discredit completely the statements that Aborigines
in Central Australia are starving as the result of drought
conditions'.[35]

This was at odds with what Cawood himself was telling the
Department of Home Affairs soon afterwards. In a report of 29
January following a visit to the Hermannsburg Mission, Cawood
noted that the mission's wells had completely given out and there
was no game to be found, 'owing to the prolonged drought'. He
was concerned about starvation among the Aboriginal people
there.[36] Hermannsburg Mission did suffer appallingly during this
period, reporting later that 85 per cent of the Aboriginal children
there had died from scurvy.[37]

M. C. Hartwig completed a detailed analysis of the causes of
the Coniston massacres for his honours thesis with the University
of Adelaide in 1960. He was convinced that the drought had
had a major influence on interracial relations in the lead-up to
the killing of Brooks and what followed, and concluded that the
board had been completely wrong to dismiss it as a factor.[38] The

Territory historian Peter Read, on the other hand, came to the opposite conclusion. In 1978 he recited a very detailed account, from the Warlpiri elder Engineer Jack Japaljarri, of the migration of the Warlmala Warlpiri from the Lander River region north to Wave Hill in 1928, just before the Coniston massacres. It had been assumed by many historians that this migration was driven by hunger, caused by the lack of water and native game in the desert. This theory had been propounded by J. W. Bleakley, the Chief Protector of Aboriginals in Queensland, in his report on Central and North Australia to the Federal Government in 1929.

Bleakley had been commissioned by the Prime Minister in May 1928 to enquire generally into the conditions of the Aboriginal people (and 'half-castes') in Central and North Australia, and delivered his detailed report in January 1929.[39] The coincidence with the Coniston events was fortuitous.

Bleakley had this to say about the drought and its significance:

Station Myalls — Conflict over Waters — Between the first of these and the stock-owners a certain conflict is always inevitable, as it is practically impossible to have cattle on country where blacks are hunting without some disturbance of the stock. During severe drought, such as has been experienced for some time, the drying up of many of the waterholes renders the situation more acute, as, naturally, the blacks have to live and the stock-owners are equally anxious to save their cattle. That the position as regards water has in some places become acute may be seen from the fact that a large party of 50 Warramulla blacks, a wild desert tribe, were seen at Wave Hill Station, where they had come, bringing their women and children, which in itself was significant, because the waterholes had dried up. Information was received that this conflict over the right to water was causing some distress amongst the natives of the Kaitish tribe in Central Australia, the scene of the murder of a white man and the unfortunate shooting of a large number of the tribe, including women, during the arrest of the supposed murderers, into which inquiry is now being held.[40]

According to Japaljarri, who had been eighteen at the time, Bleakley was completely wrong. The Warlmala branch of the Warlpiri had not moved north because of water or food, but for tobacco. It was not intended as a permanent shift, and they had to cross the territory of other hostile groups to get to Wave Hill, but the driver was a desire, rather than an existential need, for something which only white men could supply.[41]

Reconciling all of this is a frustrating business. As it turns out, there is precious little evidence of actual starvation or severe deprivation among the Aboriginal people of Central Australia during the drought, and none of that evidence comes from Aboriginal sources. It seems clear that there were serious shortages of food and water in and around some of the missions, including Hermannsburg and particularly at Annie Lock's beleaguered post at Hardings Soak. There was undoubtedly in 1928 a part of the Aboriginal population which had been reduced to the status of beggars. Unpicking the causes of that situation is beyond the scope of this work.

Part of the confusion arises from the insistence by everyone in 1928–1929 on drawing a strict dichotomy between 'myalls' or 'bush blacks' and 'semi-civilised blacks', almost as if they were two separate races. Like all such distinctions, of course, it was a nonsense. By 1928 there were few if any Aboriginal people who had not had some interaction with whites. Trying to work out just how this influence played in the minds of the particular Aboriginal men who decided to try to kill Brooks and Morton would be a pointless exercise.

The obvious conclusion is that everyone was wrong. There was never an adequate evidentiary basis for claiming that the drought was the primary, or even a substantial, cause of the attacks by the Warlpiri in August and September 1928. At the same time, it was fanciful to totally dismiss a causal relationship, as the Board of Enquiry and most of its white witnesses were so keen to do.

The drought of 1925–1929 was extreme, and had a devastating effect on much of the supply of native food (as well as the imported rabbits) on which the Aboriginal people who were living a traditional lifestyle depended. Undoubtedly, water was much less plentiful as well. The Aboriginal people had endured drought many times before in the previous 60,000 or so years, and it makes no sense to think that they were not well equipped to deal with it in the pre-colonial environment.

However, things were different now, and the contest for water between Aboriginal people and the pastoralists' cattle was real. The truth is, no doubt, that this contest played a role in the increasing tensions that eventually boiled over near Coniston. It was neither a complete explanation nor a distracting irrelevancy.

The Board of Enquiry was done. It had definitively answered every question that had been asked of it, and several that had not. Complete exoneration of Mounted Constable Murray, the other members of his hunting parties, his superiors and the Australian Government ultimately responsible for his actions was the result. So far as officialdom was concerned, there was nothing left to say.

Looking back on the board's work with a lawyer's eye, it would be difficult to exaggerate to just how much of an extent its process bordered on farce; the result was without any doubt a travesty. From the perspective of proper legal process – that is, the way it should have been done – there is a staggeringly long list of critical defects:

- the make-up of the board, for starters – it included no members who an impartial observer would expect to be free of pro-police bias, and Cawood's inclusion was a bad joke;
- the giving to Murray of free rein to operate effectively as a de facto member of the inquiry;
- the failure to seek evidence from any Aboriginal people, particularly witnesses to either the attacks on Brooks or Morton or the reprisal killings;
- the lazy failure to get the critical testimony of Wilson, Major or Dodger;
- the failure to visit a single location where shootings had taken place, while travelling extensively between places with no relevance to the inquiry;
- the non-recording of the board's questions to witnesses.

These were all procedural flaws which undermined the credibility of the board's work from the outset. Compounding them was the sheer ineptitude of its inquisitorial functioning. The board was presented with patently concocted but still contradictory evidence from Murray and his colleagues, with gaping holes in its chronology and logical inconsistencies in the explanations of their movements. All of these would have been explored, in great forensic detail, by a tribunal doing its job – of exposing the truth – properly. The board didn't bother trying, reserving its only criticisms, which didn't even make it into its report, for Sergeant Noblet's pathetic incompetence in failing to force properly detailed reports out of Constable Murray each time he returned from a killing expedition.

Every single finding in the board's final report had inadequate foundation, and some none at all. Many of them were simply idiotic – banal, lazy propositions quite obviously composed in a hurry by men who had started their deliberations with their preferred conclusion in mind (and, in all probability, tacit if not explicit riding instructions from the government), and then justi-fied it with a random selection of half-baked nods to prevailing white prejudices.

What it all boiled down to was this: the Board of Enquiry knew what it was required to do; it was determined to deliver; and it had no fear that its work would be closely scrutinised. Therefore, it could carry out its task speedily and without much care, to produce a whitewash report of rare negligence. And so it did.

The proceedings of the Board of Enquiry were public, and initially attracted a degree of press reportage. Interest waned as the hearings went on, and the board finished its work well out of the public eye. This suited the government too; in response to an early enquiry by the Chairman, O'Kelly, as to whether the board should announce its findings publicly, a telegram came quickly back from the Department of Home and Territories with instruc-tions that the 'report be forwarded direct to Minister as soon as completed and that no information be given to press'.[42]

O'Kelly duly complied, returning to Canberra by train with the board's report once it had been completed, a journey which took a leisurely eleven days. The report was in Minister Abbott's hands on 29 January 1929, and the next day it was released in full to the national press. The newspapers ran it without comment.[43] On 7 February, the report was tabled in both the House of Representatives and the Senate, unaccompanied by any statement from the government. It likewise attracted no questions in either chamber.[44]

Justice must be both done and seen to be done, and the standard justification for the commissioning of a non-judicial proceeding such as the Board of Enquiry is to ensure that a light is shone into every dark corner and all wrongdoing exposed. Public confidence in the law enforcement and justice system requires this level of transparency. For this reason, no doubt, the board's full report was tabled in Parliament and released publicly, and all of its records including the witness statements and evidentiary exhibits were preserved on the public record, where they now live permanently, in the National Archives.

But the board had delivered a second, secret report. It is not to be found in the archives; its existence was not disclosed to the media or Parliament, or apparently to anyone outside of the Department of Home and Territories. The fact that it was created at all is established by a passing mention in a departmental memo that probably wasn't meant to make it into the public record.

It came about like this. Following the publication of the board's official report, the department was copping a barrage of criticism from the various church and welfare groups that had agitated for an inquiry in the first place. They were not happy with its outcome. Most appalled was the Rev. W. Morley, secretary of the Association for the Protection of the Native Races of Australia and Polynesia, who wrote a long letter particularising his complaints about the board's process on 20 March 1929.[45] His criticisms were extremely well made: he pointed to the absence of legal representation for the thirty-two dead Aboriginal people, the extraordinary circumstances surrounding the evidence of Lala, and the failure to secure Major as a witness.

Morley had plenty to say, noting perspicaciously, for example:

> It appears from the evidence that the Police and party were well equipped with arms and ammunition. Briscoe says (page 42) 'I had a revolver loaded in 7 chambers, and I had 30 or 40 spare cartridges, Murray had a revolver, Stafford had a revolver and rifle, Saxby had a revolver and rifle, Paddy had a revolver but no rifle, Wilson (the half-caste) had a rifle.'
>
> Having regard to such preparations it appears that something more than making an arrest of individual natives was contemplated.

Morley pointed to some of the detail of Murray and Noblet's laziness in their reporting, picking up O'Kelly's comment at one point of the hearing to Noblet that 'That is just the trouble. You regard the taking of a human life as a detail.' He objected also to the obviously malicious attacks on Annie Lock, noting that 'animus or prejudice against missionaries' was a routine reaction of white settlers 'who find themselves opposed in efforts to exploit natives, or use them otherwise unjustly'. Finally, Morley pointed to Lock's explicit evidence to the board that white men in the area had been taking Aboriginal women by force and that their men were threatening revenge:

> This aspect of the treatment of natives appears to have had little or no investigation on the part of the Board, whereas it is well known that interference of white men

with native women is one of the most prolific causes of native attacks on white men.

Given the extensive Aboriginal testimony to the effect that this was indeed a major causative factor in the attack on Brooks at least, which testimony the board did not have and never sought, Morley had a very good point. He concluded with the association's expressed hope that the Minister would 'not allow the matter to rest in the unsatisfactory condition it is left by the report of the Board of Enquiry'.

The department was unmoved, forwarding Morley's complaints to the Minister with the comment that 'it is assumed that it is not proposed to have any further investigations made into this matter'.[46] That was a safe assumption. Abbott vented his frustration in unambiguous terms to *The Sydney Morning Herald*:

> Criticism of [the board's report], he said, had been couched in language which made the task of enlisting public support for aborigines more difficult. The implication was that the board had been hostile, and that the officials were doing nothing for the blacks. The aborigines had never before been better treated, and at no time had there been made such complete measures for their advancement and uplift, he said.[47]

Adverse comment also made its way into the newspapers. The Adelaide *Register* ran detailed criticisms of the board's report made by the South Australian MP Herbert Basedow ('whose interest in the aborigines is well known'), including the illogicality of claiming that all thirty-one shootings by Murray's parties were in self-defence when Murray had admitted that at least two of the victims had been running away when fired on. Basedow was also scathing about the board's insistence that there was plenty of food and water in the Centre; he had travelled throughout the area two years before, and seen no animals larger than a lizard.[48]

This was all quite vexing for the department and the government, who were no doubt feeling the sting of criticism that they had perpetrated a cover-up, while at the same time having no intention whatsoever of doing anything more. The obvious response was to sheet home the blame, such as any justifiably could be found, to the people who really deserved it. As all of the killing had been declared lawful, attention turned instead to the failings of the administration of Central Australia. Meaning, mainly, Cawood.

On 12 March, the department issued a memorandum to His Honour the Government Resident of Central Australia, inviting his attention to certain matters arising from the board's report. Cawood was in the Minister's cross-hairs, and he copped a politely worded blast:

- He had failed to take Murray's brief reports of his shooting parties' activities sufficiently seriously, simply passing them on to Canberra without comment or insistence that Murray provide more detail.
- Murray should never have been sent off on his own and forced to 'swear-in settlers as Special Constables'; at least Noblet and another Mounted Constable should have gone too.
- As for Noblet, his conduct 'appears to indicate that he does not appreciate the responsibilities of his position and is viewed with disfavour by the Minister'.
- Murray clearly needed 'tuition in general police duties and in the writing of reports', and Cawood had better send him to South Australia for six months to get it.[49]

Ouch. Cawood, fresh from his loyal participation in the white-wash that the government had commanded, would no doubt have been furious that he was now being officially hung out to dry by the same masters. He responded on 8 April, with cross-eyed civility, to each charge: there was nothing he could have added to Murray's reports, containing as they did 'the fullest and only information' available and he having no reason to doubt their veracity; more carefully, he noted that 'Murray's capabilities as a Police Officer are not below the calabre [sic] of any present member of the Central Australia Police Force'; Noblet could answer for himself. Finally, Cawood elected to throw someone else under the approaching bus, in his place:

> M C Murray did not swear in any settlers and I know of no authority whereby he could do so. The settlers volunteered to assist Murray so that no time would be lost in getting on the tracks of the aboriginals concerned in [Brooks'] murder.[50]

Back in Canberra, Carrodus at the department remained unamused, issuing a terse memo for the file repudiating Cawood's arguments. But Cawood's barb about the non-deputising of Murray's hunting companions had struck a bureaucratic nerve:

> The law provides that special constables may be sworn in by a Special Magistrate or any two Justices.
> The advice now received is the first intimation the Department had that the settlers were not sworn in. Mr O'Kelly, in his confidential report, referred to 'swearing in settlers as Special Constables', and stated that had regular police been used instead of special constables 'it

was more than probable that there would not have been the killing of blacks, at least not to the same extent'.[51]

There, in this passing mention in a departmental memo, was the smoking gun. Chairman O'Kelly had written a separate, confidential report, now in the hands of the department, in which he had said god only knows what, but it included an opinion that was not only incendiary but directly contradictory of what the board's official report had concluded. If the hunt for Brooks' killers had been conducted by police instead of just Murray and his posse of irregulars, O'Kelly believed, then fewer Aboriginal people would have died. Perhaps, even, none at all.

The board had conducted its proceedings with a high degree of legal inappropriateness, but this revelation took matters to a whole new level. It had, as it turned out, at least in one critical respect, formed opinions that were diametrically opposed to those that it published. If the shootings had to any extent been the unnecessary consequence of an improper police response, which was exactly what O'Kelly was saying had happened, then it could not be said that they were legally justified.

Not only had the board suppressed its own true findings, but the government was in possession of a secret report revealing what O'Kelly and his fellow board members had really concluded. The board had undermined its own integrity by producing a report filled with holes, but here was the proof that it had participated in a conscious public deception, and the government was complicit.

Mind you, nobody outside the government knew this, and the government was not about to tell them. O'Kelly's 'confidential' report quietly disappeared.

All that remained was to offer a tasty honorarium to the members of the Board of Enquiry – the substantial sums of £100 for O'Kelly and £50 for Giles – in recognition of their services. Cawood, however, was not so honoured.[52]

Still, the critics were unsatisfied and continued to make their voices heard. Annie Lock's reply to the savage attacks on her, which the board's report had validated, was publicised via a letter she wrote to Dr Basedow and he released to the Adelaide *News*. She maintained her key arguments: the Aboriginal people were being chased from the waterholes and their women were being interfered with by the white settlers, so it was understandable that they had finally retaliated with violence.

Lock explained to Basedow, as she had not done (or had the opportunity to do) to the board, her theory that the trouble had all been caused by the older Aboriginal men who had worked on the cattle stations and lost touch with their hunting and other traditions. They had become accustomed to beef, and had become recalcitrant:

> when I would give my Sunday morning lecture to the aborigines on how to behave on stations, and anywhere else they went, with special reference to stealing the cattle, sheep and goats of the white man, I would see by their faces that it was the stockmen 40 or 50 years of age who were the leaders in the troubles created. They would never come to a second lecture. They would say to the children 'Mummy too much sabbee alonga us'. If a few of the ringleaders had been sentenced to heavy punishment over a long period and taught that stealing was wrong it would have prevented much trouble.

There was one more thing that needed clearing up:

> As for saying that I would be happy to marry a black
> man, all I can say is that I am strongly opposed to
> anyone who is any way free with a native. I always keep
> them well in their place. What I did say was that I could
> not understand how any white person could marry a
> black.[53]

The Australian Board of Missions, National Missionary Council,
Presbyterian Assembly and Association for the Protection of the
Native Races passed resolutions criticising the Board of Enquiry
report and calling for more action, and the major city newspapers
continued to give them prominence.[54]

This persistent criticism from Christian institutions would
have been deeply irksome for the government, which had more
than enough political problems on its plate and was no doubt
extremely keen to be rid of this issue once and for all. In an
attempt to placate the righteously angry ministers and missionaries,
Abbott announced on 11 April 1929 that he had a plan: a special
conference in Melbourne, convened by him and attended by
'Representatives of Missions, Societies, and Associations interested
in the welfare of Aboriginals to consider the report and recommendations submitted to the Commonwealth Government by
J. W. Bleakley Esq.'[55]

The news of Abbott's announcement broke on 20 April, but
the conference had in fact already taken place, way back on the
12th. No media had been informed or invited ahead of time. Still,
the Minister made it clear in his statement what he was expecting
to achieve:

My idea is to educate the blacks to be better black men.
I do not propose to educate them as bachelors of arts and
barristers, but as good stockmen and men of the land, as
they are meant to be by Nature.[56]

The conference called by Abbott met in the Masonic Hall
in Melbourne on 12 April. Apart from the Minister and departmental officials, thirty-three delegates attended, representing all of
the major missionary and Aboriginal welfare bodies and a number
of women's rights organisations. The proceedings lasted less than
five hours – not a lot of time for so many interested parties to
debate the questions that confronted them.

Abbott opened the conference by remarking that it was
the first such gathering ever called to talk about the welfare of
the Aboriginal people of Central and North Australia. Framing
the issue, he noted that the Aboriginal population of Australia
was estimated at some '50,000 full-bloods and, 17,000 half-
castes'.[57] In North and Central Australia, there were about 20,000
'full-bloods' and 800 'half-castes', significantly more than in any
of the states.[58]

The Minister articulated the task of the conference: 'we have
to secure the aboriginals from privation, protect their hunting
grounds wherever possible, and relieve sickness and destitution.
We also desire to advance their moral and material welfare.' Not
that the government had been remiss: Abbott noted that it had
spent a total of £7,942 on Aboriginal welfare in the Territory in
the previous year. The Minister also wanted it clearly understood
what would and would not be on the table for debate:

There are, in the pages of the history of Australia, epi-
sodes which reflect credit on nobody; but we cannot

erase the past so we must look to the future with hopeful aspirations for better things to come. The history of Australia, in connection with the settlement of this vast area, is very much the same as that of every country in the world, where settlement has progressed. We have the slowly advancing tide of resolute white settlers, and a receding tide of natives, sullen and naturally resentful. That position has been the same in Africa, America, Australia, and the Pacific. We have had massacres and ill-treatment, and there has been the same trouble, where aboriginals were concerned, all over the world. I say it quite frankly, these things end in the same way – in the domination by the whites. We then get the problem of the half-castes, and the demoralisation of the native races, and a certain amount of degradation of those races. We are not concerned with what has happened in the past; what we want to do is to make things better for the future.

In case anyone had missed the point with respect to more recent events:

I want to hear from you concrete suggestions. Do not let us go back into criticism. I may have to refer later to the very severe criticism which has been levelled by certain societies on the killing of seventeen aboriginals in the Territory; but let us get down to concrete facts, and endeavour to reach a solution.

The delegates, who included the previously outspoken Rev. Morley, meekly complied. Not a word about the Coniston killings or the Board of Enquiry was spoken all day. Instead, the conference busied itself, under the heavy guiding hand of Abbott, with a series of resolutions regarding the general welfare of Aboriginal people. These included, after a long debate about the hardships afflicting white pastoralists in the Territory which made it impossible that they should be obliged to pay Aboriginal workers a living wage, the resolution 'That this Conference agree to the principle of the payment of aboriginals employed but it is considered desirable that such payments shall be usually otherwise than in cash'.[59]

As the conference meandered to a close, Miss Matthews from the Goulburn Island Mission ventured her first contribution of the day:

> I heard somebody remark, 'It will all fizzle out again'.
> This is an exceptional opportunity to prove that we are
> in earnest, and I would suggest that a day be set apart
> once a year, called 'Aboriginal Day', which will speak
> for itself.

Having effortlessly dismissed this silly proposition – 'I would put your motion, but I would be sorry to see it lost, because it might give a wrong impression of this Conference', he explained to Miss Matthews – the Minister closed the conference with his promise to 'give close consideration' to all that had been said and his 'hope I will be able to do something to bring them into being'. None of the resolutions survived longer than the end of that sentence.

The government had done its bit; every do-gooder in the country had had their opportunity to be heard, and not one had spoken up. The conference had, in practical terms, achieved nothing other than ensuring that no such experiment would be attempted again. In 1933, with a different party in power, the Department of the Interior was being pressed by welfare groups to do exactly that. A departmental memo was definitive:

> The experience of [the 1929] Conference, at which I was present, does not justify confidence in any success being achieved by a similar assembly of representatives. It was quite evident that many of the speakers had no first hand knowledge of aboriginals, particularly the aboriginals of the Northern Territory.[60]

By the end of May 1929, the newspapers had lost interest. The church and welfare groups had either been satisfied by their special day with the Minister, or had given up on the hope of forcing the government to address their dissatisfaction with the Board of Enquiry's proceeding.

For the Bruce government, Minister Abbott and the Department of Home and Territories, the Coniston story was over and the official file closed. Nothing more was said.

Chapter 10

DISPERSAL

While the furore over the Board of Enquiry was firing up and fizzling down through the first half of 1929, the central players in the drama that had triggered it were busily engaged in their usual activities back at the Centre. There, from a white perspective, whether or not justice had been seen to be done, the pragmatic object of 'quietening the natives' had certainly been achieved. The emergency was over.[1]

Mounted Constable Murray returned to normal duties. In February 1929, he was called upon one more time to hunt for an Aboriginal killer: Willaberta Jack, who had allegedly murdered Harry Henty back in December at Hatches Creek. In the immediate aftermath, Constable Johnson (who had replaced Murray at the Barrow Creek Police Station) had deputised (lawfully) two settlers and had since then been hunting for Willaberta Jack with no success. The legendary capabilities of Murray were now called upon instead.

Murray was despatched from Alice Springs on 15 February to join Johnson on the hunt.[2] He told Cawood that he expected to be absent for some weeks.[2] In fact he would be gone until late June, covering thousands of kilometres west of the telegraph line and checking in occasionally with progress reports.

By May, word had got out that Murray was again on a man-hunt, and Rev. Morley of the Association for the Protection of the Native Races was writing to the Minister for Home Affairs, Abbott, asking a very pertinent question:

> whether the Minister considers in view of the recent shootings of at least 31 natives in which Murray was so deeply concerned that he should have been sent by the Commissioner of Police on this further duty into remote country away from any possibility of control or supervision?[3]

It was even more pertinent than Morley knew, because Murray had still not received any of the remedial training which the Minister had directed Cawood to make sure he got, following the Board of Enquiry's criticisms.

It was, objectively, a pretty extraordinary thing for Cawood to have done. Nerves were well on edge in Canberra with the knowledge that Murray was back out in the bush once more, ostensibly on a mission identical to those that had so recently caused so much fuss. Whatever he was doing, it was too late to stop it, and there was no way that the news could be suppressed.

With this in mind, the department took the obvious active step, and telegrammed Cawood to peremptorily ask: 'When sending police in search Willaberta Jack were any instructions given regarding shooting aboriginals.'[4] Cawood replied five days later:

> instructions to police bring prisoner in if possible but knowing he was armed with rifle no undue risks were to be taken with assisting settlers lives if he attempted use rifle.[5]

This was typical Cawood, disingenuous to the end. As he knew, the Minister's question concerned Murray, who had discharged the deputised settlers when he arrived to take over the hunt. There was no doubt, in any event, that Cawood had given no such instructions to any of his officers. Was Cawood hoping that Murray would commit another massacre, in a sort of career-suicidal payback gesture to the government which, surely, he felt, had thrown him to the wolves? If it wasn't that, then Cawood must have been every bit as negligently incompetent as the department had already concluded.

Still, the Minister was content to repeat the lie to Morley, assuring him that Murray had been instructed to arrest Willaberta Jack 'if possible' and noting that, since there was only one suspect in the Henty case, 'I do not think that there is any cause for fear that aboriginals will be shot in connection with the arrest of Willaberta Jack.' Furthermore, the Minister was 'giving this matter my personal attention, and feel sure that the arrest will be effected without recourse to the use of firearms'.[6] He could always hope.

To everyone's relief, on 21 June a telegram arrived in Canberra confirming that Willaberta Jack had been arrested by Murray, without injury to anyone.[7] If not for the recent history, the tale of this hunt might have become the stuff of legend.

Willaberta Jack's trial for the murder of Harry Henty kicked off at the Supreme Court in Darwin on 31 July 1929. There was an air of familiarity to proceedings, with Judge Mallam presiding once more and Mr Asche prosecuting, while Constable Murray's now infamous presence loomed over the court.[8]

The prosecution case hinged entirely on the testimony of the 'half-caste' Jack Spratt, who had seen Henty get shot and supposedly told the police that Willaberta Jack had fired without warning or provocation from a concealed position inside his hut. On the stand being led by the prosecutor, Spratt told a slightly different story:

> I remember the trouble between Willaberta Jack and Henty just before Xmas it was. Me and Henty ride up to Willaberta's hut: when we came near the hut about 10 yards away from the door, we saw Willaberta Jack inside his house. Henry Henty said 'Have you seen my boy?' and Jack said 'I seen him three days ago.' Henty then said 'Do not tell me any lies.' Willaberta Jack got inside his hut and picked up a boomerang and came back standing at his door. Henty went to his rifle loaded it up and I saw Willaberta Jack drop the boomerang and shut the door. I heard him sing out 'Come on you white bastard I will fight you.' I saw the rifle came through a hole in the door, there was a little one in the corner of the door. The rifle was a 32. I heard the shot go off from Willaberta's rifle. Henty was about three yards away. A shot was fired from the hut. Henty dropped and I could see the blood outside his head. I jump on my horse and trotted away.

Under cross-examination by Willaberta Jack's barrister, Spratt added even more detail:

> Henty loaded to try to shoot Willaberta Jack, when he was standing at the door with a boomerang...Henty went round the hut and came back to where he was shot. He went round the hut to try to get a shot at Willaberta Jack...If Willaberta Jack wanted to live he had to shoot first.

226

Next witness for the prosecution was Lizzie, Willaberta Jack's 'gin', who the reporter described as 'a beautiful mixture of red, green and black and bone'. She claimed, to the prosecutor's dismay, that Henty had in fact fired first. Judge Mallam interrupted her evidence midstream and took the unorthodox step of both excusing her on the basis that her language was proving 'rather hectic', and informing the jury that he thought she was telling the truth.

Constable Murray described his arrest of Willaberta Jack and fended off an allegation that he had given him a beating in the Alice Springs lock-up. Had he struck Willaberta Jack two or three times and threatened to shoot him? 'The witness denied both and said that he believed in treating the natives kindly.'

The verdict was fast and a surprise: the jury found justifiable homicide, meaning it believed that Willaberta Jack had acted in self-defence, and the accused was a free man. He was still in police hands, and within a month he was dead, supposedly of pneumonia. The ever-helpful Donald Campbell, JP, happily signed the death certificate and dispensed with the need for an inquest.[9]

From Fred Brooks' lonely death to the suspicious demise of Willaberta Jack, the western frontier of Central Australia had been witness to a bloody tumult for a full year. There would be more killings, including murders unavenged, to come; but the Coniston massacres were already history.

———

The Coniston massacres were soon forgotten, but their perpetrators and enablers lived on. For the government, there was a lingering embarrassment which might re-enter the public debate at any time, and therefore some cleaning up still to do.

Emblematic of the whole debacle was the Government Resident and Police Commissioner in Alice Springs: Cawood. As it happened, his term was due to expire in December 1929. The Minister, Abbott, issued a detailed report on conditions in North and Central Australia that August, and took the opportunity to dump on Cawood from a great height. Noting that the Resident needed to be an 'active, energetic man and a good disciplinarian', he archly added, 'which Mr Cawood is not'. Criticising every aspect of his administration and blaming 'a great deal of the inefficiency in Central Australia' on his laxness, Abbott recommended to Cabinet that Cawood not be considered for re-appointment.[10]

Despite strenuous efforts by Cawood to once again leverage his political connections to resurrect his chances, the die had been cast and his time was up. He left Central Australia before Christmas in 1929, and never obtained another government appointment.[11] His replacement was his secretary, Victor Carrington, who served as Government Resident until the post was abolished in 1946.

By the end of the year, Sergeant Noblet was gone too. Severely criticised during the Board of Enquiry's hearings and by the Minister himself for his failure to exercise any control over Murray, Noblet copped another official reprimand in October 1929 over a minor matter.[12] Perhaps reading the writing on the wall, Noblet tendered his resignation soon after. The department gratefully accepted, noting for the record that Noblet 'has not proved a success'.[13] Like Cawood, he disappeared into obscurity, but both men lived very long lives (Noblet died at eighty-six; Cawood at ninety).

Saxby and Briscoe stayed on in the Territory, Saxby apparently becoming a prospector and Briscoe making an aborted attempt to take up his own pastoral lease near the Sandover River away to the east.[14] Morton and Tilmouth gave up on the Lander region in 1930, supposedly because of continuing trouble with the local Aboriginal people.[15] All of these men eventually melded into the vastness of the outback, leaving no positive legacy but a grim residue of viciousness and mistrust.

Only Stafford stayed on at Coniston, until he sold the leasehold to Brian Bowman in 1946 and retired to Adelaide.[16] It had never been more than marginal as a cattle station, and it remained that way.[17] It continued to play host to tragedy as well; in about 1943, while Stafford was on holiday in Adelaide, he left two white stockmen in charge. After an argument, said to be over Stafford's de facto wife, Alice, one of the men shot the other, set the buildings on fire and then shot himself too. This may have been the final straw for Stafford and Coniston.[18]

Morton's name would reappear in the records a couple more times. In 1937, T. G. H. Strehlow, then a Patrol Officer, reported to the Chief Protector in Alice Springs that Morton (who now owned Anningie Station), his nephew and a man named Nicker were 'ill treating' Aboriginal people. This accords with Strehlow's diary notes that the men were keeping underage Aboriginal girls for sex. Strehlow warned that they should be approached carefully as they were 'very rough types indeed and might easily produce guns'.[19] There is no indication that any action was taken.

Paddy, who the Aboriginal people caught up in the Coniston shootings considered to be a violent killer, continued his work with the Central Australian police. In August 1929, he was tracking for Mounted Constable McColl near the Kernot Range when he shot and killed an Aboriginal man called Junbuna and wounded another called Cundergin. Carrington, acting as Coroner, accepted Paddy's claim that he had been acting in self-defence, and that was that. As usual, there was no attempt to inspect the body or consider explanations other than that provided by the officer who had done the shooting. The official report was received in Canberra without comment.[20]

Alex Wilson recovered from the illness which had kept him away from the Board of Enquiry, and lived into the 1970s. In 1945 he was charged with assaulting an Aboriginal man, but acquitted.[21]

In October 1929, the Bruce government itself was gone, despatched in a landslide Labor victory which also ended the Prime Minister's six and a half years of office with the unprecedented loss of his own seat. The cause was industrial relations, which had become an explosive issue in Australian politics in the darkening interval before the Great Depression crashed through the nation's postwar torpor. As in the 1928 election, Aboriginal affairs played no part in the policy debate.[22]

Along with Bruce, the Minister for Home Affairs lost his seat as well. Abbott came back to Parliament two years later, and in 1937 was appointed Administrator of the Northern Territory, where he established a reputation as a solid friend of the pastoralists with at best an indifferent attitude to Aboriginal affairs. To anyone who had been witness to his involvement in the Coniston affair, that would have been no surprise.

In 1950, Abbott collected all of his thoughts about the Northern Territory in a book called *Australia's Frontier Province*. His many years up north had not tempered the attitudes which had been hardwired into him from his time as a Queensland cattleman. These were still representative of white Australia generally: the Aboriginal people were a 'diminishing race'; they were 'childlike', although Abbott considered them 'the most interesting of all the primitive peoples' and, racially, 'caucasian'.[23] Abbott was certainly one of the many in government over the years who believed that Australia's responsibility to its first peoples extended no further than to 'smooth the dying pillow' of that doomed race.[24] Abbott had a revealing reflection to share on the significance of the Coniston massacres:

> The last stand of the Northern Territory natives against the white man was in Central Australia in 1928, when they killed a white settler named Brooks at Coniston Station, 200 miles north-west of Alice Springs. A punitive expedition was sent out and between twelve and fifteen natives were shot. There was an outcry, and a court of inquiry investigated the circumstances and found that the action was justified on the whole. Brooks' partner, Randall Stafford, erected a monument to his memory at the scene of the killing, which is on the road to the Granites, probably one of the loneliest tracks in the world. It is fitting that this white marble column should rise out of the mulga and spinifex on this track and that it should be the last memorial marking the strife between the white and the black in Australia.[25]

Halving the official death toll was more likely due to Abbott's carelessness about the details of the incident twenty years after the fact than a conscious deceit. But his admission that Murray's expeditions were punitive (and therefore necessarily unjustifiable), probably equally lazy rather than deliberate, did much to fill in the gap which his manipulations back in 1929 had left behind. Not that anyone noticed; Abbott's book wasn't exactly a best seller, and Coniston had by 1950 been long forgotten.

Murray, the man in the centre of everything, went on as he had before. The Willaberta Jack controversy died down as quickly as its forebears. Murray's violent assault on Willaberta in the Alice Springs lock-up had enjoyed passing mention at the

Darwin trial, but there was a postscript. In June 1929, Cawood 'conducted an enquiry' into the charge, and found Murray guilty of striking Willaberta Jack. Murray was fined £5, Cawood noting that he had taken into account the 'arduous tasks allotted to Mounted Constable Murray during the previous twelve months' as a mitigating factor.

As usual, it was only an enquiry from Rev. Morley of the Association for the Protection of Native Races, in February 1931, which elicited any kind of reaction from the government. In response, the department assured Morley that the Minister had told Cawood that he considered Murray's penalty too lenient and instructed him 'to inform [Murray] that, if any further charge of maltreatment of aboriginals was proved against him, prompt disciplinary action would be taken'.[26] This was a lie; it had issued no such instruction.

It was also contradicted by the department's own earlier statement to Morley in May 1930, responding to another complaint about Murray's continuing involvement in dealings with Aboriginal people. On that occasion, the department had told Morley that his request for Murray's removal 'is one which it is extremely difficult to comply with', for two reasons. First, there was no place in North or Central Australia to which Murray could be sent where he would not be in contact with Aboriginal people; second, 'since the unfortunate incident in which he was implicated, his conduct has been quite satisfactory.' It would be unfair to punish him for something of which the Board of Enquiry had determined he was innocent.[27]

The reality was that Murray had been let back off the leash. He never received the training which the Minister had insisted upon after the board's hearings. Instead, he was posted to Arltunga, even further away from supervision. He remained in the Territory police force until his retirement in about 1940.

The public resurrection of Murray's character began as soon as the Board of Enquiry had completed its work. A hagiographic piece appeared in the Adelaide *Register* in February 1929, under the headline 'RIDES ALONE AND GETS HIS MAN ALWAYS – POLICEMAN HERO OF CENTRAL AUSTRALIA DOES MANY JOBS'. Written by an unnamed correspondent who said he had travelled with the Board of Enquiry, it did not hold back on the superlatives. 'Mounted Constable Murray is the hero of the Central Australians', it began, and went on in the same tone. Describing Murray in elegiac terms as a quintessential bushman, dead shot, a better tracker than 'the blacks', knowledgeable of 'native lore', taciturn, hard and unrelenting, the reporter related one incident during their travels when Murray spent four hours single-handedly conducting major mechanical repairs on his car during a scorching dust storm.

The reporter explained that Murray had returned from World War I 'with nothing more serious than a taste for more adventure'. The Territorian police service had offered just this, and Murray was the man for the job: 'That is the other side of the man, the side Central Australians know. That is why Murray is their hero.'[28]

When Strehlow met Murray at Arltunga in 1932, he had been told by his Aboriginal guide to expect something very different from what Murray's reputation might suggest: 'That man Murray is today a peaceful man who never harms anyone any longer.' Strehlow was impressed:

> Murray conveyed the impression of being a placid, almost an easy-going and kindly man; and there could

be no doubt about the affectionate glances which he gave to his wife and young son as he entered at the door. He gripped my hand warmly as I rose, and expressed the hope that I would be able to stay at Arltunga for several days.[29]

The government's hopes that Murray would cause it no more trouble were disturbed in 1933, when a piece appeared in the Sydney *Sunday Sun and Guardian*, written by the journalist Ernestine Hill and clearly with the close cooperation of Murray himself. It carried a compelling headline: 'MURRAY – SCOURGE OF THE MYALLS'. Hill set the tone with her opening line:

> To whisper the name of 'Murri' to the blacks of the Lower Territory today is enough to turn the stock-boys pale with fright and send the myalls in a wild scatter for the bushland.
>
> Leader of the last of the great punitive police raids that alone have made for the safety of the white man in a black man's country, Murray is stationed with his wife and family at a lonely little police station in the ranges, 100 miles north-east of Alice Springs, alone among uncivilised blacks, and unafraid.

Murray had given Hill a detailed account of the Coniston killings, differing in major respects from all of his official reports and sworn testimony to the Board of Enquiry. The telling was sensational, and Murray was not apologising for any of what he had done. 'It was a drastic case and it called for a drastic remedy. There are times when the natives understand nothing else, as history will show you.' Hill rounded out with a description of

Murray's tracker, 'Murdering Bob', so named for his reputation as a serial killer of Aboriginal people in earlier times but, according to Murray, since reformed.

> Nevertheless when the word is out that 'Murri' and 'Murdering Bob' are on the warpath, it is a noteworthy fact that all the bucks of the district fade out of the landscape and a curious lubra will put her head round the homestead door, three shades lighter from a guilty conscience, to ask in a frightened whisper, 'What name Murri come up?'[30]

Rev. Morley, of course, complained about the article, and Murray received a caution for his indiscretion.[31] His active participation in the attempt to restore his public reputation would also have rankled his old hunting comrades, who knew exactly what Murray had done in the bush in 1928. Randal Stafford unloaded some of this perspective onto Strehlow:

> As for that chap Murray's yarns about his heroic single-handed encounters with the Lander blacks, no one up here's going to swallow any of the silly bragging yarns he brought up before the Board of Enquiry in The Alice. What real bushman, I ask you, would believe Murray's evidence when he told the Board how he grabbed a spear from one of the attacking blacks and drove it through the chest of the attacker, or how he killed another black with the boomerang he had wrenched out of his own hands? Those silly Wild West yarns may take in the city mugs down south, but I know Murray far too well for that. He may be a killer, but he'd never rush into any

real danger all on his own: the man's far too cunning for that.[32]

There were to be no more massacres; or were there? History records nothing definitely lethal regarding Murray's later encounters with Aboriginal people, except for an intriguing passage in a memoir published in 1992 by Kurt Johannsen, who lived in the Territory his whole life and was a pioneer of the road train industry there. He wrote of an incident in 1934, when his travels took him to Arltunga:

> A less pleasant character along the run was the policeman there, George Murray, who was in charge of the eastern district. He was rather crude and very tough, especially on the aborigines.

He then described the rationing system the government had introduced for old and infirm Aboriginal people, administered by the police.

> The rations were intended to be free but Murray was alleged to have been an 'aboriginal hater', and I was told by Walter Smith, who had lived in the area for many years, that out there at the goldfields Murray refused to issue rations unless they brought in a bit of alluvial gold. This meant he was actually selling rations to them.
>
> 'Nugget' Morton, who owned Ammaroo Station, and Murray were also allegedly involved in the 'Sandover Massacre' where 100 or more aborigines were either shot or poisoned after it was alleged the aborigines had

speared some cattle. Apparently strychnine was put in the soakage of the Sandover River.[33]

There is no way of verifying the Sandover River story; it will have to remain no more than an intriguing possibility. Murray was, however, the subject of an official investigation in 1937 into allegations that he had been selling rations to Aboriginal people for gold.[34] The result was inconclusive, but Murray's career as a police officer ended without much credit to show for his years of service.

Embarrassment to his government employers, mass murderer to those white people who cared, and a bragging big-noter to his white contemporaries in the Centre, for Murray there would be no redemption. Least of all in the eyes of the Warlpiri and Kaytetye people who had experienced the full effect of his capabilities; to them, he was a killer whose cold eyes they should do all they could to never meet.

EPILOGUE

White man got no dreaming, him go 'nother way. White man, him go different. Him got road belong himself.[1]

Forty years after Coniston, a social worker visited George Murray at a public hospital in Adelaide.[2] Murray was the patient – he had been admitted after a fall – but the visit was for Mrs Murray's benefit.

> Mrs Murray has been seen several times whilst visiting her husband. She is much younger than her husband (who is 85 years), although she does not look it. She has a tired look about her and a slight tremor in her hands. She is determined to look after her husband at home. She said that she thought she would be able to manage him and was prepared to try.
>
> During these visits, however, Mr Murray has not said anything. He has always been lying in bed looking very morose. Mrs Murray said that her husband was a mounted trooper in the Northern Territory before he retired. This was his first spell in hospital and he didn't like it.

Murray had retired to Adelaide after his police service, apparently working for some years as a church caretaker but nothing more strenuous than that. By the 1960s he was suffering the usual physical ailments of old age, and was maintaining a vigorous correspondence with the Repatriation Commission claiming that these were all consequences of his wartime injuries. Eventually the commission relented, agreeing to pay his medical expenses related to the osteoarthritis which was severely incapacitating him.

The Murrays soldiered on at home in suburban Adelaide for as long as they could. In 1973, when Murray was eighty-nine, a rehabilitation specialist visited a desolate scene. Murray, he reported,

> passes the day sitting in the lounge-room of his large comfortable bungalow style home, looking into the street. Mrs Murray said that he was too embarrassed by his 'poor hearing and slow movements' to go with her to the Senior Citizen Club, and didn't like visitors…
>
> When showing me to the door [Mrs Murray] became upset and tearful expressing much sympathy for [Murray] and saying that he had been a proud capable man who now felt humiliated by his handicaps.

A year further on, a social worker recorded that Murray now 'rarely talks to his wife'. When he was admitted again to hospital in 1975, the doctors noted that he was 'a surly old man', 'difficult and demanding'. Murray did not return home from that stay. Two months later he was dead, passing away quietly at St Louis Nursing Home on 2 December 1975. He was ninety-one.

A few days later, Edith Esme Murray completed in her spidery handwriting an official Application for Grant Towards Funeral and Burial Expenses on behalf of her dead husband. The form required her to disclose the deceased's assets: the marital home valued at $35,000; some government bonds, $9,400; and $11,320 savings in the Commonwealth Bank. The funeral had cost her $508.

Properly assessed as eligible under Reg. 1791(a), Mrs Murray was awarded $100 by a grateful nation for the burial of her war hero. The final item on George Murray's service file is a polite letter from the Repatriation Commission to his widow, asking if she would kindly return the hearing aid which it had loaned him and which, presumably, he no longer required.

For Murray's uncounted victims in the creek beds of the Lander and Hanson rivers and among the hills to the west, there is no government file. Coniston, described by white men as the last battle stand of the Aboriginal people, was in reality the nameless and unremembered decimation of the societies of the Warlpiri and the Kaytetye. There was no war on this frontier in 1928; there was just a killing. The last great killing, as it happened, but that was no comfort to the dead.

I am unequipped to convey the meaning of country in the Aboriginal sense. The loss which the Coniston massacres entailed was so much more than the toll of the dead; the country was soaked in their blood and had become enveloped in a sadness eternal. An unidentified elder, on the eightieth anniversary of Coniston, spoke to the hurt: 'We can't go back there. You know why? Too many spirits around that place. I know I can go back, but I don't like to look at that country.'[3]

NOTES

Prologue
1   Alice Springs Police Station Day Journal, 11 August 1928.
2   M. Terry, *War of the Warramullas*, Rigby Ltd, Adelaide, 1974, p. 1.
3   ibid., p. 4.
4   S. Traynor, *Alice Springs: From Singing Wire to Iconic Outback Town*, Wakefield Press, Mile End, South Australia, 2016, p. 274.
5   B. Henson, *A Straight-out Man: F. W. Albrecht and Central Australian Aborigines*, Melbourne University Press, Carlton, 1992, p. 29. Albrecht confirmed this story in a letter to Hartwig in 1960 – he recalled Cawood as saying, 'It's time that something is done and I shall see that they are taught a lesson.' Letter from Albrecht to M. C. Hartwig, 18 April 1960, South Australian Museum, AA 662/49/27.

1   Central Australia, 1928
1   Diary of John McDouall Stuart, 23 April 1860, on planting the British flag at Central Mt Stuart, the geographic centre of Australia.
2   F. E. Baume, *Tragedy Track: The Story of the Granites,* North Flinders Mines Ltd, Wayville, South Australia; Hesperian Press, Carlisle, Western Australia, 1994, p. 2.
3   ibid., p. 21.
4   ibid.
5   ibid., p. 25.
6   ibid., p. 27.
7   ibid., p. 31.
8   ibid., p. 37.
9   T. G. H. Strehlow, *Land of Altjira* (unpublished manuscript), original held at The Strehlow Research Centre, Alice Springs, 1959, pp. 49–50.
10   For example, another series of punitive expeditions in the Daly River area in 1884 resulted in an unknown number of Aboriginal deaths; see

W. R. Wilson, *A Force Apart? A History of the Northern Territory Police Force 1870–1926*, PhD thesis, Northern Territory University, 2000, p. 271. Corporal Montagu, who led the killing, notoriously reported back that 'one result of the expedition has been to convince me of the superiority of the Martini Henry rifle, both for accuracy of aim and quickness of action'. The various massacres during the period of South Australian governance are fully described in T. Austin, *Simply the Survival of the Fittest: Aboriginal Administration in South Australia's Northern Territory 1863–1910*, Historical Society of the Northern Territory, Darwin, 1992, chapter 2. See also A. Searcy, *In Australian Tropics*, George Robertson & Co., London, 1909, pp. 173–4, 247–8.

11   T. Roberts, 'The Brutal Truth: What Happened in the Gulf Country', *The Monthly*, November 2009.

12   See Wilson, chapter 8, pp. 304ff.

13   Strehlow, pp. 118–19.

14   ibid., p. 121.

15   A. McGrath, *Born in the Cattle – Aborigines in Cattle Country*, Allen & Unwin, Sydney, 1987, p. 6.

16   M. C. Hartwig, *The Coniston Killings*, BA (Hons) thesis, The University of Adelaide, 1960, p. 3.

17   Coniston was on the Warburton River, a tributary of the Lander.

18   *Northern Standard*, 17 January 1928, p. 1; 17 February 1928, p. 6; M. Terry, *Hidden Wealth and Hiding People*, Putnam, London, 1931, p. 235.

19   NAA: A461, G300/1; also *The Aboriginals and Half-castes of Central Australia and North Australia: Report by J. W. Bleakley, Chief Protector of Aboriginals, Queensland*, Government Printer, Melbourne, 1928, p. 5. The estimated total 'full-blood' Aboriginal population of Australia at the time was about 60,000, including 20,000 in the Northern Territory. This was more than likely to be an underestimate, but less than half the NT total would have been in Central Australia, hence my guess of around 10,000. The number of part-Aboriginal people in Central Australia would have been a few hundred at most.

20   As a strong indication of how little significance the Commonwealth Parliament attached to its new responsibility for the Northern Territory, it formally delegated *all* of its lawmaking power in relation to the Territory to the executive branch, which then governed it by Ordinance, *The Northern Territory (Administration) Act 1910 (Cth)*, section 13.

21   *An Act to Make Provision for the Better Protection and Control of the Aboriginal Inhabitants of the Northern Territory and for Other Purposes*, no. 1024 of 1910; Aboriginals Ordinance 1911.

22 T. Austin, *Never Trust a Government Man: Northern Territory Aboriginal Policy 1911–1939*, NTU Press, Darwin, 1997, p. 5.

23 For an excellent exposition of the significance of this theory to Australian race relations, see T. Austin, *Simply the Survival of the Fittest: Aboriginal Administration in South Australia's Northern Territory 1863–1910*, Historical Society of the Northern Territory, Darwin, 1992, chapter 1, p. 7.

24 Ironically, the legal position in the Territory clearly favoured the Aboriginal people; all of the pastoral land was Crown leasehold, and all such leases expressly preserved Aboriginal rights to enter the land, hunt and gather and take surface water: J. Summers, *The Parliament of the Commonwealth of Australia and Indigenous Peoples 1901–1967*, research paper 10 2000–01, Department of the Parliamentary Library, Canberra, 2000, p. 26; Austin, *Simply the Survival of the Fittest*, p. 3; McGrath, *Born in the Cattle*, p. 16. Of course, this was universally ignored.

25 Austin, *Simply the Survival of the Fittest*, pp. 7–8; for as good an explanation as any of the contemporary white perspective, see J. Collier, *The Pastoral Age in Australasia*, Whitcombe & Tombs, London, 1911, chapter XV. His evocation of the 'vague terror' which afflicted white people on all the frontiers is compelling (p. 121); so too is his conclusion that the Aboriginal people's 'disappearance was a natural necessity' (p. 130). Inevitability has been a persistent theme in white observers' reflections on the Aboriginal frontier experience, always rooted in racism. Writing in 1839 during an overland trek from New South Wales to South Australia, James Coutts Crawford explained that 'like a wild beast an Australian native is not to be played with. The result of a culpable want of firmness in checking their first crimes, namely attacks on the stock of the settlers, was soon followed by the murder of several whites.' In D. H. Pike (ed.), 'The Diary of James Coutts Crawford: extracts on Aborigines and Adelaide, 1839 and 1841', *South Australiana*, vol. IV, no. 1, March 1965, p. 12.

26 The subject of 'black velvet' is well explored in McGrath, *Born in the Cattle*, chapter 4, pp. 68ff.

27 W. J. Sowden, *The Northern Territory As It Is*, W. K. Thomas & Co., Adelaide, 1882, pp. 19, 42.

28 See, for example, Barrow Creek Police Station Day Journal entry for 4 December 1927, in which Constable Murray casually noted that he had 'dispersed' a large group of Aboriginal people from Merino Well and a nearby camp, for no reason other than that they were in the way. Not that they knew it, but by law they had every right to continue their traditional customs of obtaining food and water even on pastoral leaseholdings.

29 W. E. H. Stanner, the legendary anthropologist, posited that the contest for food was a two-sided thing; when the usual substantial fauna was in short supply, the Aboriginal people tended towards what he regrettably labelled as 'intelligent parasitism', but might more appropriately have been called the obvious alternative: poaching and eating pastoral stock, the very animals that were crowding out both the native fauna and their hunters. It's unfortunate that this notion of parasitic behaviour, benignly intended as it was, has stuck and tended to obscure the practical and inevitable realities. See, for example, 'Durmugam: A Nangiomeri', in W. E. H. Stanner, *The Dreaming & Other Essays*, Black Inc. Agenda, Melbourne, 2010, p. 25.

30 Barrow Creek Police Station Day Journal.

2 The murder of Fred Brooks

1 F. Merlan, '"Making People Quiet" in the Pastoral North: Reminiscences of Elsey Station', *Aboriginal History,* vol. 2, no. 1, 1978, p. 78.

2 D. Kimber, 'Real True History: Coniston Massacre', *Alice Springs News*, vol. 10, issue 32, 10 September 2003 to vol. 11, issue 3, 4 February 2004; Strehlow, diary (unpublished), p. 314; Hartwig, *The Coniston Killings*, p. 20. A note about Kimber: His Coniston history was serialised in the *Alice Springs News* in 2003–2004, written with a journalistic eye and entirely unreferenced. However, he knew personally and interviewed a number of significant participants in the relevant events and was himself deeply knowledgeable of Territory history, and is therefore a credible source.

3 Hartwig, p. 20; Cawood to DHT, 11 October 1928, NAA: A431, 1950/2768 part 1, p. 206.

4 NAA: A431, 1950/2768, part 1, p. 206.

5 Stafford's version of the story as told to Strehlow, p. 314.

6 It was sometimes referred to as Brooks' Soak after his murder, but the Warlpiri name was Yurrkuru and I have used that throughout.

7 Strehlow, p. 315.

8 ibid.

9 Baume, p. 58.

10 Terry, *War of the Warramullas*, pp. 7–9.

11 There is no record of Stafford having ever said that Coniston came under attack; it certainly never happened.

12 J. A. Carrodus, memorandum dated 19 November 1928, NAA: A431, 1950/2768 part 1, p. 121.

13 Cawood to DHT, 30 August 1928, NAA: A431, 1950/2768 part 1,
    p. 238.

14 NAA: A431, 1950/2768 part 1, p. 239.

15 Kimber, part 4.

16 William Briscoe, who was working for Stafford on Coniston and
    camped some distance away from the homestead at the time, gave
    evidence to the later Board of Enquiry that Chapman had come past
    his camp on his way to Coniston and told him Brooks had been killed.
    NAA: A431, 1950/2768 part 2, p. 64.

17 Murray to Commissioner of Police, 2 September 1928, NAA: A431,
    1950/2768 part 1, p. 25.

18 According to Kimber, he received the note on 11 August. Hartwig says
    that one of Stafford's boys had ridden to Chapman's camp to give him
    the news on 7 August; Chapman went to Coniston, wrote his note
    and gave it to one of the station hands called 'Old Percy', who rode
    overnight to Ti Tree, arriving there on the morning of the 11th. Neither
    Hartwig, nor Kimber gives a source for this story; Kimber interviewed
    Alex Wilson, who would have known, but actually copied the story
    from Hartwig, who hadn't met Wilson at all. It seems most likely
    the source was Stafford, who Hartwig did interview. Hartwig, p. 21;
    Kimber, part 4.

19 *The Advertiser*, 13 August 1928, p. 15; *The Register*, 13 August 1928, p. 9.

20 *The Advertiser*, 14 August 1928, p. 15; *The Register*, 14 August 1928, p. 9;
    Northern Territory Times, 14 August 1928, p. 3; *The Sydney Morning Herald*,
    14 August 1928, p. 11.

21 3 September, according to Terry and Kimber, or 6 September according
    to Cawood. Terry, *Hidden Wealth and Hiding People*, pp. 243–4; Kimber,
    part 4; Cawood to DHT, 22 November 1928, NAA: A431, 1950/2768
    part 1, p. 90.

22 Testimony of Noblet to Board of Enquiry, 7 January 1929, NAA: A431,
    1950/2768 part 2, p. 100.

23 Testimony of Annie Lock to Board of Enquiry, 8 January 1929, NAA:
    A431, 1950/2768 part 2, p. 58.

24 G. Koch and H. Koch (trans.), *Kaytetye Country*, Institute for Aboriginal
    Development Publications, Alice Springs, 1993, p. 70.

25 P. Vaarzon-Morel (ed.), *Warlpiri Women's Voices: Our Lives Our History*,
    Institute for Aboriginal Development Press, Alice Springs, 1995, p. 36.

26 T. Japangardi, *Yurrkuru-Kurlu: Coniston Story*, Yuendumu School,
    Yuendumu, NT, 1978, p. 18.

27 P. Rockman Napaljarri and L. Cataldi (trans.), *Warlpiri Dreamings and*

Histories, AltaMira Press, Walnut Creek, CA, 1994, p. 163.

28 Japangardi and Japaljarri referred to here are different people to the Tim Japangardi mentioned earlier and Jack Japaljarri, who is mentioned later.

29 P. Read and J. Read (eds), *Long Time Olden Time: Aboriginal Accounts of Northern Territory History*, Institute for Aboriginal Development, Alice Springs, 1991, pp. 35–7.

30 Searcy, *In Australian Tropics*, p. 173. W. E. H. Stanner held the view, like many of his contemporaries, that Aboriginal men routinely offered their women for 'casual affairs', and that the women were eager participants. For both, the motivation was materialistic. Stanner believed that the attack on Brooks was no doubt due to a concern by the Aboriginal men involved that 'they had been bilked of due payment' for their women's services. 'Durmugam: A Nangiomeri', in *The Dreaming & Other Essays*, p. 29.

31 A large part of the 'problem' in reality was caused by the obsessive insistence that racial classification is an actual thing; as the real-life consequences of mixed couplings kept complicating this desire, increasingly idiotic labels such as 'quadroons' and 'octaroons' (respectively, to denote one-quarter and one-eighth Aboriginal blood) had to be used for the head-counts.

3 The hunters

1   S. Downer, *Patrol Indefinite: The Northern Territory Police Force*, Rigby, Adelaide, 1963, p. 13.

2   'William George Murray', in Carment, D., Maynard, R., and Powell, A. (eds), *Northern Territory Dictionary of Biography*, Charles Darwin University Press, Darwin, 2008, p. 457.

3   *Sunday Sun and Guardian*, 5 February 1933, p. 19.

4   Murray's service record, NAA: D363, M39423.

5   P. L. Murray, *Official Records of the Australian Military Contingents to the War in South Africa*, A. J. Mullett, Government Printer, Melbourne, 1911.

6   NAA: D363, M39423.

7   J. O'Brien, *'To Infuse an Universal Terror': The Coniston Killings of 1928*, thesis, Northern Territory University, 2002, p. 36.

8   *Sunday Sun and Guardian*, 5 February 1933, p. 19.

9   Barrow Creek Police Station Day Journal.

10 Koch and Koch, *Kaytetye Country*, p. 71.

11 Barrow Creek Police Station Day Journal.

12 ibid.

13 ibid.

14 Alice Springs Police Station Day Journal. The police force incorporated officially designated Aboriginal 'trackers' who were usually armed. Paddy, it seems, was not an official police tracker but was certainly treated as such.

15 C. A. Noblet testimony to Board of Enquiry, 17 January 1929, NAA: A431, 1950/2768 part 2, p. 102.

16 Cawood to DHT, 8 September 1928 (handwritten notations), NAA: A431, 1950/2768 part 1, p. 230.

17 NAA: AP613/7, Noblet C H.

18 NAA: A1, 1929/1064, p. 21.

19 Strehlow, p. 47.

20 NAA: A431, 1946/676, p. 134.

21 ibid., p. 111.

22 ibid., p. 40.

23 ibid., p. 108.

24 Alice Springs Police Station Day Journal; Cawood to DHT, 30 August 1928, NAA: A431, 1950/2768 part 1, p. 238.

25 Board of Enquiry Exhibit 13, NAA: A431, 1950/2768 part 2, p. 117.

26 NAA: A431, 1950/2768 part 1, p. 238.

27 Hartwig concluded that it was Stafford himself, but his evidence for this is unsupportive; he cites Murray's record of movements, but it doesn't mention Stafford or anyone else. Hartwig, p. 20.

28 Descriptions of Stafford and Coniston mostly from Strehlow, pp. 306–13; Baume, pp. 54–8.

29 Strehlow, p. 313.

30 ibid., p. 312.

31 ibid., pp. 293–4.

32 However, no record of these interviews appears to exist either.

33 Kimber, parts 1, 6.

34 ibid., pp. 3–4.

35 Chapman note, NAA: A431, 1950/2768 part 1, p. 239.

36 Read and Read, p. 38, story told by Tim Japangardi; Kimber, part 4.

37 Kimber, part 4.

38 Terry, *Hidden Wealth and Hiding People*, pp. 240–4; *War of the Warramullas*, p. 13.

39 Billy Briscoe claimed that Chapman was at Coniston on 19 and 20 August, but surely Murray would have mentioned this in at least one of his many versions of the events if it were so. Briscoe testimony to Board of Enquiry, 13 January 1929, NAA: A431, 1950/2768 part 2, p. 64.

40 Kimber, part 6.

41 Terry, *Hidden Wealth and Hiding People*, p. 228.
42 Saxby testimony to Board of Enquiry, 13 January 1929, NAA: A431, 1950/2768 part 2, p. 71.
43 Saxby deposition to Coronial Inquest, 13 January 1929, NAA: A431, 1950/2768 part 2, p. 281.
44 Kimber, parts 3, 6, 16. Neither Bowman nor Terry in their writing about Coniston quote Saxby as Kimber indicates, so it isn't clear where he sourced his information.
45 Briscoe said he had been in Central Australia for twenty-four years. NAA: A431, 1950/2768 part 2, p. 64.
46 ibid.

4 August

1 Terry, *War of the Warramullas*, p. 1.
2 Murray to Noblet, 2 September 1928, NAA: A431, 1950/2768 part 1, p. 25. Most of this chapter is drawn from the various written statements made by the party's white members: NAA: A431, 1950/2768 part 1, pp. 22, 25; NAA: A431, 1950/2768 part 2, pp. 68, 71, 80, 115, 276, 279, 281, 284.
3 NAA: A431, 1950/2768 part 1, p. 25.
4 ibid; Murray testimony to Board of Enquiry, 16 January 1929, NAA: A431, 1950/2768 part 2, p. 80; *Sunday Sun and Guardian*, 5 February 1933, p. 19.
5 NAA: A431, 1950/2768 part 1, p. 25; NAA: A431, 1950/2768 part 2, p. 80; Murray deposition to Coronial Inquest, 19 January 1929 NAA: A431, 1950/2768 part 2, p. 284. Paddy, by contrast, had this incident occurring on 20 August, after the party had already been out hunting. Paddy testimony to Board of Enquiry, 31 December 1928 and 1 January 1929, NAA: A431, 1950/2768 part 2, pp. 27, 38.
6 Murray deposition to Magistrate Allchurch, September 1928, NAA: A431, 1950/2768 part 1, p. 22.
7 None of the party suggested that it went to Yurrkuru, and the Aboriginal stories make it clear that the Warlpiri had, unsurprisingly, left that place very soon after Brooks' killing.
8 All of the white members of the party were at pains in their later evidence to say that Murray had given this instruction.
9 *Sunday Sun and Guardian*, 5 February 1933, p. 19.
10 The Alice Springs Police Station Day Journal records that Tracker Tommy was despatched on 14 August for Stafford's place, and remained at Coniston until 1 September when he returned to Alice Springs with

Murray, Lala and the prisoners. It doesn't explain why Tommy was sent. Presumably Murray's reference to 'Tracker Jack' was mistaken, or Tommy was addressed by more than one name (not an unusual circumstance for 'civilised blacks' at the time).

11 Paddy's two statements to the Board of Enquiry were given on 31 December 1928 and 1 January 1929; Murray did not give his evidence until 16 January.

12 NAA: A431, 1950/2768 part 1, p. 247.

13 ibid.

14 ibid., p. 246.

15 ibid., p. 240.

16 ibid., p. 238.

5 September

1 Vaarzon-Morel, p. 34; Hartwig, p. 4.

2 Strehlow, pp. 43–8.

3 Kimber, p. 6.

4 Strehlow, pp. 103–4, 44.

5 Strehlow (who was then a patrol officer), diary begun 1 April 1937, entry 28 April 1938.

6 Vaarzon-Morel, p. 37.

7 Read and Read, pp. 40–1.

8 Kimber, p. 32.

9 Strehlow, p. 45.

10 Morton statement to Board of Enquiry, 17 January 1929, NAA: A431, 1950/2768 part 2, p. 109.

11 Terry, *War of the Warramullas*, p. 12.

12 NAA: A431, 1950/2768 part 1, p. 21.

13 Alice Springs Police Station Day Journal.

14 NAA: A431, 1950/2768 part 1, p. 232.

15 ibid., p. 230.

16 Alice Springs Police Station Day Journal.

17 NAA: A431, 1950/2768 part 1, pp. 234–7.

18 Terry, *Hidden Wealth and Hiding People*, pp. 227–9.

19 Alice Springs Police Station Day Journal.

20 ibid.

21 Board of Enquiry exhibit 13, NAA: A431, 1950/2768 part 2, p. 117.

22 Kimber, p. 33.

23 Because of this difficulty, I have chosen to deal with the Aboriginal stories about the Coniston massacres together – see chapter 7.

24 NAA: A431, 1950/2768 part 1, p. 243.
25 ibid., p. 242.
26 ibid., p. 241.
27 ibid., p. 233.
28 *The Advertiser*, 16 January 1932, p. 17.
29 NAA: A431, 1950/2768 part 1, p. 213.
30 ibid., p. 214.
31 ibid., p. 216.
32 ibid., p. 218.
33 ibid., p. 219.
34 *The Advertiser*, 17 September 1928, p. 13.
35 Alice Springs Police Station Day Journal, 15 September 1928.

6 'A disgusting creature'

1 Rev. Samuel Marsden, commenting on Aboriginal people around Sydney in 1819; quoted in W. J. Lines, *Taming the Great South Land: A History of the Conquest of Nature in Australia*, Allen & Unwin, Sydney, 1991.
2 *The Register*, 16 August 1928, p. 11.
3 ibid.
4 ibid., 18 August 1928, p. 7.
5 ibid., 21 August 1928, p. 8.
6 ibid., 22 August 1928, p. 8.
7 ibid., 24 August 1928, p. 10.
8 ibid., 25 August 1928, p. 11.
9 ibid., 27 August 1928, p. 8; 30 August 1928, p. 13.
10 *The Advertiser*, 3 September 1928, p. 13; *The Register*, 3 September 1928, p. 9.
11 *The Register*, 5 September 1928, p. 9.
12 *The Advertiser*, 8 September 1928, p. 19.
13 *The Register*, 8 September 1928, p. 11.
14 ibid., 11 September 1928, p. 9.
15 ibid., 12 September 1928, p. 12.

7 October

1 Strehlow, p. 48.
2 Alice Springs Police Station Day Journal, 16, 19, 20 September 1928. Paddy didn't accompany him for this expedition.
3 Strehlow, p. 292.
4 ibid., p. 294.

5   ibid., p. 292.

6   Hartwig, p. 3.

7   ibid., p. 11, map p. 23; Strehlow, pp. 44, 314.

8   Strehlow, p. 293.

9   Tilmouth statement at inquest, NAA: A431, 1950/2768 part 2, p. 79; testimony to Board of Enquiry, 12 January 1929, NAA: A431, 1950/2768 part 2, p. 63.

10 Strehlow, p. 292.

11 NAA: A431, 1950/2768 part 2, p. 79.

12 NAA: A431, 1950/2768 part 1, p. 201.

13 NAA: A431, 1950/2768 part 1, p. 20; NAA: A431, 1950/2768 part 2, p. 86, 110, 296, 300.

14 *Sunday Sun and Guardian*, 5 February 1933, p. 19.

15 NAA: A431, 1950/2768 part 1, p. 201.

16 *Sunday Sun and Guardian*, 5 February 1933, p. 19.

17 Strehlow, pp. 47–8.

18 NAA: A431, 1950/2768 part 1, pp. 201, 202.

19 Alice Springs Police Station Day Journal, 20 October 1928; Barrow Creek Police Station Day Journal, 25 October 1928.

20 T. Japangardi, *Yurrkuru-Kurlu: Coniston Story*, pp. 19–20.

21 Rockman Napaljarri, *Warlpiri Dreamings and Histories*, p. 169.

22 Read and Read, p. 45.

23 ibid., p. 47.

24 Vaarzon-Morel, p. 43.

25 Read and Read, p. 49.

26 Koch and Koch, p. 72.

27 McCarthy, 'Remembering the Coniston Massacre', Northern Territory Library, 2008.

28 Northern Territory Archives Service, NTRS 226, TS 348 – Ada Wade.

29 One hundred was accepted as the likely tally by Mr Justice Olney in his report on the Native Title claim to the land around Yurrkuru in 1992: *Yurrkuru (Brookes Soak) Land Claim*, report no. 43, AGPS, Canberra, 1992, paragraph 6.1.5.

30 The Wikipedia 'List of disasters in Australia by death toll', which is quite comprehensive and includes incidents of all kinds including massacres and mass killings down to single-digit fatalities, does not include Coniston. Mind you, it also omits all of the other known mass killings of Aboriginal people, apart from the Myall Creek massacre. Wikipedia has a separate 'List of massacres of Indigenous Australians' (which does include Coniston), as an unconscious reminder that the colonial

genocide is even today still not thought about as an integral part of the Australian experience but something quite separate.

8 Heat on the home front

1   *The Advertiser*, 13 September 1928, p. 13.
2   NAA: A431, 1950/2768 part 1, p. 225.
3   ibid., p. 222.
4   DHT to Cawood, 2 November 1928, NAA: A431, 1950/2768 part 1, p. 195.
5   Certification by H. Mackington JP, coroner, 7 August 1928, NAA: A431, 1950/2768 part 1, p. 32.
6   NAA: A431, 1950/2768 part 1, pp. 31, 208.
7   ibid., p. 14.
8   ibid., p. 195.
9   NAA: A431, 1950/2768 part 1, pp. 207, 196.
10 ibid., pp. 193, 200.
11 ibid., p. 204.
12 ibid., p. 190.
13 ibid., p. 16.
14 *Northern Standard*, 18 May 1928, p. 3.
15 There is no extant official record of the Supreme Court proceedings. Fortunately the *Northern Standard*'s reporter took almost verbatim notes, and I have relied on his report: *Northern Standard*, 9 November 1928, p. 1.
16 *Northern Territory Times*, 9 November 1928, p. 5.
17 The details of the second trial are taken mainly from the *Northern Standard*, 9 November 1928, p. 2.
18 The *Northern Territory Times* reporter had this admission from Murray in even more compelling terms: 'What was the use of a wounded blackfellow hundreds of miles away from civilization?' *Northern Territory Times*, 9 November 1928, p. 5.
19 NAA: A431, 1950/2768 part 1, p. 94.
20 At least, that's what Hartwig believed. Hartwig, p. 35.
21 *The Sydney Morning Herald*, 9 November 1928, p. 9; *The Argus*, 10 November 1928, p. 17; *The Register*, 9 November 1928, p. 12.
22 *The Argus*, 10 November 1928, p. 17.
23 NAA: A431, 1950/2768 part 1, p. 182.
24 ibid., p. 175.
25 ibid., p. 162.
26 ibid., p. 164.
27 ibid., pp. 155, 156.

28 ibid., p. 90.
29 ibid., pp. 211, 212.
30 ibid., various.
31 *Northern Territory Times*, 13 November 1928, p. 3.
32 *The Sydney Morning Herald*, 13 November 1928, p. 12; see also for example, *The Argus*, 14 November 1928, p. 7; *The Sydney Morning Herald*, 14 November 1928, p. 18; *The Age*, 16 November 1928, p. 13; *The Advertiser*, 22 November 1928, p. 12.
33 *The Register*, 15 November 1928, p. 8.
34 *Northern Territory Times*, 16 November 1928, p. 8.
35 NAA: A431, 1950/2768 part 1, p. 84.
36 Generally on the Bruce government, see D. Lee, *Stanley Melbourne Bruce: Australian Internationalist*, Bloomsbury, London, 2010.
37 *The Sydney Morning Herald*, 15 November 1928, p. 13.
38 *The Age*, 15 November 1928, p. 10.
39 *The Age*, 6 October 1925, p. 11.
40 Alfred Deakin, speech on the introduction of the *Pacific Islanders Labourers Bill*, 1901.
41 The continuous irritation which the Aboriginal 'problem' caused to politicians becomes obvious once it is remembered that every Australian government from Federation to the late 1960s maintained an explicit White Australia policy, with the stated intention of Australia's population ending up, literally, white. It also explains why, once it had become obvious that the Aboriginal people would not be dying out altogether, other policies, such as 'assimilation' and the forcible taking of lighter-skinned Aboriginal children from their families to be raised as whites, came into vogue. There was simply no other available solution to the conundrum.
42 NAA: A431, 1950/2768 part 1, p. 12.
43 ibid., p. 121.
44 ibid., p. 3.
45 ibid., p. 46.
46 *The Sydney Morning Herald*, 28 November 1928, p. 17; cf. *The Canberra Times*, 28 November 1928, p. 1.
47 NAA: A431, 1950/2768 part 1, p. 111.
48 ibid., p. 34.
49 ibid., p. 35.
50 ibid., p. 30.

9 The Board of Enquiry

1   *R v Sussex Justices, Ex parte McCarthy* [1924] 1 KB 256, per Lord Hewart CJ.
2   NAA: A431, 1950/2768 part 1, p. 78.
3   ibid., p. 12.
4   *The Sydney Morning Herald*, 30 November 1928, p. 11.
5   *The Sydney Morning Herald*, 5 December 1928, p. 18; 6 December 1928, p. 10; *The Register*, 6 December 1928, p. 9.
6   NAA: A431, 1950/2768 part 1, p. 69.
7   ibid., p. 80.
8   ibid., p. 37.
9   Barrow Creek Police Station Day Journal, 15 December 1928.
10 NAA: A431, 1950/2768 part 2, p. 23.
11 NAA: A1, 1929/7340, p. 30.
12 NAA: A431, 1950/2768 part 2, p. 395 (the Ordinance); p. 401 (the appointment).
13 *The Advertiser*, 18 December 1928, p. 13.
14 NAA: A431, 1950/2768 part 2, p. 11.
15 ibid., p. 3. For an evocative description of the rustic conditions endured by the board, by an unnamed special correspondent who travelled with it, see *The Register,* 11 January 1929, p. 12.
16 Oral history interview with George Birt, Northern Territory Archives Service NTRS226, TS 13.
17 All of the witness statements are in NAA: A431, 1950/2768 part 2, pp. 11–102.
18 NAA: A431, 1950/2768 part 2, p. 3.
19 ibid., p. 62.
20 ibid., p. 3.
21 ibid., pp. 3–8.
22 P. Read and E. J. Japaljarri, 'The Price of Tobacco: The Journey of the Warlmala to Wave Hill, 1928', *Aboriginal History*, vol. 2, 1978, pp. 140-8.
23 NAA: A431, 1950/2768 part 2, p. 273.
24 ibid., pp. 274, 290, 294.
25 The board's source for this finding seems to have been a sensational article published by *The Register* back in September 1928, quoting an unnamed Central Australian resident who claimed that the 'mission blacks' were being taught equality and then 'going out west to meet the uncivilized aborigines, and advise them to kill the white men's cattle, and the white men if they could'. *The Register*, 11 September 1928, p. 9.
26 NAA: A1, 1929/984, p. 57.

27 *The Register*, 8 January 1929, p. 9; 9 January 1929, p. 8.

28 This was Lock's consistent assertion; she had been complaining for a long time directly to the department about starvation and pinned it as the direct cause of Brooks' murder. See, for example, her letter to Carrodus of 17 July 1928, NAA: A1, 1929/984, p. 74.

29 *Northern Standard*, 17 February 1928, p. 6.

30 Henson, *A Straight-out Man*, p. 29.

31 Traynor, *Alice Springs*, p. 277.

32 *The Advertiser*, 13 December 1928, p. 15.

33 ibid.

34 *The Advertiser*, 18 December 1928, p. 15.

35 ibid., p. 17.

36 NAA: A1, 1929/1639, p.66. The Chief Protector of Aborigines for South Australia was also reporting through this period that drought conditions in the Centre were dire; see reports for 1927–1930.

37 F. W. Albrecht, 'Hermannsburg from 1926 to 1962', in E. Leske (ed.), *Hermannsburg: A Vision and a Mission*, Lutheran Publishing House, Adelaide, 1977, p. 46.

38 Hartwig, pp. 10–11.

39 The commissioning of Bleakley had been the Bruce government's compromise response to substantial pressure for a Royal Commission or Joint Select Committee to enquire into Aboriginal welfare throughout Australia, following a widely publicised massacre of Aboriginal people in Western Australia in 1926 by police-led parties. See Summers, *The Parliament of the Commonwealth of Australia and Indigenous Peoples 1901–1967*, pp. 27–9.

40 J. W. Bleakley, *The Aboriginals and Half-castes of Central Australia and North Australia, 1928*, Government Printer, Melbourne, 1929, p. 31.

41 Read and Japaljarri, pp. 140–8.

42 NAA: A431, 1950/2768 part 2, p. 345.

43 See, for example, *The Register News-Pictorial*, 31 January 1929, p. 9; *The Sydney Morning Herald*, 31 January 1929, p. 13.

44 NAA: A431, 1950/2768 part 2, pp. 261–2.

45 ibid., p. 196.

46 ibid., p. 194.

47 Morley was unfazed, however, replying forcefully the next day: *The Sydney Morning Herald*, 7 March 1929, p. 11; 8 March 1929, p. 10.

48 *The Register News-Pictorial*, 2 February 1929, p. 35. The reporting of criticism was widespread – see also, for example, *The Sydney Morning Herald*, 29 March 1929, p. 9; *The Brisbane Courier*, 30 March 1929, p. 20;

The Register News-Pictorial, 30 March 1929, p. 7.

49 NAA: A431, 1950/2768 part 2, p. 229.

50 ibid., p. 180.

51 ibid., p. 179.

52 ibid., pp. 150–1.

53 *News*, 14 March 1929, p. 21.

54 See, for example, *The Sydney Morning Herald*, 9 April 1929, p. 12; *The Argus*, 12 April 1929, p. 10; *The Age*, 10 May 1929, p. 9; *The Register News-Pictorial*, 11 May 1929, p. 16.

55 NAA: A1, 1933/8782.

56 *The Observer*, 11 April 1929, p. 10.

57 The latter were consistently referred to throughout the conference (as they were generally at the time) as a 'problem'. During the conference, for example, Abbott commented: 'This half-caste problem gives me a great deal of worry. We take a child, we train it, we teach it, it grows to the age of 16 or so; what then becomes of it? That is what has me worried.' NAA: A1, 1933/8782, p. 46.

58 Coincidentally, the Aboriginal population in 1929 was at about its historical nadir.

59 NAA: A1, 1933/8782, p. 35.

60 ibid., p. 8.

10 Dispersal

1 According to Sidney Downer, Murray received 'hundreds of letters applauding [his actions] on the ground that they had made the Territory a safer place for the white man'. Downer, *Patrol Indefinite*, p. 126.

2 NAA: A1, 1929/7340, pp. 54, 60.

3 ibid., p. 48.

4 ibid., p. 47.

5 ibid., p. 46.

6 ibid., p. 43.

7 ibid., p. 42.

8 Details of the case are from the report in the *Northern Territory Times*, 2 August 1929, p. 3.

9 NAA: A1, 1929/7340, p. 8.

10 NAA: A431, 1946/676, p. 48.

11 Cawood was nothing if not persistent, but it was entirely in vain. NAA: A431, 1946/676.

12 NAA: A1, 1929/1064, p. 27.

13 ibid., pp. 21, 23.

14 NAA: A1, 1930/9634; NAA: A1, 1936/1241.

15 Terry, *Hidden Wealth and Hiding People*, p. 217.

16 B. Bowman, *A History of Central Australia Volume II – The Coniston Story and Tales of the North West Sector*, Bryan Bowman, Alice Springs, 1989–1991, p. 1.

17 An official report in 1935 noted that the homestead was still just a humpy and Stafford had done 'very little in the way of improvements' in his fifteen or so years' occupation. NAA: F658, 30.

18 Bowman, p. 5.

19 NAA: A1, 1937/7761, p. 10.

20 NAA: A1, 1929/8858.

21 *Northern Standard*, 25 October 1946, p. 9.

22 Lee, *Stanley Melbourne Bruce*, p. 91.

23 C. L. A. Abbott, *Australia's Frontier Province*, Angus and Robertson, Sydney, 1950, pp. 147, 151.

24 ibid., p. 147.

25 ibid., p. 138.

26 NAA: A1, 1936/6595, p. 298.

27 ibid., p. 351.

28 *The Register News-Pictorial*, 6 February 1929, p. 7.

29 Strehlow, p. 387.

30 *Sunday Sun and Guardian*, 5 February 1933, p. 19.

31 O'Brien, p. 37.

32 Strehlow, p. 317.

33 K. G. Johannsen, *A Son of 'The Red Centre': Memoirs and Anecdotes of the Life of a Road Train Pioneer and Bush Inventor of the Northern Territory of Australia*, K. G. Johannsen, Morphetville, South Australia, 1992, p. 66.

34 O'Brien, p. 39.

Epilogue

1 Stanner, 'The Dreaming', in *The Dreaming & Other Essays*, p. 57.

2 The material in this epilogue on Murray's later years is from his military file: NAA: D363, M39423.

3 From *Coniston* (film); see also Read and Read, p. 34.

BIBLIOGRAPHY

Government records

National Archives of Australia
NAA: A1, 1929/984, Missionary Miss Annie Lock re Mission Lease in the Northern Territory.

NAA: A1, 1929/1064, Mtd. Constable C. H. Noblet Police, C.A.

NAA: A1, 1929/1639, Removal of Natives from Alice Springs to Hermannsburg.

NAA: A1, 1929/7340, H. Henty – Murder of by Aboriginals.

NAA: A1, 1929/8858, Junbuna (Aborigine), Death of – central Australia.

NAA: A1, 1930/9634, John Saxby, application for assistance to prospect Central Australia.

NAA: A1, 1933/8782, Aboriginal Welfare Conference (Melbourne – 1933).

NAA: A1, 1936/1241, William Briscoe – Application for grazing license, NT.

NAA: A1, 1936/6595, Association for Protection of Native Races – Aboriginal matters, File No. 1.

NAA: A1, 1937/7761, Alleged murder of white man by Aborigines. Press Reports re.

NAA: A431, 1946/676, J. C. Cawood, Govt. Res. Central Australia.

NAA: A431, 1950/2768 part 1, Attacks on white men by natives – Killing of natives – Central Australia [Attachment titled 'Papers returned by Mr O'Kelly'].

NAA: A431, 1950/2768 part 2, Attacks on white men by natives – Killing of natives – Central Australia [Attachment titled 'Finding of Board of Enquiry with exhibits 1–13'].

NAA: A461, G300/1, Aboriginals – Aboriginal Census 30.6.1927.

NAA: AP613/7, Noblet C H – Noblet, Charles Herbert regimental number 311 South Australian fifth contingent imperial – attestation of.

NAA: D363, M39423, Murray, William George – Service Number – 308.

NAA: F658, 30, Northern Territory Pastoral Leases Investigation Committee Report – Coniston Station.

Northern Territory Archives Service

NTRS 226 – Typed transcripts of oral history interviews:
  TS 13 – George Birt
  TS 248 – Tim Langdon Japangardi
  TS 348 – Ada Wade
  TS 486 – Clarence Smith
  TS 643 – Sandy Anderson

NTRS 2211 – Reference copy of staff files 'P' (Police) single number series, P17 – William George Murray.
  Alice Springs Police Station Day Journal, 1928–1929
  Barrow Creek Police Station Day Journal, 1927–1929

South Australian Museum Archives

AA 662/49/27, letter from Albrecht to M. C. Hartwig, 18 April 1960.

Reports

The Aboriginals and Half-castes of Central Australia and North Australia: Report by J. W. Bleakley, Chief Protector of Aboriginals, Queensland, Government Printer, Melbourne, 1928.

Kaytej, Warlpiri and Warlmanpa Land Claim, Report by the Aboriginal Land Commissioner, Mr Justice Toohey, to the Minister for Aboriginal Affairs and to the Administrator of the Northern Territory, AGPS, Canberra, 1982.

Reports of the Chief Protector of Aborigines, for the years ended June 30, 1925, to June 30, 1930, Government Printer, Adelaide, 1925–1930.

Sowden, W. J., *The Northern Territory as It Is: A Narrative of the South Australian Parliamentary Party's Trip, and Full Descriptions of the Northern Territory; Its Settlements and Industries*, W. K. Thomas & Co., Adelaide, 1882.

Yurrkuru (Brookes Soak) Land Claim, report no. 43, Findings, Recommendations and Report of the Aboriginal Land Commissioner, Mr Justice Olney, to the Minister for Aboriginal and Torres Strait Islander Affairs and to the Administrator of the Northern Territory, AGPS, Canberra, 1992.

Books

Abbott, C. L. A., *Australia's Frontier Province*, Angus and Robertson, Sydney, 1950.

Austin, T., *Simply the Survival of the Fittest: Aboriginal Administration in South Australia's Northern Territory 1863–1910*, Historical Society of the Northern Territory, Darwin, 1992.

Austin, T., *Never Trust a Government Man: Northern Territory Aboriginal Policy 1911–1939*, NTU Press, Darwin, 1997.

Basedow, H., *The Australian Aboriginal*, F. W. Preece & Sons, Adelaide, 1925.

Baume, F. E., *Tragedy Track: The Story of the Granites*, North Flinders Mines Ltd, Wayville, South Australia; Hesperian Press, Carlisle, Western Australia, 1994.

Bleakley, J. W., *The Aborigines of Australia*, The Jacaranda Press, Brisbane, 1961.

Bowman, B., *A History of Central Australia Volume II – The Coniston Story and Tales of the North West Sector*, Bryan Bowman, Alice Springs, 1989–1991.

Collier, J., *The Pastoral Age in Australasia*, Whitcombe & Tombs, London, 1911.

Cribbin, J., *The Killing Times: The Coniston Massacre 1928*, Fontana Books, Sydney, 1984.

Downer, S., *Patrol Indefinite: The Northern Territory Police Force*, Rigby, Adelaide, 1963.

Durack, M., *Kings in Grass Castles*, Constance & Co., London, 1959.

Elder, B., *Blood on the Wattle: Massacres and Maltreatment of Aboriginal Australians since 1788*, 3rd edn, New Holland Publishers, Sydney, 2003.

Henson, B., *A Straight-out Man: F. W. Albrecht and Central Australian Aborigines*, Melbourne University Press, Carlton, Victoria, 1992.

Johannsen, K. G., *A Son of 'The Red Centre': Memoirs and Anecdotes of the Life of a Road Train Pioneer and Bush Inventor of the Northern Territory of Australia*, K. G. Johannsen, Morphetville, South Australia, 1992.

Koch, G., and Koch, H. (trans.), *Kaytetye Country: An Aboriginal History of the Barrow Creek Area*, Institute for Aboriginal Development Publications, Alice Springs, 1993.

Lee, D., *Stanley Melbourne Bruce: Australian Internationalist*, Bloomsbury, London, 2010.

Lines, W. J., *Taming the Great South Land: A History of the Conquest of Nature in Australia*, Allen & Unwin, Sydney, 1991.

Lockwood, D., *Crocodiles and Other People*, Cassell, London, 1939.

Lockwood, D., *Up the Track*, Rigby, Adelaide, 1964.

McGrath, A., *Born in the Cattle – Aborigines in Cattle Country*, Allen & Unwin, Sydney, 1987.

Making Peace with the Past: Remembering the Coniston Massacre 1928–2003, Central Land Council, Alice Springs, 2003.

Murray, P. L., *Official Records of the Australian Military Contingents to the War in South Africa*, A. J. Mullet, Government Printer, Melbourne, 1911.

Powell, A., *A Short History of the Northern Territory*, Charles Darwin University Press, Darwin, 2009.

Read, P., and Read, J. (eds), *Long Time, Olden Time: Aboriginal Accounts of Northern Territory History*, Institute for Aboriginal Development, Alice Springs, 1991.

Reid, G., *A Picnic with the Natives: Aboriginal-European Relations in the Northern Territory to 1910*, Melbourne University Press, Melbourne, 1990.

Reynolds, H., *Forgotten War*, NewSouth Publishing, Sydney, 2013.

Rockman Napaljarri, P., and Cataldi, L., (trans.), *Warlpiri Dreamings and Histories*, AltaMira Press, Walnut Creek, CA, 1994.

Rowley, C. D., *The Destruction of Aboriginal Society*, Australian National University Press, Canberra, 1970.

Rowley, C. D., *The Remote Aborigines*, Australian National University Press, Canberra, 1971.

Searcy, A., *In Australian Tropics*, George Robertson & Co., London, 1909.

Stanner, W. E. H., *The Dreaming & Other Essays*, Black Inc. Agenda, Melbourne, 2010.

Strehlow, T. G. H., *Land of Altjira* (unpublished manuscript), original held at The Strehlow Research Centre, Alice Springs, 1959.

Stuart, J. M., *Journal of Mr Stuart's Fourth Expedition – Fixing the Centre of the Continent. From March to September, 1860*. Available at: <www.johnmcdouallstuart.org.au>.

Terry, M., *Hidden Wealth and Hiding People*, Putnam, London, 1931.

Terry, M., *War of the Warramullas*, Rigby Ltd, Adelaide, 1974.

Traynor, S., *Alice Springs: From Singing Wire to Iconic Outback Town*, Wakefield Press, Mile End, South Australia, 2016.

Vaarzon-Morel, P. (ed.), *Warlpiri Women's Voices: Our Lives Our History*, Institute for Aboriginal Development Press, Alice Springs, 1995.

Willshire, W. H., *The Land of the Dawning: Being Facts Gleaned from Cannibals in the Australian Stone Age*, W. K. Thomas & Co., Adelaide, 1896.

Chapters, journals, articles and theses

Albrecht, F. W., 'Hermannsburg from 1926 to 1962', in E. Leske (ed.), *Hermannsburg: A Vision and a Mission*, Lutheran Publishing House, Adelaide, 1977.

Carment, D., Maynard, R., and Powell, A. (eds), *Northern Territory Dictionary of Biography*, Charles Darwin University Press, Darwin, 2008.

Cataldi, L., 'The End of the Dreaming? Understandings of History in a Warlpiri Narrative of the Coniston Massacres', *Overland*, no. 144, Spring 1996, pp. 44–7.

Northern Territory Dictionary of Biography, entry for William George Murray.

Deakin, A., speech on introduction of the *Pacific Islanders Labourers Bill*, Hansard, 1901.

Hartwig, M. C., *The Coniston Killings*, BA (Hons) thesis, The University of Adelaide, 1960.

Hartwig, M. C., *The Progress of White Settlement in the Alice Springs District and its Effects upon the Aboriginal Inhabitants, 1860–1894*, PhD thesis, The University of Adelaide, 1965.

Japangardi, T., *Yurrkuru-Kurlu: Coniston Story*, Yuendumu School, Yuendumu, NT, 1978.

Kimber, D., 'Real True History: The Coniston Massacre' (serialised in 18 parts), *Alice Springs News*, vol. 10, issue 32, to vol. 11, issue 3, 2003–04.

McCarthy, T., 'Remembering the Coniston Massacre', Northern Territory Library, 2008.

Merlan, F., '"Making People Quiet" in the Pastoral North: Reminiscences of Elsey Station', *Aboriginal History*, vol. 2, no. 1, 1978, pp. 70–106.

Mulvaney, D. J., 'Barrow Creek Northern Australia, 1874', in B. Attwood and S. G. Foster (eds), *Frontier Conflict: The Australian Experience*, National Museum of Australia, Canberra, 2003.

O'Brien, J., *'To Infuse an Universal Terror': The Coniston Killings of 1928*, thesis, Northern Territory University, 2002.

Pike, D. H. (ed.), 'The Diary of James Coutts Crawford: Extracts on Aborigines and Adelaide, 1839 and 1841', *South Australiana*, vol. IV, no. 1, March 1965.

Read, P., and Japaljarri, E. J., 'The Price of Tobacco: The Journey of the Warlmala to Wave Hill, 1928', *Aboriginal History*, vol. 2, 1978, pp. 140–8.

Roberts, T., 'The Brutal Truth: What Happened in the Gulf Country', *The Monthly*, November 2009.

Summers, J., *The Parliament of the Commonwealth of Australia and Indigenous Peoples 1901–1967*, research paper 10 2000-01, Department of the Parliamentary Library, Canberra, 2000.

Wilson, B., and O'Brien, J., '"To Infuse an Universal Terror": A Reappraisal of the Coniston Killings', *Aboriginal History*, vol. 27, 2003, pp. 59–78.

Wilson, W. R., *A Force Apart? A History of the Northern Territory Police Force 1870–1926*, PhD thesis, Northern Territory University, 2000.

Film

Coniston, a film by David Batty and Francis Jupurrurla Kelly, PAW Productions, 2012.

Newspapers

The Advertiser (Adelaide)
The Age (Melbourne)
Alice Springs News

Bibliography

The Argus (Melbourne)
The Brisbane Courier
The Canberra Times
News (Adelaide)
Northern Standard (Darwin)
Northern Territory Times (Darwin)
Northern Territory Times and Gazette (Darwin)
Observer (Adelaide)
The Register (Adelaide)
The Register News-Pictorial (Adelaide)
Sunday Sun and Guardian (Sydney)
The Sydney Morning Herald

ACKNOWLEDGEMENTS

The victims of the Coniston massacre were never named. They were ridden down, slaughtered and abandoned. Their fate remains officially unacknowledged and no apology has ever been made to them or their descendants. I acknowledge their lives and owner-ship of country, and I am sorry for the way in which they died.

This is not an Aboriginal history of Coniston. I could not have written that if I tried, and I didn't try. I hope that the Aboriginal story of Coniston, yet to be written, will be too.

I came across the Coniston story by accident, became quickly obsessed by it and, when I realised that it had never been fully researched or written, felt that that needed to be done. I have tried to let the history tell itself. My perspective is in the Western historiographical tradition, based in chronology and evidence. I have drawn on the limited record of Aboriginal recollection as much as possible, and attempted to draw fair conclusions about what happened and why from an analysis of all the available material. If I got anything wrong, the responsibility is mine alone.

This story is, too, part of my history as an Australian. I share most white Australians' educational experience of learning little to nothing about Australia's history from the Indigenous perspective. It shocked me to realise that Coniston, a major mass death event in relatively recent history, has been so neglected. It's just one example of our failure to remember our shared past; until we begin to fill in those gaps, we can't have much of a shared future. The prerequisite to reconciliation is truth.

I would like to thank whoever came up with the idea of the National Archives of Australia, and the Trove at the National Library of Australia. Both are priceless resources for historians and anyone interested in the past.

I had wonderfully cheerful help with my research in Alice Springs, from Felicity Green at the Museum of Central Australia, Strehlow Research Centre, and Elisabeth Marnie at the Northern Territory Archives Service.

Professor Catherine Lumby of Macquarie University very kindly read my manuscript and helped me reshape it in a publishable form. She and Nina Funnell were invaluable in guiding me through my first experience of trying to find a publisher, with the happy result of encountering Terri-ann White at UWA Publishing. Her team has taken excellent care of me, especially Kelly Somers and Eleanor Hurt, and copyeditor Sam Trafford.

Professor Megan Davis was instantly willing to write the foreword to my book, an enormous honour for which I am very grateful.

The writing world is full of supportive people. My thanks especially to Paul Ham, a friend and a historian whose work I admire so much, for convincing me to write a book because he kept telling me I could.

Many thanks to Julian Chan for drawing the maps in the front of this book.

Finally, nothing's possible without those around you leaning in. My partners and colleagues at my firm, Marque Lawyers, are the kindest, most collaborative tribe of all. And my beautiful wife and daughters – Charmaine, Sian and Darcy – they tell me they're proud of me, and that's all I need.

www.ingramcontent.com/pod-product-compliance
Lightning Source LLC
Chambersburg PA
CBHW021137090426
42740CB00008B/822